AGAINST AID

Against Aid presents a complex and diverse history of opposition to US foreign aid spending, explaining why critics challenged aid and how they had a significant impact on US foreign policy.

Foreign aid was an integral part of US foreign policy during the Cold War. US leaders hoped aid spending could modernize other societies, create steadfast allies, and promote global stability, but there was always considerable opposition. Jeffrey F. Taffet skillfully examines aid's opponents and shows how they questioned the assumptions that the United States needed to be globally engaged. He argues that aid's opponents forced changes in US aid programs that dramatically reduced overall spending and limited support for dictatorships. Taffet also makes a larger argument, that in fighting aid, opponents were challenging essential views about the nation and its global role that transcended debates about how much to spend. They were arguing about the appropriate use of national power and the essence of the nation's purpose.

This book is essential reading for courses in American politics, international studies, and history of American foreign policy. Students will benefit from the broad, chronological scope and accessible narrative of the text.

Jeffrey F. Taffet is Professor of History at the United States Merchant Marine Academy. He is the author of *Foreign Aid as Foreign Policy: The Alliance for Progress in Latin America* (Routledge 2007) and *The United States and Latin America: A History with Documents* (Routledge 2017, with Dustin Walcher).

"Taffet's accessible and engaging study convincingly demonstrates that many Americans rejected the notion that US foreign aid during the Cold War could strengthen other societies or benefit the United States. Illuminating fierce legislative battles that frequently cut across party lines, *Against Aid* shows how opponents of foreign aid questioned the assumptions of American Cold War leadership, laying the foundation for current debates about US global engagement."

William Michael Schmidli, Associate Professor of History, Leiden University, The Netherlands

"Whether foreign aid achieves its stated goals is an open question among scholars and even among its proponents. Jeffrey Taffet shows that its skeptics rooted their doubts in a variety of soils, and their opposition to foreign aid reflected conflicting visions of the national mission in the latter half of the 'American Century.' This is a valuable volume, and is essential reading for anyone seeking to understand the 'soft power' of foreign aid in postwar American diplomacy."

Jason C. Parker, Professor of History, Texas A&M University, USA

"What is the ultimate purpose of US foreign relations? To vigorously spread US-style freedoms and democracy around the globe, and shoulder the responsibility that comes with that choice? Or pursue narrowly construed, specific US interests, cautiously avoiding possible foreign entanglements? Although the debate goes back nearly two centuries, today the conflict over foreign aid is arguably the best way of understanding it. As such, the enduring relevance of Jeffrey Taffet's excellently researched, well-written book is clear."

James F. Siekmeier, Associate Professor of History, West Virginia University, USA

AGAINST AID

A History of Opposition to US Foreign Aid Spending

Jeffrey F. Taffet

Routledge
Taylor & Francis Group
LONDON AND NEW YORK

First published 2022
by Routledge
2 Park Square, Milton Park, Abingdon, Oxon OX14 4RN

and by Routledge
605 Third Avenue, New York, NY 10158

Routledge is an imprint of the Taylor & Francis Group, an informa business

Library of Congress Cataloging-in-Publication Data
Names: Taffet, Jeffrey F., author.
Title: Against aid : a history of opposition to U.S. foreign aid spending / Jeffrey F. Taffet.
Description: Abingdon, Oxon ; New York, NY : Routledge, 2021. | Includes bibliographical references and index.
Identifiers: LCCN 2020057905 (print) | LCCN 2020057906 (ebook) | ISBN 9781138345287 (paperback) | ISBN 9781138345270 (hardback) | ISBN 9780429437984 (ebook)
Subjects: LCSH: Economic assistance, American--History. | United States--Foreign economic relations. | United States--Foreign relations.
Classification: LCC HC60 .T238 2021 (print) | LCC HC60 (ebook) | DDC 338.91/73–dc23
LC record available at https://lccn.loc.gov/2020057905
LC ebook record available at https://lccn.loc.gov/2020057906

ISBN: 978-1-138-34527-0 (hbk)
ISBN: 978-1-138-34528-7 (pbk)
ISBN: 978-0-429-43798-4 (ebk)

Typeset in Bembo
by Taylor & Francis Books

For Bertram and Barbara Taffet

CONTENTS

ILLUSTRATIONS

Figures

Tables

ACKNOWLEDGEMENTS

I would like to thank Kimberley Smith, Eve Meyer, Emily Irvine, Zoe Forbes, Gill Gairdner and Megan Hiatt at Routledge for supporting this text and helping move it forward toward publication. I received travel funding to visit numerous archives from my employer, the United States Merchant Marine Academy, and am thankful to our dean and provost, John Ballard, for his support in obtaining those funds. I would also like to thank my friends in the Humanities Department for their camaraderie and encouragement. As a faculty member at the United States Merchant Marine Academy, I am an employee of the US federal government, and need to state for the record that the views expressed in this work are not those of the United States government or any of its agencies. At the Bland Library, my institutional library, I would like to thank Donna Selvaggio, Jan Edmiston, and Jeremy Lauber for their help in obtaining sources and for access to electronic databases.

I did most of my writing in the Wertheim Study and the Allen Room at the New York Public Library, and I am thankful for all the assistance Melanie Locay and the other librarians and support staff have given me over the years. I received help from many archivists and their assistants across the United States as I did research. At the Franklin D. Roosevelt Library, Sarah Navins helped me locate sources; at the Truman Library, Randy Sowell offered guidance about using their materials; and at the Eisenhower Library, David Holbrook pointed me in the right direction. I did research at the National Archives, and am thankful to the archivists who offered useful suggestions. While there, I was fortunate to stay with my friends Mimi and Archer McCrudden and their parents Chuck and Amada in College Park, Maryland. Aya Beydoun helped me obtain materials from the Citizen's Foreign Aid Committee Collections at Wayne State University. Jacque Roether, the expert on the Wallace Papers at the University of Iowa helped me during a short visit to Iowa City. In Monroe, Louisiana, Heather

Pilcher was fantastically accommodating as I worked with the Otto Passman collection at the University of Louisiana at Monroe. Lydia Saad of Gallup offered sage advice about interpreting their historical polling data. I am thankful for the assistance I received as I worked with multiple collections at Columbia University's Rare Book and Manuscript Library, and the help Michael Koncewicz gave me at the Tamiment Library at New York University. I have been working out pieces of this text in conversations with too many historians to mention, and am thankful for the feedback and advice I've received along the way. It is a better work as a result. I have used some of this material with my students as well, and am thankful for their responses. I especially want to thank Felipe Pereira Laureiro for asking me to teach a course at the University of São Paulo based on this text.

I would like to thank my friends and family for their kindness and inspiration. My teenage sons, Benjamin and Micah, are mostly bemused by my work, and I'm thankful that they are a loving distraction. My wife, Heather Taffet Gold, is the best partner I could imagine, and has always been considerate of my scholarship-related absences. Also, as she's done in the past, she used her exceptional editing skills to improve my sometimes clunky prose, which I am thankful she sees as one of the built-in expectations of being married to a historian. I dedicate this book to my parents, Barbara and Bertram Taffet, without whose unfailing support and encouragement I never could have become a historian in the first place.

INTRODUCTION

Two Conversations

One afternoon, when I was a few months into my research for this book, I was at a large barbecue waiting in line for food. I was chatting with my friend David. He casually asked what I was working on, and before I got very far into explaining that I was writing about how people in the United States thought about foreign aid, he exclaimed, "I just don't understand why we do that!" I asked, of course, "Do what?" He replied with a long and passionate answer about how foreign aid seemed like a waste of money, and certainly not something that the United States government should do. Private charity made sense, he said, and maybe the United Nations should be fighting global poverty, but he did not think it was right that his tax dollars went overseas when there were so many people in the United States who needed help.

About two years later, when I had just about finished my initial research and was beginning to write a first draft, I had a similar experience but with a different reaction. I was at an elegant party and having a conversation over a cocktail with Mark, another friend. Like David had, Mark asked what I was working on. After I had said only a few sentences about this book, he matter-of-factly proclaimed, "I think we need to do more of that." "More of what?" I inquired. He said the United States needed to give more foreign aid. He said that aid was a way for the country to be a constructive global power. If we wanted to live in a better world and have people support us and respect us, we needed to do more to help people in other countries.

I know both David and Mark well, and I see them frequently. Both are well educated and well traveled. One is a US Navy veteran who works for a large consulting firm, the other runs a food import company. Their political views on most issues are about the same, and I am confident that they have voted similarly in every recent national and local election. Yet instinctually they had very different ideas about foreign aid.

Our short conversations helped me think about how ideas about foreign aid do not necessarily line up with political self-identifications. Throughout this text there are examples of people who had little in common, yet saw aid similarly. Conversely, like David and Mark, there are people who shared similar political outlooks, but thought about aid differently. As I worked on the text I found that I could understand each individual position, but I initially struggled to make sense of how these views connected with each other, and what those connections might mean in a larger context. I came to believe, as the text argues, that ideas about aid can explain differences in how people view the United States government's global role and the nature of its power; these differences are not always captured by more traditional political labels.

In writing this text, I thought about Mark and David as people who might want to understand the history of the national conversations about aid. With them in mind, I have tried to avoid jargon and make the text accessible to non-historians. I've also gone a bit deeper with the historical background in the initial chapter than I might have otherwise. However, I am hopeful that my arguments about opposition to foreign aid, and aid itself, will be compelling to other scholars. The narrative in this text is mostly absent from the scholarship on foreign aid, and I believe it can be valuable in developing a better understanding of the issue, and more broadly, the complexities in the relationships between domestic political life and foreign policy in the Cold War era.

This is not the book I had originally intended to write. Not that long before my conversation with David, I had begun plotting out a book about the shifts in foreign aid implementation strategies during the Cold War. I wanted to track the ways that US aid-granting bureaucracies changed over time, and I wanted to show how political leaders used economic aid to advance their foreign policy objectives. I was frustrated that an accessible one-volume introduction to the political history of US foreign aid did not exist, and figured I could write it.[1] I knew I did not know this history well enough, and that with the growing interest in development studies such a text could be valuable to other scholars. But as I started digging in, the voices that intrigued and excited me – the voices explored in this text – did not come from aid planners and politicians calling for spending programs, they came from the individuals who fought against them. I had never fully understood how many aid opponents there were or how different they were, and I had not appreciated how they had impacted the aid process. They were rarely able to completely get their way, but aid supporters always had to fight with them and often had to compromise with them. I started to see US foreign aid as a debate, rather than a policy, and that was exciting.[2]

There was something else, though. I was struck by how contemporary discussions about US global engagement sounded like what foreign aid's opponents had said from the late 1940s to the 1970s. I could see that people who challenged ideas about foreign aid's power to transform other societies shared a worldview with people who, more recently, have been critical of multilateralism and globalization. I could see that these Cold War debates helped clarify the evolution of political philosophies in the United States and how that illuminated ideas about national mission and government in the post-Cold War world. This shifted the focus of my attention toward exploring ideas about foreign aid and away from tracing policy implementation and assessing the results of aid spending. It became less important to understand what aid programs did, and more important to study how people felt about them.

Like many observers, both scholars and not, I have watched a shift in national sentiment driven by growing frustrations with internationally oriented policies. This was clearly visible in President Donald Trump's 2016 election rhetoric as he attacked trade agreements, called for limiting immigration through the construction of a border wall, and upended long-established notions about the importance of cooperating with historical allies. Trump seemed to be saying something different about the US global role, but he was not alone. As a presidential candidate in 2016, Vermont senator Bernie Sanders also challenged conventional and long-standing notions about how the United States should engage the world, as had the earlier Occupy Wall Street and anti-World Trade Association protests. These were not consensus views, to be sure, but a broad foreign policy reassessment seemed to be occurring. Ideas that called for more limited global engagement and responsibility, and that were concerned with the domestic costs of globalization, were becoming increasingly powerful.

This new approach was visible in Trump's 2017 inaugural address. He declared,

> For many decades, we've enriched foreign industry at the expense of American industry; subsidized the armies of other countries while allowing for the very sad depletion of our military; we've defended other nation's borders while refusing to defend our own; and spent trillions of dollars overseas while America's infrastructure has fallen into disrepair and decay. We've made other countries rich while the wealth, strength, and confidence of our country has disappeared over the horizon.

All this was working toward the assertion, "From this day forward, a new vision will govern our land. From this moment on, it's going to be America First."[3] His critique of US aid programs was thus embedded in a much larger rejection of US global responsibility, and it was central to his vision about how the government, under his leadership, would approach the rest of the world.

In part, Trump was obviously contrasting his views with Secretary of State Hillary Clinton's, his 2016 presidential election opponent. Clinton had argued that the United States had basic global responsibilities and needed to use its power to promote positive international change. In a campaign speech in August 2016, she had said that the United States was an "exceptional nation" and an "indispensable nation." These terms, to her, recognized the country's "unique and unparalleled ability to be a force for peace and progress, [and] a champion for freedom and opportunity." She continued, the ability to be a global leader, which the United States was, carried a "responsibility to lead," but only in a way that could improve the world; US leadership had to be humble, thoughtful, and maintain a "fierce commitment to our values." Here, and throughout the 2016 election campaign, she attacked Trump for failing to speak about the way that the United States had the power to do good on a global scale, and for his failing to recognize that without US leadership, the world would be chaotic and dangerous.[4]

Clinton's ideas were not particularly original. Most concretely she was borrowing language that Secretary of State Madeline Albright had used about US policy toward Iraq in 1998. Albright had explained in a television interview that if "we have to use force, it is because we are America; we are the indispensable nation. We stand tall and we see further than other countries into the future."[5] Clinton and Albright were both Democrats, but Republicans had said the same kinds of things. In his second inaugural address in 2005, President George W. Bush, referring to the Iraq War, insisted that the "country has accepted obligations" to spread peace and freedom "that are difficult to fulfill and would be dishonorable to abandon," and he claimed a measure of success in Iraq. He said that "because we have acted in the great liberating tradition of this nation, tens of millions have achieved their freedom." More grandly he said that the work in Iraq was just a beginning, and that with continuing effort an "untamed fire of freedom will reach the darkest corners of our world." Historian Andrew J. Bacevich argues that Bush succeeded here "quite masterfully in capturing something essential about the way Americans see themselves and their country." Bush's words, Bacevich notes, could have just as easily come from Thomas Jefferson, Abraham Lincoln, Woodrow Wilson, Franklin D. Roosevelt, John F. Kennedy, or Ronald Reagan. All expressed a belief that the United States had a global responsibility to make the world a better place.[6]

Trump, in rejecting this vision of US global responsibility, was making a substantial break with the past. His perspective, however, was not new. His vision, I argue, echoes the many critics of US foreign aid in the post-World War II period, it has a deeper foundation in debates about US global engagement dating back to the early national period, and it will be part of the national discourse well after his 2020 election defeat. That is, Trump's approach did not break new intellectual ground; it is connected to a long tradition of broadly challenging ideas about US international engagement.

Trump's rejection of global commitments raises questions about the inadequacy of political labels. Many anti-aid politicians used the term "conservative" to explain their objections to aid, and insisted they were being "economy minded" or "fiscally responsible." They said foreign aid spending was a mistake, just like domestic welfare spending; it was riddled with bureaucratic inefficiencies, implementation failures, and corruption. More philosophically, and sometimes using racial language, they talked about aid as a handout that disincentivized recipients from doing the hard work of capitalist advancement. Some self-identifying conservatives saw sinister forces at work and argued that foreign aid was part of a plot to establish a world government, undermine religious freedom, and help communists win the Cold War. For the conspiratorially minded it was treasonous. However, not all conservatives accepted these ideas or even opposed foreign aid. Many self-identifying conservatives embraced the view that the United States had an international mission and international responsibilities, and they saw foreign aid as a valuable tool in that effort.

Beyond conservatives, there was substantial opposition to aid programming from some self-identifying "liberals" who broadly accepted the idea that government had the ability and obligation to improve society. For most of the period under study in this text, liberals were considerably more likely to back foreign aid, yet many did not. Liberal anti-foreign aid politicians believed in aid's potential to help other countries develop but worried about its morality. They suggested that aid operated as an imperial endeavor that imposed US value systems on other peoples and facilitated their exploitation by US corporations. It was a new form of imperialism, gentler and more opaque, but imperialism nonetheless. These anti-foreign aid liberals also worried that US aid was strengthening repressive anti-democratic regimes. Offering loans and grants to dictators, they argued, violated the basic principle that foreign aid should make the world a better place. Liberals also shared the concerns of conservatives about bureaucratic inefficiency, implementation failures, and corruption in recipient nations; no one liked waste. Finally, liberals worried that foreign aid limited the money available for domestic social welfare programs. In an ideal world, they suggested, the United States could promote economic growth everywhere. But they knew that funds were limited, and more foreign aid meant it would be more difficult to spend at home.

Backers of aid programs often labeled their adversaries "isolationists" because of their rejection of global engagement, in an attempt to connect opposition to the pre-World War II period. In the 1930s, Isolationists had counseled staying out of international politics because they thought the United States had neither the right nor the responsibility to become involved in European and Asian disputes. Their opponents, "internationalists," argued that the nature of global community meant that international problems were inherently all-consuming and isolation was therefore foolish. In the post-World War II era, these terms do not always fit when applied to foreign aid. Some of aid's opponents did draw inspiration from Isolationists in the conventional sense that they rejected global engagement, but they also recognized that the United States could never go back to the 1930s. Most saw international Communism as an existential national threat. On the other side, as with liberals, there was opposition from people who argued, like Internationalists, that the United States should engage the world and try to make it better. They said that foreign aid was not the right way to do it; rather than helping advance US interests, in practice aid was undermining the nation's core values.

Addressing problems with these terms, H. W. Brands offered different language. He suggested that throughout US history there have been two schools of thought, "exemplarists" who believed that the United States should perfect itself and be a beacon to the world, and "vindicators" who believed that the United States needed to go out into the messy world and fight to secure its values. Both, he contends, are essentially internationalist positions in that they believe that other places matter; they essentially disagree on tactics.[7] His analytical structure can be useful for thinking about the complex ideas behind US aid policy. Aid's opponents were "exemplarists," but some were also actual Isolationists, and others were "vindicators" who wanted vindication done differently.

Broadly, these labels are unsatisfying though, because aid's opponents did not share beliefs about what to do, they shared beliefs about what not to do (or how not to do it), and they came to those beliefs on separate paths. These paths, as this work will illustrate, were not really about aid itself, they were about a vision of government and national mission. Aid's opponents fought pro-aid national leaders, who themselves operated from their own understandings of government power and national mission. Studying their disagreements helps clarify that foreign aid operated in a contested space, and in a larger context, that the collective instincts of pro-foreign aid national leaders and economists were not necessarily universal ones.

In emphasizing ideas, a significant caveat is necessary. As the following chapters will illustrate, anti-aid and pro-aid beliefs were not "either/or" propositions. Many aid opponents did not completely reject the position that government could create economic growth, or that people in other places mattered. Most argued instead that the government could not do as much as aid's advocates believed it could, or that people in other countries mattered less than aid planners seemed to believe. Similarly, many aid supporters believed in limits about what was possible and never believed that all people outside the United States mattered equally. There were not two fixed camps of opponents and supporters; instead, there was a continuum of sensibilities, and there was change over time.

One way of understanding this continuum is by exploring how conversations about aid, especially to politicians, could have a transactional quality. As the text will explain, many legislators' ideas about aid's utility and its foreign policy necessity operated alongside their understanding that aid was political (i.e. that spending needed to be governed by short-term considerations and have concrete political justifications). Legislators understandably felt uncomfortable backing aid unless they could explain to themselves, and theoretically to voters, exactly how it was an appropriate way to spend taxpayer money. Thus, debates about foreign aid spending often reflected narrow interests. Politicians from farm states, or with connections to the maritime industry, for example, wondered how aid programs might benefit their districts, and they regularly tried to modify aid legislation to help their constituents. Similarly, decisions about support or opposition operated within a political party context. Republican legislators were more likely to support plans offered by Republican leaders, just as Democrats were more likely to oppose them. These votes had little to do with aid itself. They were signs of loyalty to the leadership.

This is all to say that debates about aid operated on two levels simultaneously. Philosophical questions about aid's potential for advancing foreign policy goals (or more accurately for this text, its lack of potential for doing so) intersected with legislative priorities and a set of non-absolute ideas about foreign aid. Taken together, that adds up to a story in which opposition was a key factor in the crafting of US foreign aid programs. Supporters needed to acknowledge the opposition and offer plans that might undercut them, and officials in the aid bureaucracy needed to constantly shift their plans depending on how much money they could spend. Although the executive branch in the United States holds responsibility for developing and implementing foreign policy, Congress could wield substantial power over that implementation. Year after year, presidents told Congressional leaders that they needed a specific amount of money to advance their policies, and year after year, Congress gave them less than they wanted. That dynamic also makes this a story about Congressional power over the foreign policy process.

Felix Belair, a *New York Times* reporter who had long covered annual legislative fights over spending legislation, summed up these problems in 1963 in explaining that "almost everybody in Congress votes for foreign aid but hardly anyone likes foreign aid." He claimed few voters backed aid programs, which made it difficult for representatives to vote for them. The other problem, he said, was that "while most people will agree in principle that foreign aid is necessary to provide stability through hope for less favored people of the earth, they are not likely to agree on how much should be spent on the effort."[8] He was probably correct suggesting that "most people" believed in aid and the logic for aid, but as this text will demonstrate, "most people" is quite different than "all people." As importantly, even the ones who could agree on aid's logic could not agree on implementation and how much to spend. Belair noted that President John F. Kennedy wrote Congress asking for a 1964 aid spending bill, arguing, "there is a national consensus of many years standing on the vital importance" of aid programs. Kennedy may have been right about this. There may have been a national consensus (albeit a shaky one), but this text posits that there is a great deal to learn about the people who rejected that consensus – or at least questioned Kennedy's understanding of it. Studying them can help explain domestic politics and conflicting visions about government power and national mission in the post-World War II era. This text does not argue that understanding the debates about aid is enough to understand the totality of these complex issues, only that their contours can become clearer by addressing them.

The importance of foreign aid is far easier to perceive in the historical record than through exploring contemporary rhetoric. Unless prompted by a historian writing a book, conversations about aid are rarely part of the daily national discourse in the United States. There are, to be sure, conversations about the US role in the world and conversations about government power, but they are more often about trade and globalization, social welfare spending, and the amorphous "catch-all" concepts of national security and individual freedom.

During the period explored in this book however, discussions about foreign aid were more prominent. Newspapers and magazines extensively covered debates about foreign aid, and they reported on the multiple spending votes in Congress each year, often on their front pages. This was, in part, because President Harry S. Truman through the Marshall Plan, and President John F. Kennedy through his embrace of modernization theory, made foreign aid central to their foreign policies. Their efforts, and the need to fund those efforts, elevated foreign aid's public profile. Both left their somewhat less enthusiastic successors, Presidents Dwight D. Eisenhower, Lyndon B. Johnson, and Richard M. Nixon, managing on-going high-profile aid efforts, and trying to recast them into something they found viable. This interplay between periods of higher and lower aid enthusiasm is visible in this text, as it impacted how opponents attacked aid spending. Throughout this period though, aid opponents forced aid's advocates to sell a vision of the nation and its government and provided a countering vision that helps explain the period and its long-term impacts on the nation.

Aid opponents were initially outsiders, but over time their challenges helped transform US foreign policy, and their ideas had a powerful impact on national dialogue. They were responsible for raising concerns about the immorality of supporting repressive anti-communist dictatorships in the 1960s, which led directly to an emphasis on international human rights policy in the 1970s. More broadly, they challenged the notion that the United States needed omnipresent global engagement as well as the idea that it had the power to remake the world in its own image. Their success in making this point shifted foreign aid programming away from infrastructure spending and toward giving aid to help recipients meet their basic human needs for food, water, housing, and healthcare. In making these cases, as the initial chapter will argue, they were part of a longer national discussion about US power and globalization and carriers of pre-Cold War ideas into the Cold War era.

Notes

1 The closest thing is Vernon Ruttan's encyclopedia-like text, *United States Development Assistance Policy: The Domestic Politics of Foreign Economic Aid* (Baltimore, 1996).

2 This is mostly a story about economic aid, rather than military aid. The United States offered both kinds of assistance during the Cold War (and beyond), and there is overlap in the ways that advocates and opponents understood them, but had distinct philosophical foundations and different goals. Unless specified in the text, budget figures refer to combined military and economic spending.

3 Donald J. Trump, "Inauguration Speech 2017," *New York Times* (hereafter *NYT*), January 20, 2017.

4 Hillary Clinton, "Swiping at Donald Trump, Argues U.S. Is Vital World Leader," *NYT*, August 31, 2020; "Presidential Candidate Hillary Clinton American Legion

Speech," time.com/4474619/read-hillary-clinton-american-legion-speech (accessed August 20, 2020).

5 Madeleine K. Albright, "Interview on NBC-TV 'The Today Show' with Matt Lauer, February 19, 1998," 1997–2001.state.gov/statements/1998/980219a.html (accessed March 18, 2020).

6 George W. Bush, "Inaugural Address, January 20, 2005," Gerhard Peters and John T. Woolley, eds, The American Presidency Project (hereafter APP), www.presidency.ucsb.edu/node/214048 (accessed November 24, 2020); Andrew J. Bacevich, "Prophets and Poseurs: Niebuhr and Our Times," *World Affairs* 170, 3 (Winter 2008), 24–37; Trevor McCrisken, *American Exceptionalism and the Legacy of Vietnam* (New York, 2003).

7 H. W. Brands, *What America Owes the World: The Struggle for the Soul of Foreign Policy* (Cambridge, UK, 1998); H. W. Brands, "Exemplary America versus Interventionist America," in Robert L. Hutchings, ed., *At the End of the American Century: America's Role in the Post-Cold War World* (London, 1998), 30.

8 Felix Belair, "Congress Reflects a Growing Opposition to Foreign Aid," *NYT*, April 21, 1963.

1

FOREIGN AID IN HISTORICAL CONTEXT

Many historians have argued that studying foreign aid programs reveals essential truths about the people who constructed them; it helps explain how economists and national leaders in the United States and Europe understood Asia, Sub-Saharan Africa, Latin America, and the Middle East, and how these economists and national leaders believed those places could and should be transformed. As tellingly, it can explain how foreign aid planners understood their own societies and their own national histories.[1] Michael Latham, in writing about US aid programs in the 1960s, argued that these understandings could collectively be called an "ideology," a holistic set of ideas that led to a particular approach to the world. The foundational assumption of this ideology, for aid planners, was a belief in "development," that expertise and financing (foreign aid) coming from materially advanced societies could and should promote growth in less materially advanced societies.[2]

Development suggests a hierarchy of nations ranked from "more developed" to "less developed." The differences between them might be measured by per capita gross domestic product, or it could include factors like the opportunities for consumers to purchase factory-made goods or participation in global markets. It also might include a government's potential to fund foreign aid programs. The rungs of the ladder separate more "modern" or "advanced" or "rich" societies from ones that are "traditional" or "backward" or "poor." Movement up the ladder (more industry, more technology, more consumption, and more trade) is "progress," which makes a society better.

Latham was writing about the early 1960s, but as this chapter will argue, the roots of development ideology predated that era. At the end of World War II, as the Cold War began, US leaders already reasonably assumed their country was the wealthiest and most technologically advanced in the world, and believed it was capable of making development happen. As importantly, they determined that aid could be a weapon to fight and win the Cold War. Aid would help construct stable non-communist societies and a cohesive non-communist community of nations in which the United States could be secure and economically prosperous. They reasoned that if less developed countries became modern through US efforts, the people living in them would not be attracted to communism and their leaders would become happy and thankful friends. In this way, aid programs would be a Cold War security policy that would cost far less than war. Another advantage would be that aid-receiving nations would be willing and capable trading partners. This would strengthen the US economy in the short run and provide a foundation for global prosperity and economic integration over the long term. US leaders thus understood foreign aid both as a tactical weapon for winning the Cold War and as a tool for advancing broad US economic interests; aid was not only good for the people in poorer societies, it was good for the people of the United States.[3]

However, throughout this period, there was always substantial opposition to foreign aid programming. Critics, broadly speaking, challenged the logic of one of two interconnected ideas on which development ideologies rested (or both). Some rejected the notion that government could move other societies up a development ladder from poor to rich, traditional to modern, and backward to advanced; and that external interventions could make people's lives better. Others fought the idea that government should be involved in the lives of people outside the state. They rejected the belief that other people mattered to the people in the nation, and that helping them would strengthen the country.[4] From these opposition perspectives, foreign aid made no sense. There was no point in spending money on foreign aid if that money could not improve other societies, and there was no point in spending money on foreign aid if there was no benefit to be gained in the spending.

These opposition perspectives were not new in the Cold War period; both had roots in much older historical debates. In exploring those roots, this chapter helps explain that clashes over foreign aid were, as Latham argued, fundamentally about contested visions of the nation, the nature of society, and its purpose.[5]

The First Idea: Alexander Hamilton and Government Power

The first of these two ideas, that government could promote economic development, can be traced back to Alexander Hamilton, its most important advocate in the early national period. Hamilton was not alone in pushing this idea, and certainly not the first to advance this philosophical case, but because of his role in early national government, it makes sense to start with him. Throughout his public career, including most importantly as Secretary of the Treasury in President George Washington's cabinet, he pushed for the construction of a powerful state with a dominant executive that could spur developmental progress. Making this point, he wrote in Federalist Papers 11 that "Under a vigorous national government, the natural strength and resources of the country, directed to a common interest, would baffle all the combinations of European jealousy to restrain our growth … ."[6]

More specifically, he believed commerce and industry had to be the foundation for transformative economic progress, therefore government effort should support them in moving the nation up a developmental ladder. He wrote, again in Federalist 11, that without a powerful government, an "unequaled spirit of enterprise, which signalizes the genius of the American merchants and navigators, and which is in itself an inexhaustible mine of national wealth, would be stifled and lost, and poverty and disgrace would overspread a country which, with wisdom, might make herself the admiration and envy of the world."[7] In the following essay, Federalist 12, he argued, "The prosperity of commerce is now perceived and acknowledged by all enlightened statesmen to be the most useful as well as the most productive source of national wealth."[8]

This vision was at the core of Hamilton's much longer 1791 *Report to Congress on the Subject of Manufactures* in which he maintained that capitalists in manufacturing fields needed government backing to succeed. He wrote, "It is in the interest of nations to diversify the industrious pursuits" of non-agricultural economic activity, which was "calculated to increase the general stock of useful and productive labor." Government funding was especially important in the United States because, compared to historically wealthier European societies, there was limited private capital available for investment. Government needed to intervene, he said, to borrow money from abroad, help attract European capital, and invest in building a foundation for domestic trade and production.[9]

The radicalism of his views is most apparent when considered alongside those of contemporary theorists – most influentially, Adam Smith. In *The Wealth of Nations*, Smith argued in 1776 that

> No regulation of commerce can increase the quantity of industry in any society beyond what its capital can maintain. It can only divert a part of it into a direction into which it might not otherwise have gone; and it is by no means certain that this artificial direction is likely to be more advantageous to the society than that into which it would have gone of its own accord.[10]

That is, states should allow markets to operate without interference. Avoiding interventionism (a *laissez-faire* approach) would help businesses to grow organically and efficiently.[11] In sum, while Hamilton argued that government should and could promote economic growth, Smith argued it could not and should not.

Hamilton's views also developed in a way that set him at odds with Thomas Jefferson and James Madison. Both did agree that a powerful state was necessary to protect national independence, and that weak government had made fighting the British harder. They also embraced the idea that a vigorous government was an antidote to political chaos. Yet they understood the role of government differently. They rejected the idea that commerce and industry should be the bedrock of the national economy, and instead hoped the new government would promote an agrarian society of independent farmers. Commerce and industry were dangerous because they concentrated power in a few hands, and urban people working in shops and factories could never fully be free. Land ownership, and the autonomy that came with it, they believed, was the cornerstone of freedom; an agrarian democracy, in which independent farmers held sway, would safeguard a wide distribution of power.[12]

The essential job of government, to Jefferson and Madison, was providing order so that freedom and liberty could flourish. This built on the enlightenment idea that government was dangerous, especially if powerful and active, because it could limit basic human rights.[13] Democracy, they believed, was virtuous because it freed a citizenry from a self-interested elite while also keeping order. These concerns about government power also motivated anti-Federalists, who opposed the Constitution and hoped to preserve the Articles of Confederation. Patrick Henry of Virginia and Melancton Smith of New York both argued that real power should remain with state and local officials, as a vigorous national government, by definition, meant less local autonomy and freedom, and greatly increased the potential for dictatorship or corruption. To be clear, Jefferson, Madison, and the anti-Federalists did not see this issue as Smith had. They did not reject the notion that state power could be effective in promoting development; instead, they saw Hamilton's modernization theories as destructive to democracy.[14]

The Question of Government Power After Hamilton

Initially Hamilton seemed to have lost this debate. As Secretary of the Treasury his greatest success had been the establishment of a national bank, however this united his foes and strengthened their resolve to fight pro-industrial and pro-commerce government policy. Hamilton and his allies increasingly lost influence, and Jefferson's win in the 1800 presidential election was so complete that Hamilton's political party, the Federalists, never regained national power, and by the mid-1810s it had essentially disappeared. Its ideas were unpopular in a nation composed of farms and small towns. Andrew Jackson's presidential election victory in 1828 was a climax of anti-Hamiltonianism in its celebration of the idea that ordinary citizens living on farms and small towns should manage the state, while policies dedicated to helping business leaders get richer were dangerous to the nation's political equality.[15]

Yet Hamilton's approach never completely went away. His logic was key to New York State governor DeWitt Clinton's effort to construct the Erie Canal between 1817 and 1825 and to the multiple canal-building projects that followed. His ideas were also important in mobilizing opposition to Jackson. In 1832, the influential Kentucky senator Henry Clay proposed a Hamiltonian-like plan for internal infrastructure development. The American System, as Clay called it, envisioned government spending on roads, canals, and other infrastructure to strengthen the state and extend prosperity through increased trade and manufacturing. Clay, and others who joined him in the new Whig party, believed state spending could advance progress, and that evolution from barbarism to civilization was the goal of the human condition; small towns were not the future, they argued, cities and factories were.[16] The Whigs did not survive the tumult of the pre-Civil War period, but their ideas about a government role in helping trade and industry drove their post-Civil War successors, the Republicans, and provided them with the logic for what could be considered the first foreign aid program in US history, the post-Civil War reconstruction effort in the South.[17]

Toward the turn of the century, Progressive Era reformers similarly embraced vigorous government. Herbert Croly, the longtime editor of the *New Republic* and a leading Progressive intellectual, wrote in *The Promise of American Life* that "every popular government should in the end … possess the power of taking any action, which, in the opinion of a decisive majority of the people, is demanded by the public welfare."[18] Croly had been inspired in part by Hamilton, noting the founding father had understood "that genuine liberty was not merely a matter of a constitutional declaration of rights. It could be protected only by an energetic and clear-sighted national government, and it could be fertilized only by the efficient national organization of American activities."[19]

Woodrow Wilson, while still in academia and long before he became president, wrote about these ideas in his 1898 text, *The State: Elements of Practical and Historical Politics*. He explained that government was "the organ of society, its only potent and universal instrument" for advancing progress, and wrote that "it should be the end of government to accomplish the objects of organized society." Like Jefferson and Madison however, Wilson worried about the destructive impact of economic development. He wrote that industrialization "has so distorted competition as sometimes to put it into the power of some to tyrannize over many" and enabled the "rich and the strong to combine against the weak." But government was the solution. To protect justice, he wrote there needed to be "constant adjustments of governmental assistance to the needs of a changing social and industrial organization." The goal of these adjustments (i.e. regulations) was not interference in individual liberty, but to create the "equalization of conditions, so far as possible, in all branches of endeavor." Wilson was saying there was no way to return to a bucolic Jefferson-imagined world in which each citizen could be autonomously independent. Activist government power was the only way to advance freedom (which he thought was the core element of progress) in the industrial world.[20]

Like Wilson, Theodore Roosevelt also supported activist government in the name of national development, though he advocated for a different type of activism. In his 1912 speech offering his platform as the Progressive Party candidate for president, he argued that the whole point of elections was to place public policy experts into positions of authority. It was their job to study the matters for which the people "cannot be intimately acquainted" and then to "formulate a policy for … [the] betterment" of all. He echoed Wilson and said he worried about justice in an increasingly industrial age, and argued that only government could police business and keep it from operating "under conditions inimical to the social welfare." Without government, capitalism would create an "abnormal" and "ruthless" society that would "drag down all to the level of the least considerate." Only government by policy experts could fight industry, regulate it, and keep people free from its destructive forces. It was also, as Hamilton would have insisted, the only way to create an efficient economy that could compete with the European industrial powers.[21]

Concerns About Government Power

Ideas about the dangers of government remained popular. In his still timely classic 1963 study, *Anti-Intellectualism in American Life*, historian Richard Hofstadter tracked the ways people outside the largest US cities fearfully and emotionally responded to urbanization, industrialization, and expanding government power in the nineteenth century. He explained that people in rural communities and small towns often thought that people living in cities seemed to have lost their democratic and traditional "American" cultural values. National government, in that it was supportive of industrialization, located in urban areas and dominated by wealthy educated elites, was part of the problem. These concerns, expressed as anti-intellectualism, were not always exactly anti-government, but their instincts were similar, and they fed off a parallel skepticism that elites were controlling the country for their own good; it was government spending that only enriched officeholders and their cronies in Washington and New York. Hofstadter followed up with an essay in 1964 describing this as "The Paranoid Style in American Politics," suggesting that these conspiratorial suspicions were an integral part of nineteenth-century populist belief systems.[22]

Urban elites also attacked the idea that government could solve problems, though. The influential journalist and academic, Henry Jones Ford, worried in the early 1900s that expanding government would create an anti-democratic or non-democratic society, as a civil service dedicated to advancing government efficiency would be insulated from political processes. Ford argued this violated basic constitutional principles. The point of elections, he suggested, was for elected representatives to determine the will of the people and what the state should do.[23] He appreciated that voters were "incapable of serving as an organ of administration," but argued they could serve as "an agency of control" ensuring accountability.[24] As worrisome, and certainly connected, was his understanding that the term "reform" had "become synonymous with improvement," and therefore questioning reform meant, in a political context, that one was against the evolution of society.[25] This stifled dissent and made sure that technocrats, rather than voters, would hold the real power.

Ford was stating ideas that President William Howard Taft explained in writing about his Jeffersonian understanding of limited government. Taft argued that government's essential purpose was to preserve liberty and property, which were the basis for civilization and prosperity. He suggested, as Adam Smith would have argued, that if government could secure liberty and property, economic development would develop naturally.[26] Thus, the sole goal of the state should be establishing law and order. Taft differed from Ford by arguing that government did not need to respond to the will of the citizenry because people were often whimsical and irresponsible. A legal system with judges operating above the fray of politics would allow for incremental progress, Taft thought, which would be better than government-driven growth or chaotic democracy. "Great reforms," he said, "should not be brought about overnight. They need time. They should be marked by careful consideration." In this argument, Taft veered toward the English philosopher, Edmund Burke, who also believed that the problem with democracy was that people – ordinary and uneducated people – did not have the basic competency to manage government. In Burke's conception, as well as in Taft's, elections were for voters to choose between elites who offered competing agendas. Only the elite, Taft believed, could create stable governments and protect the rights of individuals and minority groups. This was not exactly anti-government action: Taft believed in government, but was skeptical of its ability to directly advance development or progress.[27]

The Second Idea: Washington and Entanglements

As later chapters will explain, foreign aid's opponents built on Jefferson's and Madison's ideas and Taft's perspective, and they often saw the world through the anti-intellectual lenses that Hofstadter described. But this was only one part of the argument. The second idea undergirding foreign aid's logic is that the United States government should engage with people and governments outside it; that involvement in the political, economic, or cultural affairs of other societies can strengthen them, and in turn strengthen the United States. This idea, as with the previous one, has a long contested history dating back to the creation of the republic.

Here the story starts with George Washington. In his farewell address (written in collaboration with Hamilton), he offered guidance for dealing with the rest of the world, arguing that engagement with Europe would be dangerous and that national security and development would best be secured by remaining internationally aloof. He asserted that

> The great rule of conduct for us in regard to foreign nations is in extending our commercial relations, [but] to have with them as little political connection as possible. So far as we have already formed engagements, let them be fulfilled with perfect good faith. Here let us stop. Europe has a set of primary interests which to us have none; or a very remote relation. Hence she must

> be engaged in frequent controversies, the causes of which are essentially foreign to our concerns. Hence, therefore, it must be unwise in us to implicate ourselves by artificial ties in the ordinary vicissitudes of her politics, or the ordinary combinations and collisions of her friendships or enmities.

He added, along similar lines, "Why quit our own to stand upon foreign ground? Why, by interweaving our destiny with that of any part of Europe, entangle our peace and prosperity in the toils of European ambition, rivalship, interest, humor or caprice?"[28] Four years later, in his inaugural address, Jefferson pithily restated Washington's preposition as "peace, commerce, and honest friendship with all nations, entangling alliances with none."[29]

In part because this principle stemmed from Washington and Jefferson (and Hamilton), it operated as established and core wisdom throughout the nineteenth century. It was also logical and excellent advice. The United States was weak, relative to the European powers, and its experiences in interacting with them in the early national period, including in the Quasi-War with France (1798–1800) and in the War in 1812 with the British, demonstrated the danger of getting caught up in their intrigues.[30] Further strengthening the principle, President John Quincy Adams proclaimed in his July 4, 1821 address that

> America goes not abroad in search of monsters to destroy … . She well knows that by once enlisting under other banners than her own, were they even the banners of foreign independence, she would involve herself beyond the power of extrication in all the wars of interest and intrigue, of individual avarice, envy and ambition, which assume the colors and usurp the standards of freedom.[31]

This idea resonated with small farmers and settlers in western communities in the nineteenth century as an essential part of their value systems. Far from population centers and entirely reliant on their own resources, they generally believed that self-reliance was a virtue and there were tangible dangers in the external world; they believed that engagement in the wider world could weaken their communities and was a danger to their independence. This does not necessarily mean they were entirely individualist, or that they rejected communities and community values. Communities of like-minded people could be relied upon and could be the locus of self-reliant collective action, but the larger, external world was beyond their responsibility.[32]

Complete disengagement proved impossible and impractical in the long term, though. In his 1823 State of the Union address, President James Monroe reasserted Washington and Jefferson's principle that "In the wars of the European powers in matters relating to themselves we have never taken any part, nor does it comport with our policy so to do." However, he added that this prescription was not to be applied to the Americas because the emergence of newly independent nations in Latin America required a different response. The United States was "intimately connected" with events on its side of the Atlantic Ocean, and he therefore declared, "we should consider any attempt on" the part of Europeans "to extend their system to any portion of this hemisphere as dangerous to our peace and safety." This line formed the core of the Monroe Doctrine.[33]

Nothing in the Monroe Doctrine was inconsistent with the sentiment behind "entangling alliances with none," as long as that "none" meant Europe. It asserted a new dictum, though, that things that happened outside the United States should matter to the United States government. Specifically in this case, the United States had a responsibility to its neighbors to protect them from European imperialism. It was a kind of paternalism on which foreign aid would eventually rest.[34]

In making an exception for the Western Hemisphere, the Monroe Doctrine reflected the many ways that people in the United States increasingly were engaged in external communities, despite the Farewell Address. Much of this was commercial. In the colonial era, US merchants developed a substantial maritime fleet whose total profits, by the revolution, were second only to those of tobacco production. Independence freed these merchants to explore further abroad in search of commercial opportunities. In the 1780s, for example, Elias Haskett Derby of Salem, Massachusetts, became the country's first millionaire by shipping goods to and from India.[35] Then, as Latin Americans fought for independence from Spain in the first and second decade of the nineteenth century, US merchants developed a profitable trade in arming the revolutionaries. The establishment of new republics throughout the hemisphere further opened up new ports and new opportunities to US fleets. Spanish reconquest would have destroyed that potential. Monroe and, more importantly, his Secretary of State, John Quincy Adams (the force behind the Monroe Doctrine and a New Englander closely connected to merchant families), were keenly aware that the health of the national economy depended on international trade; they determined it was necessary to use state power to advance the maritime-related commercial interests; the United States, to strengthen itself, needed to become more internationally engaged. This decision served as a precursor to other kinds of outward-oriented state behavior in the nineteenth century that included expansionism and missionary activity, which in their own ways also laid the foundation for foreign aid programs in the twentieth century.

In 1845, the journalist John Louis O'Sullivan coined the term "Manifest Destiny" following the annexation of Texas. He wrote that Texas had been "absorbed into the Union in the inevitable fulfillment of the general law which is rolling our population westward."[36] Expansion was inevitable, he had earlier written, because the United States had developed perfect governmental systems that defined the "duty of man to man, and consequently man's rights as man." Both metaphorically and literally, he thought the nation was "entering on its untrodden space, with the truths of God in our minds, beneficent objects in our hearts, and with a clear conscience unsullied by the past. We are," he added, "the nation of human progress."[37] The country would climb up a developmental ladder because God had blessed its people, because they would use new lands to establish a society better than anything then known, and because the land was empty.

The power of O'Sullivan's phrasing was not its revelation of hidden truths; it was an appealing way to describe popular ideas already widely held. Movement west in the colonial era, and the rapid expansion of migration in the early national period, accelerated by the completion of the Erie Canal in 1827, had turned a coastal nation into an increasingly continental one. O'Sullivan justified Manifest Destiny as bringing national values to the wilderness. He suggested colonization was moral because it advanced civilization. Settlement had the potential to transform and develop the world, and because adherents saw material development as inherently good, settlement was inherently good. Non-white people in the "wilderness," in O'Sullivan's judgement, were not fully realized humans. They were wild, like the lands they lived in, and thus they could not claim to own that land. They would need to be either educated and uplifted or eliminated.

James K. Polk, the most important proponent of national growth, won the 1844 presidential election on this expansionist platform. In his inaugural address in March 1845, beyond calling for the annexation of Texas, he said he would "assert and maintain … the right of the United States to that portion of our territory which lies beyond the Rocky Mountains." The country had expanded rapidly across the Mississippi valley and more recently emigrants had populated the Missouri valley and settled even further west along the Pacific Ocean. Although some of these settlers lived beyond the nation's technical boundaries, and he pledged that all treaties would "be sacredly respected," he further insisted that "the jurisdiction of our laws and the benefits of our republican institutions should be extended over them in the distant regions which they have selected their homes." The United States, he said, would be responsible for places that were outside the nation in the name of advancing civilization.[38]

Expansionism as Immoral

At every stage of this expansionism, however, there was opposition, often expressed as a violation of national values. For example, one of Abraham Lincoln's most notable actions as a young congressional representative from Illinois had been to challenge James K. Polk's justification of the war with Mexico in 1846. Polk claimed the Mexican army attacked a US unit, which was an act of war, and thus his request for a declaration of war was not an act of aggression, but one of defense. Lincoln, and others opposed to the war, suspected (correctly) that US forces had been ordered to cross into territory claimed and occupied by Mexico. If this were the case, the United States was responsible for starting the war; it was imperialism, and Mexico was acting defensively. Thus, Lincoln's famous "spot resolution" demanded that Polk provide evidence that the Mexican attacks had occurred on US soil.[39]

The writer Henry David Thoreau similarly believed war in Mexico represented a distortion of national values. In his 1849 treatise "Resistance to Civil Government" he argued with Jeffersonian logic that "Government is at best but an expedient; but most governments are usually, and all governments are sometimes, inexpedient… The government itself, which is only the mode which the people have chosen to execute their will, is equally liable to be abused and perverted before the people can act through it."[40] Personal and national greed had led to war with Mexico, and citizens who understood the injustice of an aggressive foreign policy, to Thoreau, had a responsibility to challenge US power. Expansionism by definition was imperialism, and imperialism by definition was immoral. In his own way, Thoreau was also making an argument that people in other states mattered. It mattered that they might be subject to imperialism. If they did not matter, their destiny was not meaningful and it would be acceptable to exploit them.

Implicit in this argument was the belief that the United States' founding was a moral event, and that as a democracy the nation had a greater responsibility to advance peace and freedom than states merely responsible for promoting stability and protecting their own people. The United States was supposed to be better, somehow, than amoral states. This idea had predated the revolution and was at the core of John Winthrop's oft-quoted 1630 "City Upon a Hill" sermon. Before embarking on the journey to Massachusetts, Winthrop told his followers that, like the ancient Israelites, they had made a covenant with the Lord, and the way to fulfill that covenant was to "follow the counsel of Micah, to do justly, to love mercy, to walk humbly." The way to justify their effort was by turning the new colony into a model for the rest of the world. People looking at what Winthrop's followers had done would say of their own lands, "May the Lord make it like that of New England. For we must consider that we shall be as a city upon a hill." Abraham Lincoln restated this idea in his Gettysburg Address when he proclaimed that the key question in the Civil War was if a nation "conceived in liberty and dedicated to the proposition that all men are created equal … can long endure." A Northern victory would demonstrate the affirmative, "that government of the people, by the people, for the people shall not perish from the earth."[41] The point of national power, Lincoln intoned, was not power itself but the moral purposes that would be advanced through the preservation of democratic values.

Missionaries and National Values

This connection between values and national power can also be a way of thinking about nineteenth-century missionaries. Operating globally (but primarily in Asia), Protestant missionaries were committed to improving material conditions and to development of "modern" worldviews in the service of a higher power. As such, they too were predecessors to foreign aid advocates in the post-World War II era.

There was a growing curiosity about the external world in the early part of the nineteenth century, especially in port cities, as merchants returned home with artifacts from other civilizations. Improvements in newspaper and book printing similarly exposed wide audiences to travel and exploration narratives, again often coming through sailors. Historian John Rogers Haddad argued this literature did little to teach about the reality of other cultures, but instead allowed for the construction of romantic and exotic imaginary foreign worlds of adventure, wonder, and opportunity.[42] These visions spread at the same time a social activist movement was developing, especially in religious communities. In the decades leading up to the Civil War, key northern Protestant figures including Charles Finney and Lyman Beecher had preached that slavery was immoral, which encouraged lay citizens, especially women, to form organizations to push for its abolition. Historian Patricia Hill argues that after the war, the success of abolitionism (i.e. emancipation) encouraged these same women to use their power and resources to attempt a bigger challenge, bringing the blessings of their civilization to peoples everywhere enslaved by traditional societies. They did not know much about other, non-white people, yet still determined that they needed to be helped.[43]

This impulse connected with older Protestant ideas about evangelization. As early as the seventeenth century, religious leaders in New England had worked to convert and assimilate indigenous peoples. These efforts were sporadic and disorganized. Change came with the Second Great Awakening in the early nineteenth century, which spurred evangelical fervor and led to increased missionary activity. In 1810, Congregationalists ministers created the American Board of Commissioners for Foreign Missions to sponsor the initial efforts to convert the peoples of the Sandwich Islands and Hawai'i; by the 1830s Congregationalists were setting up missions in Africa, China, and eventually in Japan. Other Protestant movements followed (Presbyterians Baptist, Methodist, Episcopalian, and Reformed) in organizing missionaries, especially in the post-Civil War era.[44]

Historian Jennifer Snow argues that Protestant missionaries differed in their approaches and goals. She wrote,

> Missionaries who believed in humanitarian and educational work, either for its own sake or as an aid to "Christianizing" the heathen culture, usually had a modernist view of the Bible, comfortable with historical criticism and the language of science. Many of them, in the early twentieth century, began to question the nature of Christian "finality" – the sense in which Christianity was superior in degree and kind to other religions … . Other missionaries continued to emphasize the oral evangelism and the translation of the Bible into heathen languages as the sole work to which missionaries should give themselves; they criticized humanitarian works as a distraction from the duty of the missionary to "make disciples," especially since there was little evidence that education and medicine led to conversion; they focused on individual sin and salvation, defined Christianity as the only religion not of

> Satan's making, and demanded allegiance among converts and missionaries, to a literal and inerrant scripture.[45]

Either way, however, missionaries shared the view that uplift of foreign peoples was a responsibility of people with means. They implicitly believed that the lives of the peoples in foreign lands mattered, and are similar, in this way, to postwar aid theorists who hoped to eliminate "backward" ways of thinking, and who wanted to bring a measure of equality to technologically and materially disadvantaged peoples. In the Cold War era, pro-aid US leaders believed, like missionaries, that non-whites the world over could become developed through the successful application of western systems. Missionaries were different only in that they thought Christianity was a prerequisite for modernization.

There was also a racial element behind these efforts. Josiah Strong, a prominent Protestant clergyman, argued in 1885 that Anglo-Saxons were the "depository" race of the blessings of civil liberty and Christian civilization, which was only possible because of their racial superiority. Anglo-Saxon supremacy, he suggested, was the product of the mixing of mostly Norman, Saxon, and Danish blood with supplemental doses of other northern Europeans peoples (Celts, Gauls, Welsh, Irish, Frisian). The resulting "unequaled energy," "indomitable perseverance," and "personal independence" meant that the Anglo-Saxon would have a "genius for colonizing," and in so doing they would improve the world.

Strong predicted that Anglo-Saxons would conquer the whole world. "Some of the stronger races," he said "doubtless, may be able to preserve their integrity; but, in order to compete with the Anglo-Saxon, they will probably be forced to adopt his methods and instruments, his civilization and his religion."

Change would not come from active missionary activity, but from a recognition among other people that they needed to abandon their own cultures. He wrote, "contact of Christian with heathen nations is awaking the latter to new life. Old superstitions are loosening their grasp. The dead crust of fossil faiths is being shattered by the movements of life underneath." In the United States, God was also at work, "training the Anglo-Saxon race for its mission." God was "preparing in our civilization the die with which to stamp the nations" and "preparing mankind to receive our impress." This, in short, was a development ideology.[46] Strong believed in national superiority and the inevitability and justice of expansion into other "uncivilized" lands. He shared, along with O'Sullivan, Polk, and missionaries, the fundamental assumption that people living in other lands were inferior and needed the guiding hand of the United States and its people.

Embracing Expansion and Responsibility

In the last years of the nineteenth century, rising US economic power allowed national leaders to think more expansively about government's potential, and simultaneously to fully explore the idea of national responsibility for others. As in earlier periods however, there was substantial opposition to global engagement because of a belief that it was neither possible to transform the world nor the responsibility of the United States government to do it. These debates, especially about joining World War I, the lessons of that war, and most importantly entering World War II, provided the framework for US Cold War engagement. In the postwar era, few people wanted to argue that joining World War II had been a mistake, and foreign aid programs came from a desire to learn from the past and do things differently.

But exploring opposition to global engagement in the pre-World War II period is helpful as more than just a case study for understanding what policymakers in the postwar era wanted to avoid. It helps clarify how ideas about opposition to foreign aid developed and helps demonstrate that, just as with postwar foreign aid, opponents of global engagement in the prewar period came from multiple sectors of society. It also raises a question about how "normal" an expansive globalist Cold War foreign policy was in the sweep of US history, and suggests the existence of a powerful long-run skepticism of global engagement that, as following chapters will explain, would later find expression in the fight against foreign aid.

In 1890, the naval theorist Alfred Thayer Mahan published the *Influence of Sea Power Upon History, 1660–1783*. The widely read book suggested that naval power was the key to national power, and led to his call in a follow-up essay, "The United States Looking Outward," for an expanded national navy and a system of worldwide bases. He argued, "Americans must now begin to look outward. The growing production of the country demands it." For Mahan, the mechanism to do this was government spending, especially on the navy. He insisted the problem holding back the country was that "We have not the navy, and, what is worse, we are not willing to have the navy, that will weigh seriously in any disputes with those nations whose interests will conflict there with our own."[47]

Mahan was mostly interested in empire and expansion in geopolitical terms, and he was not alone in calling for exercising US power beyond national borders. Rapid post-Civil War economic growth had led to growing confidence, and perhaps hubris, about the nation's potential, and a desire to look for new challenges. The historian, Fredrick Jackson Turner's arguments played into this belief, and like Mahan, he pushed expansionism. In 1893, Turner suggested that the national character had been forged through the taming and settlement of western lands. This constant return to the "primitive conditions" of the frontier, which was a "meeting point between savagery and civilization," had led to the "perennial rebirth" that made the nation's people unique. Because of the frontier they had a "coarseness and strength combined with acuteness and inquisitiveness" and a "practical, inventive turn of mind, quick to find expedients." They had a "restless, nervous energy" and the "buoyancy and exuberance which comes with freedom." The problem, as Turner identified it, was that the frontier had ceased to exist by 1890. These traits would wither away if people did not identify new areas with frontier conditions and find new challenges that would encourage rebirth cycles of national reinvention.[48]

In 1898, Charles Conant, an influential writer on economic issues, presented a simpler argument that addressed the shifting global context. He said it seemed unwise to "adhere to a policy of isolation while other nations are reaching out for the command of … new markets." He accepted that there were moral considerations involved in becoming an imperial power, but said that the United States would not actually be imperialistic as long as it was limiting itself to pushing for global free trade. This argument was central to US Secretary of State John Hay's "Open Door Note" in 1899. Hay would call upon European governments that held treaty rights in China to allow US ships to operate in their spheres of influence on terms equal to those of their own merchants. Conant also argued it would also be acceptable to establish "the direct government over groups of half-savage islands" to "safeguard and extend commercial interests." Failing to obtain outlets for US manufactured goods, or colonies, would lead to a "glut of unconsumed products, the convulsions followed by trade stagnation, and the steadily declining return upon investments" within the United States.[49]

These ideas, and public support for them, led to more global engagement. An early example came as the United States intervened in a dispute between Venezuela and Great Britain about the boundary between them (the contemporary Venezuelan-Guyana border) in 1895. President Grover Cleveland's Secretary of State, Richard Olney, insisted that the United States needed to protect Venezuela from a potential European land grab, which would be a violation of the Monroe Doctrine; he successfully pushed the British government to accept US-organized arbitration. Although the decision was ultimately unfavorable to the Venezuelans, the United States stood up for the principle that it was responsible for the people of other states.

Then, in 1898, building on the Venezuelan precedent, Republican President William McKinley inserted the United States into the Cuban independence struggle, claiming that for humanitarian reasons, war between Cuban rebels and the Spanish must end, and that intervention was necessary to protect Cuban "life and property." This action could not be defended with a Monroe Doctrine justification; Cuba was legally held by Spain. It could only be warranted on the principle that the destinies of non-citizens living outside the nation-state mattered to the United States, and that government could fix the problem. It represented a victory for belief systems about the power of government and national responsibilities for others.

Turn-of-the-Century Anti-Imperialists

Amidst these events there was opposition. Historian Robert Beisner, in his classic 1968 text, *Twelve Against Empire*, cataloged the ideas of two sets of leading anti-imperialists who attacked the shift in US policy. One key group was the Mugwumps, elite public intellectuals that included Charles Francis Adams, Jr., William Lloyd Garrison, Jr., Charles Eliot Norton, William Dean Howells, and also the more populist Mark Twain. Mugwumps lamented the nation's growing industrial culture and rising ethnic diversity, worrying that their vision of civilization was under threat. As Beisner wrote, "The more America departed from her original character, the more it seemed to the Mugwumps that she began to resemble the old nations of Europe." He continued, this "trend, if unchecked, would be fatal to a nation that had been created as an escape from and an improvement upon an imperfect European civilization."[50] Thus, a war of conquest emerging from selfish economic considerations was necessarily dangerous. It was a step that would take the United States further from its white, elitist, Jeffersonian commitment to individual and autonomous liberty over societal development.

The Yale sociologist, William Graham Sumner, shared the Mugwump view that the path to empire would lead to the long-term destruction of the United States. In an 1899 lecture published as *The Conquest of the United States by Spain*, he argued that "expansionism and imperialism are nothing but the old philosophies of national prosperity… and they will lead us to ruin unless we are hard-headed enough to resist them." One problem was the cost of empire. He noted that pro-war senators said the United States would stay in Cuba only as long as was necessary to prepare the people to manage their own government. This would cost at least $20,000,000, Sumner said, but that investment might not even have any impact. Sumner made a larger point though, that empire was, by definition, antithetical to national values. Writing about US occupation of the Philippines, he said, "we assume that what we like and practice, and what we think better, must come as a welcome blessing" to colonized people. He insisted this was "grossly and obviously untrue. They hate our ways. They are hostile to our ideas. Our religion, language, institutions, and manners offend them. They like their own ways." The fundamental problem with empire, he argued, was that it began by "saying to somebody else: We know what is good for you better than you know yourself, and we are going to make you do it." This was the opposite of liberty. He concluded, "If we believe in liberty, as an American principle, why do we not stand by it?"[51]

Beisner also explained there was a second set of national leaders opposed to McKinley's expansionist policies, and to those of his successor, Theodore Roosevelt (who even more ardently wanted the United States to embrace an imperial destiny). Exemplified by the Massachusetts senator George Frisbie Hoar and the leading industrialist Andrew Carnegie, these Republican leaders had been close allies to McKinley and Roosevelt, but objected to imperialism on more practical grounds. Hoar rejected the notion that US power was necessary to improve conditions in places like the Philippines or the Caribbean. In his view, the peoples of all races shared a "love of liberty" that would allow them to construct their own governments, and that would guarantee that they would rebel if colonized. Becoming a global imperial power would mean necessarily fighting against the forces of liberty abroad.[52]

Carnegie shared the sentiment with the Mugwumps, and with Hoar, that imperialism was incongruous with national values and would lead to a destruction of the unique character of the national democracy. He also, perhaps befitting his position as a leading industrialist, focused on the economics of an imperialistic policy. Sumner had suggested that the spending associated with empire might be a waste, but Carnegie made a more nuanced argument that expansionist and colonial ventures, especially in the Philippines, would not pay for themselves. He argued the costs of administering empire would be greater than the economic benefits derived from them, and taxpayers would end up with the bill. The United States had built its industrial trade power on the concept of an open door (the rejection of imperial preferences in global trade). In becoming an imperial power itself, it would need to either reject the open door, which would destroy US trade, or allow the open door in the Philippines. If the latter was the decision, and it was, other nations could trade more efficiently with the Philippines, meaning that there would be no economic advantage gained.[53] The United States might manage a global empire, but it should not. It would be a waste of money.

Samuel Gompers, the leader of the American Federation of Labor (AFL), also offered an economic anti-imperialist argument. He had joined the Mugwumps in founding the Anti-Imperialist League in Boston in 1898, but viewed the issue as connected to workers' livelihood. As spelled out in the AFL convention's 1898 resolution, maintaining a standing army and navy to protect an empire would "burden" workers, who would inevitably end up paying for them. He also feared industrialists might develop factories within new colonies that would drive down labor costs. Following a meeting with President Roosevelt in 1902, Gompers and the AFL changed their position somewhat. While stating they were still concerned about imperialism in general, they supported US efforts in Puerto Rico on the condition that its inhabitants obtain full citizenship and labor unions would be legal there. This would eliminate the problem of outsourced labor.[54]

A bit further outside of the national intellectual mainstream of the era, the influential African-American scholar and activist, W. E. B. Du Bois, objected to imperialism from a labor and Marxist perspective. In *The Souls of Black Folk* (1903), Du Bois emphasized that cotton production and export in the US South, its most valuable commodity, was part of an imperial capitalist system built on the exploitation of black labor that had allowed the United States to become powerful. Here he was essentially paraphrasing Karl Marx, who had written, "Without slavery you have no cotton; without cotton you have no modern industry .... Cause slavery to disappear and you will have wiped America off the map of nations."[55] In his 1920 book, *Darkwater: Voices from Within the Veil*, Du Bois expressed a more transnational critique of imperialism and labor exploitation. He wrote that, by 1900, "White supremacy was all but world-wide, Africa was dead, India conquered, Japan isolated, and China prostrate, while white America whetted her sword for mongrel Mexico and mulatto South America, lynching her own Negroes all the while." This imperialism was allowing for new and more exploitation. He wrote that "modern white civilization" could no longer be maintained through the subjugation of "white working classes" because of processes (democracy and education) that allowed for a distribution of wealth. "The day of the very rich," he wrote, "is drawing to a close, so far as individual white nations are concerned." But there was a way to avoid that outcome:

> There is a chance for exploitation on an immense scale for inordinate profit, not simply to the very rich, but to the middle class and to the laborers. This chance lies in the exploitation of darker peoples. It is here that the golden hand beckons. Here are no labor unions or votes or questioning onlookers or inconvenient consciences. These men may be used down to the very bone, and shot and maimed in "punitive" expeditions when they revolt. In these dark lands "industrial development" may repeat in exaggerated form every horror of the industrial history of Europe, from slavery and rape to disease and maiming, with only one test of success, – dividends![56]

Transnational elements of exploitation, as interpreted through a Marxist lens, also animated the labor leader Eugene Debs, who challenged US involvement in World War I. In his June 1918 Canton, Ohio, speech, he explained that "wars throughout history have been waged for conquest and plunder." In the feudal era when lords hoped to increase their power, they "declared war upon one another. But they themselves did not go to war any more than the modern feudal lords, the barons of Wall Street go to war." It was their "miserable serfs who fought all the battles… The master class has always declared the wars; the subject class has always fought the battles. The master class has had all to gain and nothing to lose, while the subject class has had nothing to gain and all to lose – especially their lives." Because war was serf against serf for the advancement of their masters, it was illogical for serfs to decide to fight; it was illogical for workers in the United States to decide to fight in Europe. The masses had no reason to engage themselves in the affairs of foreign lands. This speech resulted in his arrest, conviction, and incarceration for violating the Espionage Act of 1917 on the grounds that he had encouraged draft dodging,[57]

World War 1 and Opposition to Engagement

Debs' Canton speech occurred after Woodrow Wilson had committed the United States to World War I, and thus the courts considered it treason. However, it reflected a position that, not surprisingly, had been far more popular before US entry. Following the outbreak of fighting in Europe in 1914, evidence suggests that the vast majority of people in the United States were sympathetic to Britain and France. However, that sympathy competed with a belief that it was a war in which, in Washington's terms, the United States could become dangerously entangled. When Wilson eventually did call for war, he noted expressly (using language not that far from Debs') that "we have no quarrel with the German people. We have no feeling toward them but one of sympathy and friendship." The war was not their decision, Wilson said, rather, it was begun as wars "used to be determined upon in the old, unhappy days when peoples were nowhere consulted by their rulers and wars were provoked and waged in the interest of dynasties or of little groups of ambitious men who were accustomed to use their fellow men as pawns and tools."[58]

A key factor driving public sentiment against the war were reports that it was a bloody and useless mess. A young John Dos Passos traveling in Europe in 1916 wrote, "there is something frightfully paralyzing to me in the war … . Europe is to senselessly destroy itself … a crevasse has opened and all the fair things, all the mellow things, all the things that were to teach us in America how to live were slipping in – a sort of tidal wave of blood and fire."[59] The US ambassador in London, Walter Hines Page, echoing Washington on the constancy of European conflicts and the US interest in avoiding those conflicts, wrote, "it seems inevitable that Germany will be beaten … that England will gain even more of the Earth's surface, that Russia may play the next menace; that all Europe (as much as survives) will be bankrupt … . I thank heaven for many things – first, the Atlantic Ocean."[60] Page saw opportunities for US leadership and suggested the world had changed in a way that made full isolation impossible and unwise. Writing about the outbreak of war, he said that because the United States was not involved, it could "play a helpful and historic part at its end … . It will probably help us politically and it will surely help us economically." This was only a private thought; it would have been impossible to say this aloud in 1914.[61]

Historian Robert W. Tucker, writing about Wilson's desire to stay neutral, said it "had the simplest of explanations: he wanted to stay out of the war. He wanted to stay out of the war because, as he said on many occasions, the people relied on him to keep the nation out of war and because he himself believed to the very end that participation in the war held out the greatest threat to the nations' democratic values and institutions."[62] This was not only an issue of his personal values; it was political. The 1916 Democratic National Convention platform explicitly stated he was a peace candidate, applauding his "splendid diplomatic victories" that "preserved the vital interests of our Government and its citizens, and kept us out of war." Wilson hated the phrasing of the slogan "he kept us out of war," because he recognized that German actions might force him to alter his position (as was the case), but he appreciated it had significant popular appeal.[63] As Elihu Root, a prominent Roosevelt supporter in the 1916 presidential election also said, it was not a particularly impressive claim because every president in US history, save Lincoln and McKinley, had kept the country out of wars. Root needled that keeping the country out of wars meant merely "doing nothing."[64]

Even as the Senate debated a war declaration, following Wilson's message that German abuse of neutral shipping constituted a violation of the "humane practices of civilized nations," there was still significant opposition.[65] On the Senate floor, the Nebraska Republican George Norris echoed Debs' sentiment, suggesting it was the munitions industry leading the United States to war. Arms merchants had earned millions already, and "will make many hundreds of millions more if we get into the war." He argued, "War brings no prosperity to the great mass of common and patriotic citizens. It increases the cost of living of those who toil and those who already must strain every effort to keep soul and body together. War brings prosperity to the stock gambler on Wall Street – to those who are already in possession of more wealth than can be realized or enjoyed."[66]

This idea, or at least a variant of it, returned in victory. Through the course of World War I, Wilson had touted the construction of a new multinational League of Nations to serve as an international governmental body to promote peace. The idea emanated from Wilson's faith in government as capable of solving problems, and from his internationalist sensibilities (enhanced by the war) that suggested the United States needed to engage in the global arena to protect its own safety and prosperity. Yet the League of Nations, codified in the Treaty of Versailles (which Wilson personally negotiated) faced stiff resistance in the United States, especially from Republicans in the Senate. In part, opposition was tactical and political. Republicans were angry about the way Wilson used promises about the League of Nations in the 1918 mid-term elections, and believed that Wilson further politicized the League by failing to ask Republicans to accompany him to the peace negotiations. There were also philosophical concerns. Many Republicans, including Henry Cabot Lodge, the Senate majority leader and chair of the Foreign Relations Committee, accepted the idea that the country should play a leading international role, but they were skeptical about the League of Nations and troubled by the possibility that the United States might be surrendering a measure of its sovereignty to the organization. They hoped to develop bilateral security agreements with European states, especially France, and reduce the power of the League of Nations. Wilson opted to fight though, rather than compromise, and he lost.[67]

Objections to the treaty and international engagement partially developed through a growing understanding of the brutality of the war, especially as described by popular authors such as Dos Passos and Ernest Hemingway, who wrote about the cruelty and senselessness of the combat. The focus on the human toll made it difficult to justify anything that might lead to more global interventionism. In early 1920, this concern increased as John Maynard Keynes' *The Economic Consequences of the Peace* became a bestseller in the United States. Keynes argued that the peace treaty, especially the terms for German reparations that Wilson accepted in order to gain British and French support for the League, would make German redevelopment impossible and guarantee another war.[68]

The question about what kinds of global engagement would be appropriate after World War I was also connected to the substantial aid program constructed during the fighting. In the early part of the war, before US entry, German and French armies destroyed Belgian agricultural productivity and made it difficult for Belgians to import food. Believing that something needed to be done, and could be done, Walter Hines Page, the US ambassador in London, recruited Herbert

Hoover, then living in England, to construct and manage a private aid organization, the Commission for Relief in Belgium. Initially Hoover solicited money and food donations from the public in the United States, but following US entry into the war in 1917, the government assumed control of the organization and provided funding. After the war the commission became private again, but it still continued to receive government support. In all its incarnations Hoover remained in charge, which propelled his public career.[69]

The postwar aid was controversial on multiple fronts, as demonstrated by debates in January 1919 (not long after fighting ended in November 1918) regarding authorizing spending for Hoover's operation. Senator William Borah (R-ID) argued, as many leaders in the post-World War II period would, that aid was an irresponsible use of tax dollars. He said,

> Whatever may be the great ability of Mr. Hoover, there is one individual whom he does not know exists in this country, and that is the taxpayer. He seems to think that money comes like manna to the children of Israel from Heaven and not from the sweat and toil and sacrifice of the people. He has no conception of the existence of the taxpayer, and his distribution of foods is utterly regardless of his existence. For these reasons … under the present circumstances, with no information, no restrictions, no safeguards, no directions, no limitations, we are turning over a hundred million dollars to be distributed and I cannot endorse it. In the name of common honesty, of common fairness with those whom we represent, in the name of those who are now positively discouraged by reason of the taxes imposed upon them, to wit, the business men of this country, in the name of the poor, the prices of whose food will be raised by this bill, let us throw around the undertaking the ordinary safeguards of a sane transaction.[70]

Montana Senator Henry Myers (D) had a different concern. He worried that aid might go to Germans, or to other people who had fought the United States. It made no sense, he thought, that the United States might pay to help feed people who merely a few weeks earlier had been trying to kill US soldiers, and he called for a bill that would only support people in allied countries.[71]

Utah senator Reed Smoot (R), one of Hoover's powerful supporters, rejected these criticisms and said that the United States needed to think about using aid in a tactical way. He rejected Borah's concerns about tax dollars, and as aid advocates would later suggest in the post-World War II period, argued that aid needed to be understood as part of a geopolitical strategy that would ultimately save money and lives. He said he wanted aid to help "quiet the people in the countries in which Bolshevism is rampant." He posited that hungry people would be far more likely to embrace radicalism than well-fed ones, and given that radicalism in postwar Europe was not in the national interest, feeding people made sense.[72] Smoot's colleague from Utah, Senator William King (D), similarly saw aid as a strategic issue, but talked about different goals. He hoped aid could make it easier for the United States to disengage from Europe. It needed to be understood as a "war measure," albeit funded after the war, to create enough stability that US forces could come home. He explained that if people had no food, "there will be unrest, internecine strife, revolution, and warfare" in Europe. He added, "there might be a recrudescence" that could include attacks on allied governments, which "would necessitate our government retaining troops in Europe for a longer period of time." Aid would create order; it would not be possible to get out without it.[73]

A Return to Normalcy

In terms of an overall policy, Republicans challenging Wilson's policy offered an easier path, a "return to normalcy," which proved more popular than ideas about long-term and permanent involvement in global affairs. Borah, who led the fight against the treaty and aggressively campaigned for Warren G. Harding in 1920, gloated after the election that the "overwhelming and engulfing vote for the Republican ticket was the judgment of the American people against the League or any political alliance or combination with European powers." This was, he said, "the re-dedication of this nation to the foreign policy of George Washington and James Monroe, undiluted and unemasculated." Harding similarly explained in his 1921 inaugural address, that the United States was not responsible for people in other parts of the world and sought to return to an earlier stance on global engagement. "Confident of our ability to work out our own destiny, and jealously guarding our right to do so," he said, "we seek no part in directing the destinies of the Old World. We do not mean to be entangled. We will accept no responsibility except as our own conscience and judgment, in each instance, may determine." The country would chart its own course, putting its own interests first.

This was not full isolationism. Harding said the nation "never will be blind to a developing menace" and "never deaf to the call of civilization." There was a new order in the world, and that required "fellowship, fraternity, and cooperation." It would be necessary, he noted, to "associate ourselves with the nations of the world, great and small, for conference, for counsel; to seek the expressed views of world opinion; to recommend a way to approximate disarmament and relieve the crushing burdens of military and naval establishments."[74] This second sentiment, for limited engagement necessary to promote peace, led to US involvement in organizing the Washington Naval Conference in 1921/2, substantial postwar loans to Great Britain and France, as well as the Dawes and Young Plans to help Germany pay war reparations.[75] This was piecemeal internationalism, limited to the world of elite diplomatic interaction and dedicated to the greater goal of advancing normalcy.

Republicans in the 1920s also challenged a Hamiltonian vision of an expansive government. Following his discussion of global affairs, Harding argued "that no statute enacted by man can repeal the inexorable laws of nature. Our most dangerous tendency is to expect too much of government." He continued,

> The economic mechanism is intricate and its parts interdependent... No altered system will work a miracle. Any wild experiment will only add to the confusion. I speak ... for the omission of unnecessary interference of Government with business, for an end to Government's experiment in business, and for more efficient business in Government administration.[76]

This was not a complete rejection. Harding accepted that "wise government policy" could "encourage continued progress." He also had concerns about domestic radicalism and Bolshevism, especially because of events in the Soviet Union and chaos in the postwar economy. It was necessary though, he argued, to end wartime economic regulations as part of a larger effort toward establishing a peaceful society. In May 1920, in his "Return to Normalcy Speech," he famously said that "America's present need is not heroics, but healing; not nostrums, but normalcy; not revolution, but restoration; not agitation, but adjustment; not surgery, but serenity; not the dramatic, but the dispassionate; not experiment, but equipoise; not submergence in internationality, but sustainment in triumphant nationality."[77]

Staying out of Europe's Problems in the 1930s

As Europe seemed to be lurching toward renewed conflict in the mid-1930s, questions about US global engagement emerged again. A full study of pre-World War II isolationism is not possible here, nor warranted, but some review will set the stage for seeing continuities in the foreign aid narrative during the postwar period. Many national leaders from across the political spectrum, reflecting popular opinion, asserted that the United States should stay out of European conflicts. Others went further, arguing that US fighting in the first global war had been a mistake.

The failures of the League of Nations and efforts to promote disarmament were central in raising questions about a US international role in an increasingly complex world. In May 1933, Japan withdrew from the League of Nations after the League voted to condemn the Japanese invasion of Manchuria. Then, in October 1933, Adolf Hitler recalled Germany's delegation from ongoing European disarmament talks and, like the Japanese, withdrew from the League of Nations. The obvious and increasingly severe lurches away from peaceful coexistence frustrated US leaders who had hoped the League of Nations and US interwar diplomacy might provide stability. Returning from a trip to Europe, California senator William Gibbs McAdoo, who had been among President Wilson's close allies (as well as his son-in-law) and a hearty supporter of US participation on the League of Nations, came to see the global situation as "hopeless." The European states had "repudiated their obligations without a semblance of justification, and with an utter disregard of every honorable consideration." The only logical response, he believed, was remaining aloof from foreign entanglements.[78]

Two books published in 1934, H. C. Englebrecht and F. C. Hanighen's *Merchants of Death* and George Seldes' *Iron, Blood, and Profits*, both offered an additional powerful reason to avoid European conflict. Their work collectively argued that arms merchants had been responsible for encouraging the Great War by enflaming the public and working to encourage politicians to be more combative.[79] These conclusions led the Senate to create a special committee led by the Progressive Republican senator Gerald Nye (R-ND) to investigate the claims. The committee's report echoed both books. It said the actions of "companies during the war, wherever examined, was close to being disgraceful … ." It continued,

> They made very considerable profits … . They secured cost-plus contracts and added questionable charges to the costs. They secured changes in contract dates to avoid war taxes. They bought from the Government, very cheaply, [construction] yards which had been built expensively at Government costs. In one case this was prearranged before the yard was built … . Knowingly exorbitant claims were filed against the government. Huge bonuses were paid to officers. Profits were concealed … .[80]

The report suggested that the war had not been about German militarism, but about enriching capitalists, and thus US soldiers killed in combat had not been fighting for a moral or national cause, but to line the pockets of US business leaders. Other influential scholarship, including Walter Mills' *Road to War: America 1914–1917* (1935), presented a different case, but came to the same conclusion. Mills argued that the US effort was mostly dedicated to protecting English and French economic interests. The growing consensus, stated brashly by Senator Homer Bone (D-WA), was that war had been "utter insanity" and that "we had no business in it at all."[81]

This view led directly to the neutrality bill of 1935, which aimed to prohibit the export of arms, ammunition, and other implements of war to all belligerents engaged in a war. The goal, following the logic of the Nye Committee, and from a desire to keep the United States out of another European war, was to avoid the slippery slope of engagement that might incrementally lead to greater commitments and eventually to combat. Senator Hiram Johnson (R-CA), a leading proponent of the legislation, was jubilant as it was about to pass. He said, "Never again during the generation which now lives … will we be able to be taken into European war or drawn into a European entanglement." The bill stated "a policy, the policy of minding our own business, keeping out of Europe, European controversies, foreign wars, and the like." It would be the "downfall … of the internationalist who has been devoting his gigantic energy in the last seventeen years to involving us in machinations abroad and who would take us into Europe's troubles and into Europe's difficulties."[82] Johnson's triumphal tone was warranted as the bill passed in the House without a roll-call vote, indicating its wide popularity, and passed in the Senate 77 to 2. The bill only covered a six-month period, required an affirmative presidential statement that a state of war existed before coming into force, and did not prohibit the shipment of other goods, but it was understood by its backers as a permanent step toward neutrality. Renewal of the bill in 1936, again for a limited time, led to additional bills that modified its provisions while retaining the initial aims.[83]

Keeping out of war in Europe was personal for Senator Johnson. His son Archibald had fought in France during World War I and never fully recovered from a gas attack, which led to his depression and suicide in 1933. This was a painful reminder to the California senator that the outcome had not been worth the expense, and looking at Europe in the late 1930s he saw no reason to alter that conclusion. He submitted that the fear that Hitler "will conquer Europe and we will be next" was "a perfectly idiotic assumption."[84] He said, "we could stand on our shores, with our airplanes and carriers, and a vastly superior navy, and laugh at his efforts" as Germany had little ability to project power across the Atlantic Ocean. In 1939 it had two battleships and no aircraft carriers; its smaller ships could disrupt trade, but they could not transport significant numbers of soldiers or equipment. The United States, by contrast, had 21 battleships and seven aircraft carriers. Japan was even less of a hazard. "God gave us two oceans," Johnson said, and that made the United States permanently secure.[85]

The overwhelming victory of the neutrality bill indicated the broad support for the belief that the United States needed to do everything it could to avoid getting dragged into a new war. Scholarship on Isolationism in the mid-1930s and late 1930s often highlights Nye and Johnson, who had both been leading members in the Progressive movement, as "the Isolationists." Nye, especially, served as a voice for small-town and rural Midwestern Isolationism that had roots in Jeffersonian concerns about urbanism, and ideas about the superior democratic values of self-reliant farmers. He echoed Jefferson's sentiment that "those who labor upon the earth are the chosen people" and were God's "peculiar deposit for substantial and genuine virtue." He also reiterated the idea that democracy could not survive in conditions where "people were piled upon each other," because cities created "degeneracy" that was a "canker which soon eats to the heart of its laws and constitution." Nye also followed in the intellectual wake of William Jennings Bryan, Nebraska's greatest statesman, and perhaps the most powerful Midwestern leader of the late 1800s and early 1900s. Bryan had also argued that national power rested on the shoulders of farmers, and that a natural tension existed between the interests of city and countryside. Putting this together, historian Wayne Cole explained that Nye, like Jefferson and Bryan before him, "feared bigness of almost any sort, including big military, big government, and big labor." It would be a mistake to enter any war that would necessitate more bigness, and which would be fought to advance the interests of urban anti-democratic bankers, industrialists, and politicians.[86]

Isolationism, defined here as a desire to keep the United States aloof from the conflicts in Asia and Europe, was not limited to Midwesterners. It extended across the ideological spectrum and was powerful in most sectors of society. Beyond agrarian Progressives, leading Republicans, including senators Robert A. Taft (OH) and Arthur Vandenberg (MI), also adopted isolationist postures. On entering the Senate in 1939, Taft immediately asserted his leadership within his party by challenging President Franklin D. Roosevelt's New Deal. He tried to advance what he believed were Republican Party values about less activist government and the promotion of a less regulated business climate. This was also tied to a concern that global engagement might further expand executive power, which was central to his opposition to a 1940 bill that called for a compulsory draft. Taft suggested "we should not exaggerate the character of the emergency" in Europe to US interests, but instead concentrate on the greater threat of giving a president "more and more power, until the Executive had complete discretionary power to take all property and to take all men." Framing this is as a foundational national question, he said expanded government power had been behind the establishment of the totalitarian governments of the period, and further, "the history of every tyranny in the world."[87]

Vandenberg, who served as the Republican party's institutional voice on foreign policy and had been on the Nye Committee, similarly counseled that the United States needed to stay out of European conflicts. In 1939, following the German attack on Poland, Roosevelt called for a special congressional session and asked for the repeal of the neutrality legislation. The president argued it was his "deep and unalterable conviction, based on years of experience as a worker in the field of international peace, that by the repeal of the embargo the United States will more probably remain at peace than if the law remains as it stands today." Roosevelt added that "with the repeal of the embargo, this Government clearly and definitely will insist that American citizens and American ships keep away from the immediate perils of the actual zones of conflict."[88] Vandenberg rejected this argument. He said, "this is the road that may lead to war, and I will not voluntarily take it." Any engagement of any kind would drag the United States in. He continued,

> It is entirely human – and a credit to our sensibilities – to give vent to our outraged emotions from time to time in the presence of broken liberties and broken lives beneath other flags. But surely our paramount responsibility – every minute of every hour in every day – is so to maintain our national attitudes that the wars of others do not needlessly come to us, and that whatever destruction happens elsewhere may not needlessly happen here. This is not our war. We did not start it. We have no control over its course. We cannot dictate its conclusion. We cannot order Europe's destiny, not even if we took it as a permanent assignment. It is not our war, despite our devotion to democracy. It need not – it should not – become our war.

Vandenberg later said he appreciated that it was possible that the United States might eventually need to become engaged in the fighting, but he hoped to "preserve our insulation to the last honorable degree."[89]

Idealism and Isolationalism

There was also opposition to involvement in war on the other side of the political spectrum. Charles Beard, a leading historian and public intellectual, had been an enthusiastic Roosevelt supporter and advocate of New Deal programs for alleviating unemployment and economic inequality. On these grounds he counseled isolationism and reasoned that global engagement would draw resources from addressing domestic problems. He accepted the idea that the United States had never been a "hermit" nation, and that a completely aloof policy was impossible. However, the central problem with interventionism, and what he believed World War I had amply demonstrated, was the "limited nature of American powers to relieve, restore, and maintain life beyond its sphere of interest and control." He continued that political leaders needed to recognize "the hard fact that the United States, either alone or in any coalition, did not possess the power to force peace on Europe and Asia, to assure the establishment of democratic and pacific governments there, or to provide the social and economic underwriting necessary to the perdurance of such governments." It was thus a mistake to become involved in the war, even to the point of "abstaining from denouncing" foreign governments, like Germany and Japan, with whom the United States was at peace.[90]

John Dewey, the influential public intellectual, psychologist, and educational reformer, offered a different rationale for staying out of European affairs. In "On America's Responsibility," initially printed in 1926, but reissued as part of a collection of his writings in 1939, he explained that World War I's origins and fighting reflected "the European state of mind and of politics," or as German philosophers might have put it, a particular *weltanschauung*. Looking at this in the 1920s, he saw no evidence of a "marked sign that the state of the European mind and politics has undergone any change, save as due to exhaustion." He said the United States had, through its history, developed a different system and a different tradition in international relations of "genuine practical idealism" that was based on an "immense fund of goodwill and desire to be of help to those in need." This led him to suggest, "the notion that we can really be of help to Europe by joining in their affairs on terms that are set by their unhappy international and diplomatic heritage seems to me silly. We shall be simply drawn in, and our system assimilated to theirs." Unfortunately, Europeans operated in a system characterized by "strife, intrigue, and mutual treacheries," and engaging with their systems would degrade national values. The goodness of national society would necessarily be undermined by global engagement, he said, and if the country were to remain good, it needed to stay out of the affairs of the bad.[91]

Dewey's argument about values overlapped with ideas central to the peace movement. In part because of its deep connections to the dogmas of some US Protestant denominations (Quakers, Mennonites, Brethren and others), religious pacifism had long been a factor in opposition to military spending. In the pre-World War I period, and even more so in the interwar era, the peace movement expanded to include distinct sub-communities. Women engaged in social justice work were an instrumental part of this expansion. In 1915, Jane Addams, the founder of Chicago's Hull House settlement, worked with other female reformers, including most prominently Lillian Wald of Settlement House in New York and the Suffragist Carrie Chapman Catt, to organize the Women's Peace Party, which became a branch of the Women's International League for Peace and Freedom. These women, along with similarly inclined leaders of the American Association of University Women, the General Federation of Women's Clubs, the National Federation of Colored Women, and the Women's Christian Temperance Union, all made peace advocacy central to their mission. For them, pacifism connected to their larger moral concerns about the uses and abuses of violence and a vision that war was exploitative and inherently destructive to workers and communities. This political understanding also motivated Dorothy Day, who founded the influential *Catholic Worker* in 1933. Day's power came from her use of the language of the gospels to argue that militarism and nationalism were antithetical to Christ's message and turned the poor into cannon fodder for the rich.[92]

This concern about workers and exploitation connected moral and religious pacifists with political pacifists, who most often came from socialist and labor movements. Socialist and labor pacifists usually began with secular assumptions about the necessity of promoting human equality and rights, which then led to the position, similar to that of religious and social reformer pacifists, that war would be most destructive to those with the least power and money. However, rising fascism, especially in Spain, challenged this perspective. Norman Thomas, the leader of the US Socialist movement following Debs' death, and a six-time presidential candidate, argued that pacifism could not be absolute given the stakes. The struggle for peace, he said, was "immensely complicated" and necessitated a compromise that would include pushing for neutrality while also selling weapons to anti-fascists. This would be a step toward "the establishment of a warless world." The obvious internal inconsistency foreshadowed the breakdown of left-leaning political pacifism in the late 1930s and early 1940s. Given Germany's aggression, the destruction associated with that aggression, and Hitler's lack of interest in cooperation or compromise, it was hard to see how options other than violence might lead to peace.[93]

Pro-Germany Isolationists

On the opposite side of the spectrum, there were citizens whose national origins led them to believe that the United States was backing the wrong side. Many in Irish-American Catholic communities held strong anti-British sensibilities because of the history of British occupation of Ireland, British resistance to Irish independence, and the continuing British occupation of Ulster (Northern Ireland). Although they were not particularly pro-German, they were angry about Roosevelt's pro-British leanings, and cheered as their enemy seemed to be on its heels in the early part of the war. German-Americans also viewed the war in personal-ethnic terms. Many believed that Hitler's regime was destroying their nation's historical and cultural foundations, while others applauded as their ancestral homeland was becoming a global power. A fascinating study of voting patterns in Hamilton County, Illinois, demonstrated the power of pro-Nazi and related anti-Roosevelt sentiment. In one heavily German-American voting district, Roosevelt won 79 percent of the vote in 1932 and 72 percent in 1936, but only 39 percent in 1940.[94]

Proto-fascists and xenophobic populists in the United States also advocated Isolationism. Some admired Hitler's rise in Germany and applauded his political agenda, and modeled their own populism on his successes. They argued, similarly to Nye and Johnson, that joining the war would enrich arms merchants and that US geostrategic interests were not at stake, but they spoke more critically and conspiratorially about how it might impact US society. Charles Lindbergh, the well-known aviator, was the most successful in gaining a national following for this stance. In 1939 he argued that the United States should rethink its international friendships as Germany was "growing like a giant at the side of an aged complacent England." Germany, he claimed, was best equipped to advance "Western Civilization" in Europe, and would inevitably cooperate with the United States for the mutual benefit of both.[95] In 1941, speaking to a national radio audience from Des Moines, Iowa, he famously argued that three groups, the British, the Jews, and the Roosevelt administration, were acting for their own personal reasons against the national interest and pushing the United States closer to war against Germany. The British were operating logically in "spending great sums of money for propaganda," and he said, "if we were Englishmen, we would do the same." He also noted that Jewish concerns were reasonable given persecution in Germany. This was a Jewish problem though, not one for the United States, and it represented a "danger to the country." Jews were "looking out for what they believe to be their own interests," and were influential because of their "large ownership and influence in our motion pictures, our press, our radio and our government." Antisemitically identifying Jews as foreigners within the United States, he said, "we cannot allow the natural passions and prejudices of other peoples to lead our country to destruction." Roosevelt was less complex. The perception of a war emergency kept him in power. All three, Lindbergh claimed, were behind a massive propaganda campaign in which "newsreels lost all semblance of objectivity" in an effort to enflame popular opinion and smear opponents of engagement in Europe as traitors, Nazis, and anti-Semites.[96]

Lindbergh operated as the public face of the America First Committee, the largest antiwar organization in 1940 and 1941. The committee initially served as a big tent bringing together all elements of society opposed to US involvement in war. This included religious pacifists and an ideologically broad group of supporters (though Midwestern anti-Roosevelt business leaders provided most of the funding). Lindbergh's joining of its executive committee in April 1941 shifted the organization and empowered anti-Semitic conspiracy theories among its members. Some America First Committee leaders expressed support for Father Coughlin, the fascist-enthusiast anti-Semitic priest from Detroit, Michigan. Coughlin claimed that Jews maintained a secret transnational government dedicated to the destruction of Christian civilization, and that they were responsible for the spread of communism. His newsletter, *Social Justice*, argued that Jewish influence was everywhere, even in the efforts of Jewish greeting card manufacturers in England trying to take "Christ out of Christmas." Coughlin thus applauded German efforts to end Jewish power, and he argued, as Lindbergh would, that people in the United States did not have a true understanding of the war. He wrote, "we have a gross exaggeration of the negatives and a gross underestimation of the positives put into practice by … Germany, thanks to the Jewish influence in government, journalism, and finance in our own country."[97]

This short survey of anti-engagement ideas in the United States demonstrates vast differences in the underpinnings of opposition. Pacifists, Progressives, and proto-fascists all traveled different paths to arrive at a similar conclusion, that the United States must stay out of the war. This is significant, moving forward, because their ideas and perspectives never went away, despite immediate near-consensus about joining the war following the Pearl Harbor attacks. In the late 1940s, and into the 1950s and 1960s, many of the same people (and their intellectual and political heirs) made similar arguments about US foreign aid. They were not responsible for the only objections, but they used much of the same logic in opposing the Marshall Plan and the corpus of institutional aid programs that followed. In doing so, they built on the longer history of antagonism to domestic government-led development efforts and to ideas about global responsibilities. They were rehashing arguments that went back to the nation's founding about the nature of government and its role in the world.

Notes

1 Hilde Eliassen Restad, "Old Paradigms in History Die Hard in Political Science: US Foreign Policy and American Exceptionalism," *American Political Thought* 1, 1 (May 2012), 53–76; John G. Ikenberry, *After Victory* (Princeton, 2001); Henry Nau, *At Home Abroad: Identity and Power in American Foreign Policy* (Ithaca, 2002); Jeffrey Legro, *Rethinking the World* (Ithaca, 2005); Melvyn Leffler, "9/11 and American Foreign Policy," *Diplomatic History* 29, 3 (June 2005), 395–413; John Ruggie, "The Past as Prologue?: Interests, Identity, and American Foreign Policy," *International Security* 21, 4 (Spring 1997), 89–125; Michael Desch, "America's Liberal Illiberalism: The Ideological Origins of Overreaction in U.S. Foreign Policy," *International Security* 32, 3 (Winter 2007–8), 7–43.

2 Michael E. Latham, *Modernization as Ideology: American Social Science and "Nation Building" in the Kennedy Era* (Chapel Hill, 2003).

3 US visions of development were not particularly different to communist ones. Communists believed in a development hierarchy based on material advancements, the potential for the application of knowledge and money to make material change happen, and that development would be good for the people experiencing it.

4 Adam Smith, *An Inquiry into the Nature and Causes of the Wealth of Nations*. S. M. Soares, ed. (Amsterdam, 2007); César A. Hidalgo and Ricardo Hausmann have used the term "economic complexity" to refer to the diversity and scope of productive inputs that exist within a nation's economy as a way of determining the strength of that economy. While this idea, as a predictive and quantifiable index may be new, the larger idea, that industry and commerce are the building blocks of a powerful economy can be traced back to Smith. César A Hidalgo and Ricardo Hausmann, "The Building Blocks of Economic Complexity," *Proceedings of the National Academy of Sciences* 106, 26 (June 2009), 10570–10575.

5 Samuel Hale Butterfield suggests that a more complex but not altogether different set of assumptions guided the development of US foreign aid, especially in its initial phases. These assumptions were: (1) that the United States could only encourage development elsewhere and that local governments needed to be committed to the process, (2) that experts in the United States had the technical solutions to make development happen, (3) that US experts were capable of working aboard effectively, (4) that technical assistance would be more important than money, (5) "That population growth was not a problem," (6) that economic growth would promote wealth creation across all sectors of recipient nations, (7) that aid recipient nations would be thankful and that this would result in stronger international friendships, (8) that aid programs could and would be temporary. Samuel Hale Butterfield, *US Development Aid – An Historic First: Achievements and Failures in the Twentieth Century* (Westport, CT 2004), 29–34.

6 Alexander Hamilton, "The Utility of the Union in Respect to Commercial Relations and a Navy/Federalist Papers Number 11," Primary Documents in American History, Library of Congress, guides.loc.gov/federalist-papers (accessed October 11, 2020). The framework here is not dissimilar to the one developed by Walter Russell Mead, in *Special Providence: American Foreign Policy and How It Changed the World* (New York, 2001). Mead suggests four elements of US foreign policy, Hamiltonian, Jeffersonian, Jacksonian, and Wilsonian.

7 Hamilton, "Federalist Papers Number 11."

8 Hamilton, "Federalist Papers Number 12."

9 Alexander Hamilton, "Report on the Subject of Manufactures, December 5, 1791," Founders Online, National Archives, founders.archives.gov/documents/Hamilton/01-10-02-0001-0007 (accessed August 23, 2019).

10 Adam Smith, "Book IV, Chapter II," *Wealth of Nations* (1776), www.econlib.org/library/Smith (accessed August 23, 2019).

11 Smith did believe that some forms of state interventionism could be necessary or even beneficial to regulate trade, manage courts, and educate youth. Smith, *Wealth of Nations* 356, 556–558, 605; Adam Smith, *An Inquiry into the Nature and Causes of the Wealth of Nations*, S. M. Soares, ed., (Amsterdam, 2007).

12 Thomas Jefferson, *Notes on the State of Virginia* (Philadelphia, 1788); A. Whitney Griswold, "The Agrarian Democracy of Thomas Jefferson," *American Political Science Review* 40, 4 (August 1946), 657–681; Shlomo Slonim, *Forging the American Nation, 1787–1791: James Madison and the Federalist Revolution* (New York, 2017).

13 Andrew Shankman, *Original Intents: Hamilton, Madison, and the American Founding* (New York, 2018), 1–22; Johnathan Israel, *Democratic Enlightenment: Philosophy, Revolution, and Human Rights, 1750–1790* (Oxford, 2013); Henry F. May, *The Enlightenment in America* (Oxford, 1978).

14 J. R. Pole, *The American Constitution For and Against: The Federalists and Anti-Federalist Papers* (New York, 1987); David J. Siemers, *The Antifederalists: Men of Great Faith and Forbearance* (Lanham, MD, 2003).

15 Sean Wilentz, *Andrew Jackson* (New York, 2005); Robert Remini, *Andrew Jackson* (New York, 2008); John Belohlavek, *Andrew Jackson: Principle and Prejudice* (New York, 2016).

16 Songho Ha, *The Rise and Fall of the American System: Nationalism and the Development of the American Economy, 1790–1837* (London, 2008); Gillis J. Harp, *Positivist Republic: Auguste Comte and the Reconstruction of American Liberalism, 1865–1920* (State College, PA, 1995).
17 Daniel Walker Howe, *The Political Culture of the American Whigs* (Chicago, 1979), 21.
18 Herbert Croly, *The Promise of American Life* (Norwood, MA, 1909), 35–36.
19 Harp, *Positivist Republic*, 196; David W. Levy, *Herbert Croly of the New Republic: The Life and Thought of an American Progressive* (Princeton, 1985).
20 Woodrow Wilson, *The State: Elements of Practical and Historical Politics* (Boston, 1889), 659–661; Scot J. Zenter, "Liberalism and Executive Power: Woodrow Wilson & the American Founders," *Polity* 26, 4 (Summer 1994), 597–599; Robert M. Saunders, *In Search of Woodrow Wilson: Beliefs and Behavior* (Westport, CT 1998), 13.
21 Theodore Roosevelt, "Theodore Roosevelt's Confession of Faith before the Progressive National Convention, August 6, 1912" campaign pamphlet (New York, 1912); Claudio J. Katz, "Syndicalists Liberalism: The Normative Economics of Herbert Croly," *History of Political Thought* 22, 4 (Winter 2001), 669–702.
22 Richard Hofstadter, *Anti-Intellectualism in American Life* (New York, 1963); Richard Hofstadter, *The Paranoid Style of American Politics and Other Essays* (New York, 1964).
23 Henry James Ford is not to be confused with the automotive pioneer, Henry Ford. Henry James Ford, "Political Evolution and Civil Service Reform," *The Annals of the American Academy of Political and Social Science* 15 (March 1900), 159. Lonce H. Sandy-Bailey, "Ideological Dissention in the Progressive Era: Uncovering the Challengers to Direct Democracy Reforms." Doctoral Dissertation, University of Massachusetts – Amherst, 2006.
24 Henry James Ford, "Municipal Corruption," *Political Science Quarterly* 19 (December 1904), 681.
25 Henry James Ford, "The Results of Reform," *The Annals of the American Academy of Political and Social Science* 21 (January-June 1903), 223.
26 William Howard Taft, *Address of President Taft in front of the State House at Concord, New Hampshire, March 19, 1912* (Washington, 1912); Sandy-Baily, "Ideological Dissention," 102; Donald F. Anderson, *William Howard Taft: A Conservative's Conception of the Presidency* (Ithaca, 1968).
27 William Howard Taft, *Popular Government: Its Essence, Its Permanence and Its Perils* (New Haven, 1913), 90; Richard Leopold, *Elihu Root and the Conservative Tradition* (Boston, 1954), 9; Sandy-Baily, 105, 161–162.
28 George Washington, *Farewell Address*, September 17, 1796 (New York, 1861).
29 Thomas Jefferson, "First Inaugural Address," Papers of Thomas Jefferson, Princeton University, jeffersonpapers.princeton.edu/selected-documents/first-inaugural-address (accessed October 11, 2020); Lawrence S. Kaplan, *Entangling Alliances with None: American Foreign Policy in the Age of Jefferson* (Kent, OH, 1987); Christopher McKnight Nichols, *Promise and Peril: America at the Dawn of a Global Age* (Cambridge, MA, 2011), 1–6.
30 Bemis, Samuel Flagg. "Washington's Farewell Address: A Foreign Policy of Independence." *The American Historical Review* 39, 2 (1934), 250–268; Jeffrey Malanson, *Addressing America: George Washington's Farewell and the Making of National Culture, Politics, and Diplomacy, 1796–1852* (Kent, OH, 2015); *Samuel Flagg Bemis, "Washington's Farewell Address: A Foreign Policy of Independence," American Historical Review* 39, 2 (January 1934), 250–268.
31 John Quincy Adams, "July 4, 1821: Speech to the US House of Representatives on Foreign Policy," Miller Center, University of Virginia, millercenter.org/the-presidency/presidential-speeches/july-4–1821-speech-us-house-representatives-foreign-policy (accessed October 11, 2020).
32 Stacy Smith "Beyond North and South: Putting the West in the Civil War and Reconstruction," *Journal of the Civil War Era* 6, 4 (December 2016), 566–591; Christopher Ryan Pearl, "'Our God, and Our Guns': Religion and Politics on the

Revolutionary Frontier," *Pennsylvania History: A Journal of Mid-Atlantic Studies* 85, 1 (Winter 2018), 58–89.

33 James Monroe, "Seventh Annual Message to Congress, December 2, 1823," The Avalon Project, avalon.law.yale.edu/19th_century/monroe.asp (accessed October 11, 2020).

34 Jeffrey F. Taffet and Dustin Walcher, *The United States and Latin America: A History with Documents* (New York, 2017), 4–12.

35 Alex Roland, W. Jeffrey Bolster, and Alexander Keyssar, *The Way of the Ship: America's Maritime History Reenvisioned, 1600–2000* (New York, 2008), 10, 102.

36 John Louis O'Sullivan, "Annexation," *The United States Magazine and Democratic Review* 17, 85 (July and August 1845), 5–10, 7.

37 John L. O'Sullivan, "The Great Nation of Futurity," *The United States Democratic Review* 6, 23 (November 1839), 426–430; This is a variant of the argument William Appleman Williams pioneered in *The Tragedy of American Diplomacy* (New York, 1959).

38 James K. Polk, "Inaugural Address of James Knox Polk, March 4, 1845," The Avalon Project, avalon.law.yale.edu/19th_century/polk.asp (accessed December 8, 2020).

39 Abraham Lincoln, "Lincoln's Spot Resolution, December 22, 1947," United States House of Representatives, history.house.gov/Records-and-Research/Listing/lfp_037 (accessed October 11, 2020). See also Caleb Smith, *Speech of Mr. Caleb B. Smith, of Indiana, on the Mexican War, Delivered in the House of Representatives of the United States, July 16, 1846* (Washington, 1846).

40 Henry David Thoreau, "Resistance to Civil Government," The Walden Woods Project, The Thoreau Institute, www.walden.org/collection/essays (accessed October 11, 2020).

41 Abraham Lincoln, "The Gettysburg Address, November 19, 1963," The Avalon Project, avalon.law.yale.edu/19th_century/gettyb.asp (accessed November 4, 2020).

42 John Rogers Haddad, *The Romance of China: Excursions to China in US Culture* (New York, 2008), xi–xix; Brian Rouleau, "Maritime Destiny as Manifest Destiny: American Commercial Expansionism and the Idea of the Indian," *Journal of the Early Republic* 30, 3 (Fall 2010), 377–411.

43 Patricia Hill, *The World Their Household: The American Woman's Foreign Mission Movement and Cultural Transformation, 1870–1920* (Ann Arbor, 1985).

44 Jennifer Snow, *Protestant Missionaries, Asian Immigration, and Ideologies of Race in America, 1850–1924* (New York, 2007), 4–7.

45 Ibid.

46 Josiah Strong, *Our Country: Its Possible Future and its Present Crisis* (New York, 1885); Ray Allen Billington, *The Protestant Crusade, 1800–1860* (New York, 1938); Kyle E. Haden, "Anti-Catholicism in U.S. History: A Proposal for a New Methodology," American Catholic Studies 124, 4 (Winter 2013), 27–45; Justin Nordstrom, *Danger on the Doorstep: Anti-Catholicism and American Print Culture in the Progressive Era* (South Bend, Indiana, 2006); David H. Bennett, *The Party of Fear: From Nativist Movements to the New Right in American History* (Chapel Hill, 1995); Dale T. Knobel, "America for the Americans": The Nativist Movements in the United States (New York, 1996); John Higham, *Strangers in the Land: Patterns of American Nativism, 1860–1925* (New Brunswick, NJ, 1955).

47 Alfred Thayer Mahan, *The Influence of Sea Power upon History, 1660–1783* (Boston, 1890); Alfred Thayer Mahan, "The United States Looking Outward," *Atlantic Monthly*, December 1890, reprinted in Alfred Thayer Mahan, *The Interest of America in Sea Power, Present and Future* (Boston, 1897).

48 Frederick J. Turner, "The Significance of the Frontier in American History," *Annual Report of the American Historical Association for the Year 1894* (Washington, 1894), 197–227.

49 Charles A. Conant, "The Economic Basis for Imperialism," *North American Review* 167, 502 (September 1898), 326–340.

50 Robert L. Beisner, *Twelve Against Empire: The Anti-Imperialists, 1898–1900* (New York, 1968), 15; David Tucker, *Mugwumps: Public Moralists of the Gilded Age* (Columbia, MO, 1998).

51 William G. Sumner, *The Conquest of the United States by Spain: A Lecture before the Phi Beta Kappa Society of Yale University, January 16, 1899* (Boston, 1899), 3, 6, 9–10.
52 Beisner, *Twelve Against Empire*, 160.
53 Ibid., 165–185.
54 *Report of the Proceedings of the 18th Annual Convention of the American Federation of Labor* (1898); Horace B. Davis, "American Labor and Imperialism Prior to World War I," *Science & Society* 27, 1 (Winter 1963), 70–76.
55 W. E. Burghardt Du Bois, *The Souls of Black Folk: Essays and Sketches* (Chicago, 1904), 135–162; Karl Marx, *The Poverty of Philosophy* (Moscow, 1955), 96.
56 W. E. Burhhardt Du Bois, *Darkwater: Voices from Within the Veil* (New York, 1920), 42–44.
57 Eugene Debs, "The Canton Ohio Speech," *The Call*, June 16, 1918; Ernest Freeberg, *Democracy's Prisoner: Eugene V. Debs, The Great War, and The Right to Dissent* (Cambridge, MA, 2008).
58 Woodrow Wilson, "Address to a Joint Session of Congress Requesting a Declaration of War Against Germany" Gerhard Peters and John T. Woolley, eds, APP, www.presidency.ucsb.edu/node/207620 (accessed October 14, 2020).
59 John Dos Passos to Walter Rumsey Marvin, December 12, 1916, in Townsend Ludington, ed., *The Fourteenth Chronicle: Letters and Diaries of John Dos Passos* (Boston, 1973), 40; Kenneth Rose, *The Great War and Americans in Europe, 1914–1917* (New York, 2017), 3.
60 Walter Hines Pages to Woodrow Wilson, August 9, 1914, in Burton J. Hendrick, ed., *The Life and Letters of Walter Hines Page* (Garden City, 1923); M. Ryan Floyd, *Abandoning American Neutrality: Woodrow Wilson and the Beginning of the Great War, August 1914 – December 1915* (New York, 2013).
61 Walter Hines Page "Memo, August 2, 1914," in Hendrick, ed., *The Life and Letters of Walter Hines Page.*
62 Robert W. Tucker, *Woodrow Wilson and the Great War: Reconsidering America's Neutrality, 1914–1917* (Charlottesville, VA, 2007), 10; Trygve Throntveit, *Power Without Victory: Woodrow Wilson and the American Internationalist Experiment* (Chicago, 2017); Arthur Link, *Wilson: The Struggle for Neutrality, 1914–1915* (Princeton, 1960).
63 Manfred Berg, "He Kept Us Out of War: A Counterfactual Look at American History," *The Journal of the Gilded Age and Progressive Era* 16, 1 (January 2017), 2–23; James Allen Beatson, "The Election the West Decided: 1916" *Arizona and the West* 3, 1 (Spring 1961), 39–58.
64 "Wilson a Failure, Says Elihu Root," *NYT*, October 6, 1916. He overlooked James K. Polk (Mexican-American War) and James Madison (War of 1812).
65 Woodrow Wilson, "Address to a Joint Session of Congress Requesting a Declaration of War Against Germany," Peters and Woolley, eds, APP, www.presidency.ucsb.edu/node/207620 (accessed October 14, 2020).
66 George Norris, "Against Entry into War, 1917," reprinted in Andrew J. Bacevich, ed., *Ideas and American Foreign Policy: A Reader* (New York, 2018), 152–154.
67 Throntveit, *Power Without Victory*; Ronald Powaski, *Toward an Entangling Alliance: American Isolationism, Internationalism, and Europe, 1901–1950* (New York, 1991); John Milton Cooper, *Breaking the Heart of the World: Woodrow Wilson and the Fight for the League of Nations* (New York, 2001); Thomas Knock, *To End All Wars: Woodrow Wilson and the Quest for a New World Order* (New York, 1992); Lloyd Ambrosius, *Woodrow Wilson and the American Diplomatic Tradition: The Treaty Fight in Perspective* (New York, 1987).
68 Powaski, *Toward an Entangling Alliance*, 23; John Dos Passos, *Three Soldiers* (New York, 1921); Ernest Hemingway, *A Farewell to Arms* (New York, 1929); John Maynard Keynes, *The Economic Consequences of the Peace* (New York, 1920); Paul Fussell, *The Great War and Modern Memory* (New York, 1975).
69 Matthew Lloyd Adams, "Herbert Hoover and the Organization of the American Relief Effort in Poland (1919–1923)," *European Journal of American Studies* 4, 2

(Autumn 2009), 1–18; Bertrand M. Patenaude, *The Big Show in Bololand: The American Relief Expedition to Soviet Russia and the Famine of 1921* (Stanford, 2002), 30–31, 33–35, 644–653; Benjamin Weissman, *Herbert Hoover and Famine Relief to Soviet Russia: 1921–1923* (Stamford: 1974); H. H. Fisher, *The Famine in Soviet Russia 1919–1923: The Operations of the American Relief Administration* (New York, 1927).

70 *Congressional Record*, January 18, 1919 (Washington, 1919), 1664 (hereafter *CR*).

71 *CR*, January 18, 1919, 1655.

72 *CR*, January 18, 1919, 1555–1556; Charles E. Strickland, "Aid to Germany, 1919 to 1921," *The Wisconsin Magazine of History* 45, 4 (Summer 1962), 256–270.

73 *CR*, January 18, 1919, 1658.

74 Warren G. Harding, "Inaugural Address, March 4, 1921" Peters and Woolley, eds, APP, www.presidency.ucsb.edu/node/206688 (accessed October 14, 2020).

75 Thomas N. Guinsburg, *The Pursuit of Isolationism in the United States Senate from Versailles to Pearl Harbor* (New York, 1982), 55; Brooke Blower, "From Isolationism to Neutrality: A New Framework for Understanding American Political Culture, 1919–1941" *Diplomatic History* (April 2014), 345–376.

76 Warren G. Harding, "Inaugural Address, March 4, 1921" Peters and Woolley, eds, APP, www.presidency.ucsb.edu/node/206688 (accessed October 14, 2020); Robert K. Murray, *The Politics of Normalcy: Governmental Theory and Practice in the Harding-Coolidge Era* (New York, 1973).

77 Warren G. Harding, "Back to Normal: Address before the Home Market Club, May 14, 1920", in Frederick E. Schortemeier, ed., *Rededicating America: Life and Recent Speeches of Warren G. Harding* (Indianapolis, 1920), 223–229.

78 "McAdoo Sees Snag in Sinclair's Plan," *NYT*, September 5, 1934; Thomas Guinsberg, *The Pursuit of Isolationism in the United States Senate from Versailles to Pearl Harbor* (New York, 1982), 150–151.

79 H. C. Englebrecht and F. C. Hanighen, *Merchants of Death* (New York, 1934); George Seldes, *Iron, Blood, and Profits* (New York, 1934); Charles Chatfield, *For Peace and Justice: Pacifism in America, 1914–1941* (Knoxville, 1971), 122.

80 US Senate, *Preliminary Report of the Special Committee on Investigation of the Munitions Industry* (Washington, 1935), 9.

81 Bone quoted in Guinsberg, *The Pursuit of Isolationism*, 152; Walter Mills, *The Road to War: America 1914–1917* (Boston, 1935); Warren I. Cohen, *The American Revisionists: The Lessons of Intervention in World War One* (Chicago, 1967).

82 *CR,* August 24, 1935, 14430.

83 *CR,* August 24, 1935, 14362, 14434; "Parley at the White House," *NYT*, August 22, 1935; Powaski, *Toward an Entangling Alliance*, 67–83.

84 Peter G. Boyle, "The Roots of Isolationism: A Case Study," *Journal of American Studies* 6, 1 (April 1972), 41–50.

85 *CR,* October 20, 1939, 631; *CR,* January 15, 1935, 498.

86 Thomas Jefferson, *Notes on the State of Virginia* (Philadelphia, 1788), 175; Wayne S. Cole, "Gerald P. Nye and Agrarian Bases for the Rise and Fall of American Isolationism," in John N. Schacht, ed., *Three Faces of Midwestern Isolationism: Gerald P. Nye, Robert E. Wood, and John L. Lewis* (Iowa City, 1981); Kendrick Clements, *William Jennings Bryan: Missionary Isolationist* (Knoxville, 1982).

87 *CR,* August 14, 1940, 10300; *CR,* February 22, 1940, 1277–1278; James T. Patterson, "Alternatives to Globalism, Robert Taft and American Foreign Policy, 1939–1945," *The Historian* 36, 4 (August 1974), 670–688; Geoffrey Matthews, "Robert A. Taft, The Constitution and American Foreign Policy, 1939–53," *Journal of Contemporary History* 17, 3 (July 1982), 507–522.

88 Franklin D. Roosevelt, "Message to Congress Urging Repeal of the Embargo Provisions of the Neutrality Law, September 21, 1939," Peters and Woolley, eds, APP, www.presidency.ucsb.edu/node/210082 (accessed October 14, 2020).

89 *CR,* October 4, 1939, 99; Hank Meijer, "Arthur Vandenberg and the Fight for Neutrality, 1939," *Michigan Historical Review* 16, 2 (Fall, 1990), 1–21.
90 Charles A. Beard, *A Foreign Policy for America* (New York: Knopf, 1940), 152–153; A. J. Bacevich, "Charles Beard, Properly Understood," *The National Interest* 35 (Spring 1994), 73–83.
91 John Dewey, "On America's Responsibility," *The Christian Century*, December 23, 1926, reprinted in Joseph Ratner, ed., John Dewey, *Intelligence in the Modern World* (New York, 1939), 503–508; John Narayan, *John Dewey: The Global Public and its Problems* (Manchester, UK, 2016); Charles F. Howlett and Audrey Cohan, *John Dewey, America's Peace-Minded Educator* (Carbondale, IL, 2016).
92 Chatfield, *For Peace and Justice*, 15–41; Marian Mollin, *Radical Pacifism in Modern America: Egalitarianism and Protest* (Philadelphia, 2006), 29–48.
93 Norman Thomas, "The Pacifist's Dilemma," *The Nation* 144 (January 16, 1937); Chatfield, *For Peace and Justice*, 287–328; Mollin, *Radical Pacifism in Modern America*, 13; James C. Duram, "Norman Thomas as Presidential Conscience," *Presidential Studies Quarterly* 20, 3 (Summer 1990), 581–589; Andrew Alexandra, "Political Pacifism," *Social Theory and Practice* 29, 4 (October 2003), 589–606.
94 Howard W. Allen, "Isolationism and German-Americans," *Journal of the Illinois State Historical Society* 57, 2 (Summer 1964), 143–149. Overall in Illinois, Roosevelt won 55% in 1932, 57% in 1936, and 51% in 1940. Nationally he won 57% in 1932, 61% in 1936, and 55% in 1940.
95 Charles Lindbergh, "Neutrality and War, 1939," reprinted in Bacevich, ed., *Ideas and American Foreign Policy*, 215–220.
96 Charles Lindbergh, "The Des Moines Speech, 1941," reprinted in Bacevich, ed., *Ideas and American Foreign Policy*, 227–220.
97 *Social Justice*, February 13, 1939; Justus D. Doenecke, ed., *In Danger Undaunted: The Anti-Interventionist Movement of 1940–1941 as Revealed in the Papers of the America First Committee* (Palo Alto, 1990); Ronald Modras, "Father Coughlin and Anti-Semitism: Fifty Years Later," *Journal of Church and State* 31, 2 (Spring 1989), 231–247.

2

FIGHTING THE MARSHALL PLAN AND POINT FOUR

In the early Cold War era, specifically through the Marshall Plan and President Harry S. Truman's Point Four initiative, foreign aid became a permanent and institutionalized part of US foreign policy. US officials thought that aid would help create a global environment conducive to promoting lasting security and domestic economic growth. They believed that aid spending could transform other societies, and that the United States had no choice but to act for its own good and for the good of the world.

For advocates of these early aid programs, the connections between aid and foreign policy goals appeared self-evident. They were sure that the United States had made grave mistakes following World War I and throughout the 1930s, mistakes responsible for setting the course to World War II and keeping the country from developing an early and effective response to European and Asian aggression. The Isolationists had been wrong, listening to them had been dangerous, and the United States should not make these mistakes again; the country had to adopt a more proactive, internationally oriented approach that would include rebuilding programs for war-torn Europe and Asia and development assistance for other parts of the world.

These connections between aid and policy were not self-evident to all, especially not to people who thought that the United States had neither the power nor the responsibility to remake the world. To investigate this idea, in August 1947 the *New York Times* sent a reporter to Rushville, Indiana, to survey attitudes about US foreign policy. Rushville was in many ways a typical Midwestern town. The reporter, Gilbert Bailey, wrote, "Standing on the court house square, looking down Main Street, it is hard to believe that the war ever happened – or that it could ever happen, for Rushville, no matter what happens to the rest of the world calmly obeys the natural inclination to mind its own business." Rushville was special though, and its insularity worth noting. It was the hometown of Wendell Willkie, the 1940 Republican candidate for president who, like Franklin D. Roosevelt, advocated for greater US global engagement. Bailey found few traces of Willkie's internationalism in Rushville. When he asked locals about world problems he was told, we should "tend to our own knitting," and, just as people in small Midwestern towns might have said in the 1930s and earlier, "Europe should take care of itself."[1]

An editorial response in the *Chicago Tribune* to the *New York Times* story complained that Bailey seemed "rather depressed by the outlook" in Rushville, but did not explain what was wrong with local attitudes: "He just deplores." Bailey did not understand that the people of Rushville believed national leaders had "turned the country over to the intellectuals, the dreamers, and the radicals," and they refused to go along with internationalism. The *Tribune* editors wrote it was characteristic of New Yorkers to believe they knew better than Midwesterners what was best. "New Yorkers are New Yorkers, not Americans," and Bailey and his readers needed to learn that what they instinctually assumed to be obvious, self-evident, or apparent was not necessarily so.[2]

The Assumptions of the Marshall Plan

On June 5, 1947, Secretary of State George C. Marshall delivered a speech at a Harvard University graduation event that included the initial call for a comprehensive European reconstruction program. He explained that Europe remained devastated and its economies had not been able to transition to a peacetime footing. This led to shortages of essential goods that kept markets from working efficiently. It was "apparent to all intelligent people," he said, that the "world situation is very serious." Later in the speech, again using the word "apparent," he argued that because of "the demoralizing effect on the world at large, and the possibilities of disturbances arising as a result of the desperation … the consequences to the economy of the United States should be apparent to all." The United States had to do whatever it could to "assist in the return of normal economic health in the world, without which there can be no political stability and no assured peace."[3] He did not justify the statement about consequences for the US economy, or the notion that the United States had to act. It was clear to him, indeed thoroughly obvious, that US economic strength and security required a healthy and secure Europe.

Marshall argued that victory in war carried a responsibility to clean up the mess afterwards. The United States had, as noted in the previous chapter, offered humanitarian assistance to Europeans in the wake of World War I, and Marshall said the United States needed to do more in the late 1940s. World War II had been brutal. Belligerents targeted civilian populations and infrastructure more aggressively than in any previous war in history. As Marshall explained, there had not only been a "visible destruction of cities, factories, mines and railroads," but a more wholesale "dislocation of the entire fabric of [the] European economy." The United States had to revive Europe "so as to permit the emergence of political and social conditions in which free institutions can exist." Aid should not be on "a piece-meal basis," it needed to be "a cure rather than a mere palliative."[4]

In his speech at Harvard, Marshall purposely did not mention the spread of communism as a threat. This similarly seemed self-evident to officials in the Truman administration, who agreed among themselves that the Soviet Union was a danger to the United States. They viewed Soviet efforts to assert their power in Eastern and Southern Europe as a first step toward the construction of an anti-capitalist global empire, and they similarly worried that Soviet-inspired and Soviet-controlled communist parties in Western Europe might take advantage of local economic instability to gain power and join the emergent Soviet bloc. It was unnecessary to say all this, however, at least at Harvard. Marshall – and his advisors helping construct the speech, Charles "Chip" Bohlen and George Kennan – thought the productive and constructive message about recovery might be lost with a focus on enemies. Furthermore, the anti-communist message about reconstructing markets was embedded in the speech, making its geopolitical intent clear.[5]

Despite their sense that aid programming was the obvious way to advance US interests, Marshall and his advisors recognized that not everyone would share their understanding, and that the connections he made might not be universally self-evident. Marshall said, "the problem is one of such enormous complexity that the very mass of facts presented to the public by press and radio make it exceedingly difficult for the man in the street to reach a clear appraisement of the situation." Ordinary people, unlike those at Harvard, might not be able to see through all the detail and come to the conclusions he deemed "apparent." He explained that "the people of this country are distant from the troubled areas of the earth and it is hard for them to comprehend the plight and consequent reactions of the long-suffering peoples, and the effect of those reactions on their governments in connection with our efforts to promote peace in the world." Ordinary Americans, he believed, like those in Rushville, might not recognize that Europe mattered, and that for their own benefit their country needed to do something.[6]

In retrospect, the speech and the construction of the program it called for, the Marshall Plan, was a defining milestone in the early Cold War and in the history of US foreign aid programming. For the first time, the United States committed itself to long-term peacetime engagement in Europe and, more broadly, to using foreign aid systematically to advance its international interests. At the time, it was similarly obvious that the Marshall Plan represented something new, a bigger commitment to extended global responsibility. Yet, the Marshall Plan was also an evolutionary step in US postwar policy rather than a departure from it. It was not the first postwar aid effort, but a juncture in which the Truman administration indicated that aid needed to be more significant and organized, and that it needed a long-term approach.

Pre-Marshall Plan Aid

In 1942, the Roosevelt administration had created the Office of Foreign Relief and Rehabilitation to manage aid and reconstruction efforts in US-controlled war-torn areas, a step similar to Hoover's work in Belgium during World War I. The next year that agency became a foundational part of the United Nations Relief and Rehabilitation Administration (UNRRA). Although technically a multilateral organization, the United States provided the bulk of the UNRRA's $3 billion budget, and it was initially managed by former New York governor Herbert Lehman, and then by former New York City mayor, Fiorello La Guardia, both of whom reported directly to Roosevelt. The UNRRA operated throughout Europe, but was most active in China, employing a staff of almost 13,000 people at its peak in June 1946. Following victory in Japan and Germany, there were additional humanitarian crises, and the Roosevelt administration constructed a separate agency, US Government Aid and Relief in Occupied Areas, initially dedicated to providing short-term emergency services. Over time it became involved in reconstruction, eventually operating alongside the Marshall Plan and US aid efforts in Japan.[7]

Other relief spending went to the British and other European governments, which desperately needed money to begin reconstruction and pay wartime debts. In the Anglo-American Financial Agreement of 1945, the United States government offered Great Britain a $3.75 billion loan, while forgiving $20 billion in war debts. Similar agreements with France and Italy followed. Yet, by 1947, it appeared to many observers that economic conditions in Europe, and by extension political conditions, were not improving.[8]

Greece was an area of particular concern as a civil war between an irregular communist-inspired militia and a royalist government began as soon as Nazi occupation troops left, and it seemed the communists might win. In the initial postwar period the British government had been assisting the royalists, but in February 1947 they reported to Truman administration officials that they had "already strained resources to the utmost," and "it [was] impossible to grant further financial assistance to Greece." Marshall and others in the Truman administration decided that the United States needed to step in and assume the British financial role.[9]

In a speech to Congress on March 12, 1947, Truman asked for $400 million for aid, explaining that Greece was "without funds to finance the importation of those goods which are essential to bare subsistence." More pressingly, its government was facing a civil war. The United States had to help because there was "no other country to which democratic Greece can turn." While asking Congress for funds, Truman made an additional request for aid to Turkey. That country, he noted, was just as vital as Greece, and though not facing a civil war, it also needed economic assistance. He said his goal was "the creation of conditions in which we and other nations will be able to work out a way of life free from coercion." It was also geopolitical, as a "glance at a map" suggested that if either Greece or Turkey fell under communist control, "Confusion and disorder might well spread throughout the entire Middle East." Victory in war, he explained, and national strength, had brought "great responsibilities" to the United States, and he was confident that US aid could have decisive political and economic impacts.

In the midst of the speech, Truman made a series of statements that transcended the Greek and Turkish issues and pledged larger and deeper US global responsibility; they immediately became known as the Truman Doctrine. Setting the stage for the Marshall Plan, he said,

> I believe that it must be the policy of the United States to support free peoples who are resisting attempted subjugation by armed minorities or by outside pressures. I believe that we must assist free peoples to work out their own destinies in their own way. I believe that our help should be primarily through economic and financial aid, which is essential to economic stability and orderly political processes.[10]

Both houses of Congress took up bills to provide Truman funds for this effort, and at a remarkable pace they moved his request through the legislative process, passing a final authorization on May 15; the Senate vote was 67 to 23, and in the House, it was 287 to 105.[11]

Although this was a victory for Truman, the limited debates in Congress about the Truman Doctrine foreshadowed objections to the Marshall Plan, and suggested how prewar ideas about US global engagement would provide the foundations for those objections. Democratic senator Edwin Johnson of Colorado said that his colleagues needed to understand the risks involved. He told his colleagues, "Twice I have seen the United States drift into a European bloodbath. I know the signposts." Truman's aid to Greece and Turkey would "pave the road to war." He added poetically, "Everything is running true to form. Not one fatal criterion is missing. Once again without their approval and against their will the American people are being sold down the river of blood." The Tennessee Democrat, Senator Kenneth McKellar, went back even further and referenced Washington's Farewell Address, insisting "Our Government's old foreign policy of not interfering with the internal affairs of other nations is too just a policy, too fine a policy, too honest a policy, too successful a policy, too profitable a policy, too tried-and-true a policy to be forsaken at this time when we are now at the very zenith of success in our history." The United States needed to avoid entangling alliances and return to its isolationist roots. Senator John J. Williams of Delaware (R) worried the request was only the "small beginning" of a policy that was "conceived in haste, without adequate consideration or appreciation of its ultimate effect." Like McKellar and Johnson, he thought the risks of engagement were too great. Truman was committing "the United States to a program which we are not powerful or rich enough to carry out without ourselves becoming financially and morally bankrupt." Rather than helping the rest of the world, it would more likely destroy the nation.[12]

In the House, there was also deep opposition, and the final vote was not indicative of the broader negative sentiment about the spending request. Francis Case (R-SD), who had been the floor manager for the bill, noted in a letter to Truman that "Very,

very few spoke of the bill with enthusiasm. Support was reluctant." He guessed that at least seventy-five members, himself included, would have voted against the bill, but that would have meant its likely defeat, and they worried it would be "pulling the rug out from under you."[13] Ellsworth Foote, a Republican from Connecticut, expressed a similar sentiment on the floor. He was not enthusiastic about Truman's policy, saying "it is anybody's guess as to what will happen," but admitted he would vote for the aid because failure to pass it "would be interpreted as an abandonment of free people everywhere to whatever fate may befall them." Truman had "left us with little choice except to go forth. It is a difficult, but now, apparently, a necessary course that we pursue."[14]

The Marshall Plan moved through Congress on a much slower timeline. Though Marshall made his call for an aid program in June 1947, Congress would not pass a bill authorizing the program until the following April, and did not actually allocate money for it until June 20, 1948, more than a full year after the Harvard speech.[15] This long time lag was only in part a result of opposition, it was more significantly a function of the time needed to develop a comprehensive bill, and then of the slowness of the legislative process. The timing provided an opportunity for the Truman administration to increase awareness of the program and build support for it. But it also provided Marshall Plan skeptics an opportunity to make their case and fight against its passage.

Communist Opposition to the Marshall Plan

Some of the earliest and most adamant critiques of the Marshall Plan came from communists and affiliated labor organizations that rejected the notion that the Soviet Union was a threat to US interests and therefore argued that cooperation rather than confrontation would lead to lasting peace in Europe. They claimed that, rather than a plan to help with reconstruction, the Marshall Plan would only help US business leaders dominate global trade and exploit workers. Joseph Starobin, the foreign editor of the Communist Party newspaper, *The Daily Worker*, explained that, "The men who run our country didn't like the fact that in Eastern Europe, a new type of government was coming to be – anti-fascist governments, led by the workers themselves who had nationalized the big industries and were beginning to do some real planning." Starobin added that the men in Washington and on Wall Street "didn't like the fact that the people of Italy and France were bidding for power, and that Communists were in the governments of those countries. They didn't like the fact that Soviet Russia was holding the United States to the war-time agreements as far as Germany was concerned." More bluntly, he said, essentially correctly, "The idea was to threaten the Soviet Union and her allies" and to weaken the communists' ability to trade in Western Europe and have a say in its political and economic development.[16]

Throughout 1947 and 1948 *The Daily Worker* attacked the Marshall Plan in these terms. In a long essay summarizing its position, Communist Party chairman,

William Z. Foster, argued that "the Marshall Plan is not a program of economic recovery. The essence of it is an attempt of the big corporations of this country, who rule both the Republican and Democratic Parties, to establish their control over Europe, as part of their larger scheme to dominate the entire world. It is a war plan." Truman administration officials claimed that they were trying to help Europe, using "the Hitlerite slogan of saving the world from Communism," but it was really just a new type of imperialism.[17]

These positions, especially the attack on anti-communism, were not particularly surprising. However, Communist Party leaders also attempted to make an economic argument similar to the position fiscally minded conservatives would make. They argued that aid would hurt the US taxpayer struggling to make ends meet. Foster's essay on the Marshall Plan explained its imperialist aspect and emphasized how it would increase the cost of living by "creating a drunken spree of profiteering" and "hurling this country into a great economic crisis." Starobin wrote similarly, that the Marshall Plan had "direct costs, the *pork-chop account*," which meant that taxes would be "way higher than ever." Ordinary people would suffer, he explained, as they financed corporate growth.[18]

Henry Wallace and the Marshall Plan

There is no evidence that anyone in the Truman administration took communist views seriously at the time, but Henry Wallace, who made similar attacks, was a far more potent and less easily dismissible critic. Founder of a successful seed business and editor of a farm periodical in Iowa, Wallace joined Franklin D. Roosevelt's administration in 1933 as Secretary of Agriculture, and served as vice president in Roosevelt's third term (1941–1945). During the war, he thought about how best to secure and maintain peace after the fighting ended, and vigorously argued that the United States needed to develop a stronger and warmer relationship with the Soviet Union, as that nation would obviously be powerful at the war's end. Wallace also pushed Roosevelt to contemplate enacting a global New Deal, essentially like the Marshall Plan, in which the United States would offer loans to help rebuild war-ravaged countries.

Wallace was skeptical about the Soviet Union's economic model, but admired its rapid post-revolutionary advances in agricultural output, their emphasis on the glorification of ordinary workers, and their efforts to advance social justice. He became even more convinced at the potential for cooperation during an extended goodwill trip he took to Siberia in 1944. The abundant consumer goods and the friendly reception offered by ordinary people (much of which he later learned was staged) led him to conclude that the Soviet Union was advancing toward prosperity, and that the two nations could work together if their people and leaders got to know each other better. In its own way, Wallace believed, the Soviet Union was attempting to advance the interests of the "common man," and the United States needed to respect its different path to that end.[19]

This position alienated most Democratic Party leaders, who saw the Soviet Union as dangerous and who were more fearful about communist ideology, and it became part of their substantial opposition to Wallace's 1944 candidacy as Roosevelt's vice-presidential running mate (and thus likely successor if the aging president died). It was not the only factor though in their opposition, however. Wallace had done little to ingratiate himself with party officials, urban leaders, or legislators from Southern states, and they all pushed Roosevelt to select a more reliable and conventional candidate. Roosevelt, hoping to unite the party, agreed to drop Wallace, and instead selected Harry Truman. This, understandably angered and disappointed Wallace, but he accepted Roosevelt's subsequent offer to serve as Secretary of Commerce, which kept him in the administration and gave him substantial power over recasting the postwar economy.[20]

Wallace continued as Secretary of Commerce following Roosevelt's death and into the Truman presidency, but was increasingly out of step with other Truman administration officials because of his Cold War foreign policy views and his own sense that he was speaking for Roosevelt's authentic vision about constructing a collaborative postwar community.[21] In a wide-ranging speech in September 1946 about promoting global peace, he said relations with the Soviet Union should be "put on a friendly basis" and that he was "neither anti-Russian nor pro-Russian." He conceded that the Soviets were partly to blame for increased global tension, but he suggested the United States also bore responsibility for the budding Cold War. "The Russians," he argued, "should stop conniving against us in certain areas of the world just as we should stop scheming against them;" they "should stop teaching that their form of communism must, by force if necessary, ultimately triumph over democratic capitalism." But, he added, "we should close our ears to those among us who would have us believe that Russian communism and our free enterprise system cannot live, one with another, in a profitable and productive peace."[22] He made similar arguments in private. In a lengthy letter to Truman in June 1946, he suggested that the United States, as a nation, and the administration in particular, had not self-critically tried to "get an honest answer" about what caused the Soviets to distrust the United States or "what factors lead us to distrust Russia." He argued that the long history of prewar conflicts drove the antagonisms, and those prewar issues were getting in the way of global peace. The only way forward, he believed, was to "allay any reasonable Russian grounds for fear, suspicion and distrust." The United States needed to take a "fresh point of view" about Soviet security concerns "as a prerequisite" for "cooperation in the construction of a world order."[23]

His September 1946 speech led to a minor crisis within the Truman administration as Marshall's predecessor, Secretary of State James Byrnes, who advocated taking a much tougher position against the Soviets, threatened to quit if Wallace continued to discuss foreign policy. Truman felt he had little choice but to side with Byrnes and force Wallace to resign.[24] Wallace had encroached on Byrnes bailiwick, but more importantly, he was out of step with Truman's own thinking, which made it easier, and perhaps even necessary, to push him out. In a way, though, the firing enhanced Wallace's reputation and gave him a wider independent platform to argue for moderation and cooperation. He had stood up for peace and suffered for it, and the following month the *New Republic*, then an influential liberal political magazine, offered him their editorship, which he accepted. This helped Wallace remain a public figure and gave him a platform to publicize his views, many of which dealt with foreign aid as the centerpiece of US foreign policy.

Initially, Wallace tentatively supported the Marshall Plan and even claimed to be one of its intellectual fathers. As noted, he had proposed this kind of program to Roosevelt during the war, and in January 1947, wrote to Marshall, just before he replaced Byrnes as Secretary of State, making the same case. He told Marshall that if the United States hoped to retain its position as a world leader, it needed to develop a "mobile offensive in our foreign policy" that would affirm the country's "revolutionary tradition" in helping fix the "wrecked societies of Europe and Asia." He insisted that the United States had clumsily "yielded to the Russians the loyalty of millions of workers and peasants in Europe because they believe that the Russians and not ourselves are their only guarantors against hunger and war." Aid was necessary because "Wherever we meet Russia in Europe, it is not Russia that is the enemy, but the devastation itself."[25]

Truman's plan to send money to Greece and Turkey was another matter. In a nationally broadcast radio speech on March 13, 1947, just a day after Truman's speech to Congress, Wallace said Truman had "proposed, in effect, that America police Russia's every border" thus expanding a "contest which may widen until it becomes a world war." Aid, he insisted, made no sense in either case. Greece was still in the midst of a civil war and did not have a democratic government, and Turkey had done little in the fight against Germany. Wallace then pointed to the much bigger economic problems elsewhere. Explaining that he did not want communism to spread, he argued, "You can't fight something with nothing." That is, if the United States was serious it needed to make a bigger, Marshall Plan-like commitment. He concluded that by failing to offer aid where it was most necessary, Truman was "acting as the best salesman Communism ever had" and "betraying the great tradition of America and the leadership of the great Americans who preceded him."[26]

He was thus pleased, initially, with Marshall's speech. In late June 1947 Wallace suggested optimistically that it made "me begin to think the Truman administration realized the unwisdom of the earlier policy [the Truman Doctrine] and was prepared to forget it." He also said, rehashing his idea that the Soviet Union was not the fundamental problem in Europe, that he hoped concerns about growth, not anti-communism, would drive the policy, and that the United Nations would play a central role in its administration. A multilateral organization in charge would show that the United States was attempting to serve humankind, not merely itself. It would be the best way to engage the Soviet Union and encourage them to be a cooperative player in European life and also build up Poland and Czechoslovakia as counterweights to inevitable German reindustrialization. Laying out this tactical strategy, he explained: "World peace demands that the industries of these two countries [Poland and Czechoslovakia], and particularly their heavy industry, be at least doubled if a rebuilt Germany is not to dominate Europe." This was "the key to the success or failure of the Marshall program."[27]

But as it became obvious through the summer and early fall of 1947 that the Marshall Plan would not engage communist countries, Wallace became more critical and he began to find flaws elsewhere. One new objection, echoing the concerns of both the Nye Committee in the 1930s and the communists, was that the Marshall Plan unilaterally expanded US economic power and, more disturbingly, enriched politically connected elites. One *New Republic* article, in which Wallace's influence was clear, made this point by explaining the links between Truman's top-level appointments and the financial community, highlighting the many conflicts of interest. The article explained that Undersecretary of State Robert Lovett and Secretary of Commerce W. Averell Harriman (Wallace's successor) were both partners in the Wall Street banking firm Brown Brothers, Harriman; and Secretary of Defense James V. Forrestal and Undersecretary of the Army William H. Draper were both executives at another Wall Street firm, Dillon, Read & Co. The *New Republic* argued that these men had already worked to help US companies gain control over German reindustrialization, and in so doing had enriched their former colleagues. The Marshall Plan would expand their power and allow them to gain even more control over European economies, thus making investment bankers even richer. This was not an accusation of direct corruption; rather, it was a suggestion that the values and interests of the financial industries and their elite executives were not the same as the interests of the people of the United States.[28]

Wallace's message resonated with a subset of Democrats who thought Truman had abandoned Roosevelt's foreign policy. Roosevelt, of course, died at a moment when it was too early to know precisely how he would have handled the postwar world, yet many liberals thought that his pro-labor sentiments and his wartime commitment to working with Stalin would have led to a policy that saw the Soviet Union as a collaborator rather than a competitor. Roosevelt had pushed for the United Nations' construction as a way to keep the United States globally engaged and was willing to share global management responsibilities with other world powers (the Soviets, the British, the French, and the Chinese).[29] As historian Richard Walton argued, Roosevelt's death "left a void," encouraging individuals who thought of themselves as his true heirs to fight to rescue his legacy. This led to the founding of the Progressive Citizens of America (PCA) in December 1946 and the Americans for Democratic Action (ADA) in January 1947. Both unified smaller organizations with the hope of creating a mass movement; both were interested in more than foreign policy and also pushed for a continuation of New Deal-style policies through which the government would resume its prewar efforts to fight poverty and inequality. ADA leaders opted to remain connected to the Democratic Party, hoping to push it toward pro-labor and internationalist positions. The PCA (which included some communists) regarded Truman and the Democratic Party as hopelessly compromised by its senseless anti-communism and by its connection with Southerners who rejected racial equality and blocked civil rights legislation.[30]

Wallace was not involved in the organization of the PCA, but its construction encouraged him to contemplate his relationship to the Democratic Party. Throughout the summer and fall of 1947, he toured the country, speaking to large and enthusiastic audiences in an attempt to build momentum for a presidential campaign in 1948.[31] Truman administration officials privately worried that Wallace needed to be taken seriously, and that he could become a real threat to the president, as it seemed his criticisms of their foreign policy resonated with the public. They believed his rallies were "stage-managed" by communists, and that crowds were mostly "rabid left-wingers," but many neo-Isolationists, conservatives, and veterans also attended. For all these supporters, Wallace's approach seemed more likely to lead to peace, while Truman's approach seemed to be leading back to war. There was so much enthusiasm for Wallace that Truman's advisors were amazed that not only were his events packed, but people were paying as much as $3.60 per seat to attend. Political rallies were traditionally free, so the idea that someone might pay to see a candidate was impressive – and concerning.[32]

Wallace remained cagey about his loyalty to the Democratic Party through the summer of 1947, which encouraged state party leaders like the former California attorney general, Robert W. Kenny, to create a California Democrats for Wallace organization. Only Wallace, Kenny argued, would provide a "real choice" to the voter on both domestic and foreign policy, because Republican and Democratic leaders seemed committed to similar goals and similar methods. An election between a Republican candidate and Truman, he said colorfully, "would be as phony, and as meaningless, as one of those wrestling matches in which both contestants grunt and groan for an hour and a half, and then ride home in the same automobile."[33] Yet Wallace seemed to be leaning toward an independent campaign by September, recognizing that he had little chance of convincing Democratic Party bosses to drop Truman. In a speech to 20,000 people at Madison Square Garden in New York City, Wallace said that "If the Democratic party is a war party, if my party continues to attack civil liberties, if both parties stand for high prices and depression … then the people must have a new party of liberty and peace."[34] Given this sentiment, in December 1947 Wallace announced he would quit the Democratic Party and, with PCA support, run for president as an independent.

In his initial campaign speech, Wallace reiterated his opposition to the Marshall Plan and US aid. He said, "I have fought and shall continue to fight programs which give guns to people when they want plows. I fight the Truman Doctrine and the Marshall Plan as applied because they divide Europe into two warring camps." The problem, he continued, was that "Those whom we buy politically with our food will soon desert us. They will pay us in the base coin of temporary gratitude and then turn to hate us because our policies are destroying their freedom."[35] He said that after the war the United States had an opportunity to deal with hunger in a non-political way, and in a way that would have helped "build an expanding economy of abundance." But anti-communism blocked that, and the United States gave "guns to reactionary regimes instead of food to hungry peoples." The Marshall Plan, he said, would "freeze wages," create "inflation and high taxes," "drive independent businesses to the wall, squeeze the farmers, and increase corporate taxes." Ultimately it would "take the nation down the road to World War III."[36]

Wallace's campaign started with optimism in early 1948, especially as Idaho senator Glen Taylor agreed to be his running mate and as he began collecting endorsements. Rexford Tugwell, a key architect of the New Deal, served as a chair of his national committee, and a long list of celebrities and public intellectuals backed him. However, his lack of an effective national organization, and the power of the extant parties ensured the campaign had little chance. There were also questions, continually raised in the press, about the role of communists running his campaign. In a June 1948 Gallup poll, 51 percent of those surveyed assumed that his campaign was managed by communists, and only 21 percent indicated they thought this was not true (with the rest indicating no opinion).[37]

In the end, Wallace's campaign failed badly. He earned 2.37 percent of the national vote, 44 percent of which came from New York. Part of the defeat was connected to the difficultly of mounting a third-party campaign in US politics, but the failure also demonstrated the power of anti-communism as an organizing principle and a lack of interest in approaching the Soviet Union in a nuanced way.[38] Nevertheless, it would be a mistake to read his failure as a rejection of his ideas about foreign aid. He said that foreign aid was being misspent, which would have negative consequences for the national economy, that it could operate as a kind of imperialism potentially leading to violations of basic national principles and, ultimately, to war. All these ideas would re-emerge in future debates about aid, and many would be adopted by critics across the political spectrum.

Republicans and the Marshall Plan

Criticism of the Marshall Plan also played a role in Republican Party politics in the lead-up to the 1948 election. Ohio senator Robert Taft, a leading prewar Isolationist, had been positioning himself in 1947 to run for president, and was reticent to say much of substance about the Marshall Plan. On one hand, he needed to draw distinctions between himself and the Democrats and to explain how his foreign policy might be better. On the other, he needed to appeal to the many Republicans who had come out in support of Marshall's plan.

When Taft finally started talking about foreign aid, in a speech in Tacoma, Washington, in late September 1947, he was skeptical but non-committal. He suggested Republicans needed to be deferential to Truman and said that Congress should "hesitate to interfere with the President's foreign policy" unless it would lead to the "danger of an unnecessary war." He claimed it was important to make sure that foreign countries did not see a divided US government, and that cooperation between different branches and parties (which he thought was not happening effectively) should be the rule. This was only tentative implicit support. He shared criticisms about international engagement in a wider sense, though, and insisted, as he had before the war, that the United States needed to play a smaller role in the world. He said the "guiding principle of any foreign policy should be the maintenance of peace so long as conditions do not threaten the freedom of the people of the United States." He added his opinion that this had not been "the guiding principle of our foreign policy in the last fifteen years," suggesting, possibly, he thought World War II was a mistake.[39]

A substantial problem with the Marshall Plan, Taft continued, was its grounding in ideas about expansive government power. He said he opposed "the 'Mr. Fix-It' philosophy of the New Deal," now spreading to foreign policy, and argued that "Just as the New Dealers wanted to control the lives of all citizens and improve them whether they wished to be improved or not, so have they tried to use our financial resources" to try to control the rest of the world. It would be better and certainly "reasonable" if the United States encouraged the Europeans to "help each other before asking the United States for help," and that they should consider a European customs union. Still, he agreed that something did need to be done, but added: "we cannot afford to go on lending money on a global scale." Instead, "our loans should be made to specific countries for specific purposes and only to pay for goods shipped from the United States."[40]

By November, continuing to try to build support for his candidacy, Taft spoke in New York City and seemed to have a clearer sense of what he wanted to argue about the Marshall Plan, abandoning his tacit support and coming out more aggressively in opposition. He said there had been extensive pressure as part of a "carefully planned propaganda" effort "stimulated by the State Department by widespread publicity and by secret meetings" to build support for the Marshall Plan, but he would not be swayed. He again conceded that there was a place for "aid to Western Europe in reasonable amounts," but that these amounts needed to be small as they represented a "present to other people of the fruits of our labors." He focused on the idea that aid would be a burden on US taxpayers, and also argued that the government spending would be inflationary and destabilize the US economy, along with European economies. Sending goods abroad would cause shortages in the United States, leading to increased prices as demand remained constant. In Europe, the influx of money would also mean increasing prices as people would suddenly have the means to buy things. Further, because there were widespread production problems and shortages, prices would also rise as consumers competed for goods.

Drawing on his general understanding of government power, Taft contended that the Truman administration was overestimating the impact US dollars might have. European economic problems were a function of their political problems, he said, and aid would not force them to follow what he saw as historically sound, US-style, limited government fiscal policy. The spending would instead create chaos, in both the United States and Europe, which would encourage the Truman administration to be even more interventionist in the economy. It would "force the reimposition" of wartime price controls, which would be a "major calamity."[41]

A few weeks later, on the Senate floor, Taft turned his opposition into an early campaign speech and was even more aggressive. Europe was a mess and needed aid, not because of the war, he insisted, but because the Truman administration had bungled postwar politics so badly. It had yielded to Soviet demands at the end of the war, which had allowed them to become powerful in Eastern Europe. That, in turn, had allowed them to "interfere with and prevent the cure" of Western European problems. Attacking, he said, "I think we can say that we ourselves are to a large extent responsible, through our policy, for the condition which now exists, and which calls for this relief."[42]

Taft did not speak for all Republicans, however. Most notably, Michigan senator Arthur Vandenberg, chair of the Senate Foreign Relations Committee, opted to back Truman's plan. Both Taft and Vandenberg were among the most prominent Republican figures of the day and influential in determining the party's course. Taft generally led on domestic issues, while Vandenberg led on international ones. In the prewar era, Vandenberg had been among the most vocal Isolationists in Congress, leading the unsuccessful fight in 1939 against Roosevelt's efforts to revise the Neutrality Act of 1937 and repeal the embargoing of arms trading with nations at war. He had told a crowd in Michigan in late 1939 that he and the nation wanted "nothing of Europe's war, troubles, or fears," but he also worried that the United States could be dragged into war. In May 1940, according to his biographer, Lawrence S. Kaplan, Vandenberg conceded "isolation is impossible in this foreshortened world. But insulation continues to be entirely practical." That meant that if Hitler's Germany won the war, the United States needed to be prepared to deal with such a new world order. After the Pearl Harbor attack, though, despite believing that Roosevelt had pushed the United States toward war, Vandenberg shifted. He claimed he realized Isolationism had to die, and that his job as a Republican leader was helping the Democratic president win the war.[43]

In the aftermath of the war, as the Cold War developed, Vandenberg did not revert to Isolationism and remained committed to global engagement; this included working with the Truman administration as part of what the press and politicians termed a "Bipartisan Foreign Policy." On funding for Greece and Turkey, Vandenberg came out strongly for the request, saying that Truman had been realistic in assessing the threat and that Congress needed to do the same. He was upset that Truman was not cooperative and consultative in developing his proposals, but he still fought for the funding.

Recognizing the challenge of passing the Marshall Plan, the Truman administration handled Vandenberg far more carefully in the weeks before and after the Marshall Plan speech, even allowing him to believe that his thinking had, in part, driven the speech. Vandenberg then met frequently, and privately, with administration officials to receive briefings, and over time to craft the details of the legislation. Instead of feeling like he was pushing Truman's policy through Congress, he believed he was pushing his own vision, thus dividing Republicans into two camps: Vandenberg/internationalist and Taft/isolationist. Vandenberg, like Taft, also fancied himself a viable presidential candidate for 1948, and saw his leadership on the Marshall Plan as enhancing his national stature and, likely, undermining Taft's. Neither would earn the nomination in the summer of 1948, though. Vandenberg ultimately was too close to Truman, and enough Republican Party leaders rejected Taft's positions as divisive and wrongheaded. This opened up a path for New York governor Thomas Dewey, who had also run against Roosevelt in 1944, to represent an anti-Taft and pro-internationalist platform.[44]

But back in late 1947 and into 1948, Vandenberg's backing was vital to the Marshall Plan as it divided the Republican Party and offered its senators and representatives a choice. Democrats also had a choice. While some immediately backed Truman, others expressed Wallace-like sentiments, and a third group expressed concerns, as Taft did, about spending and unprecedented peacetime international engagement. Given these divides, the Truman administration needed to sell the plan.

Selling the Marshall Plan

Truman administration officials determined that they needed to launch a two-part effort to build support for Marshall Plan spending. They tried, first, to lobby congressional leaders, as well as less powerful members, to explain European needs and the stakes involved. Their most successful effort was encouraging legislators to travel to Europe to meet political and business leaders and see the suffering for themselves. At least 215 representatives made a European junket in late 1947, and in most cases they returned home more concerned about European economic conditions and more supportive of the plan than before they left.[45]

These junkets took many forms. Massachusetts representative Christian Herter, the chair of the House Select Committee on Foreign Aid, an ad hoc 19-member committee charged with studying the Marshall Plan, led the most extensive trip. Herter and the other members – including Richard Nixon, then in his initial term as a representative – spent over a month in Europe, starting in London as a group, then breaking up into smaller cohorts to travel the continent. Working on their report on their return voyage aboard the liner, *Queen Mary*, many initially skeptical members reported they had changed their minds and unanimously agreed to back some kind of plan (though they differed greatly on what that plan should look like).[46] Encouraging travel did not always work perfectly, though. John Taber of New York, chair of the House Appropriations Committee and a consistent foe of government spending, visited Rome, Athens, Istanbul, Ankara, Trieste, Vienna, and Berlin and said he did not think conditions were that bad. He claimed he had not seen any Europeans that looked underfed, even though, he noted, "I have specifically looked for it." But he also conceded that he would "favor reasonable cooperation in trying to rebuild the devastated areas of the world within the limits of the American capacity to pay." It was not a ringing Marshall Plan endorsement, but still evidence that travel had an impact.[47]

A second strategy was trying to build public support for the plan by engaging influential citizens and business leaders, who, in turn, would pressure senators and representatives to back the program. One example of this effort was an administration-planned conference at the White House in late October 1947. Truman invited executives from major corporations including Chase Bank, Standard Oil of New Jersey, American Home Products, Bristol-Meyers, B. F. Goodrich, General Foods, Eastman Kodak, and R. J. Reynolds Tobacco, along with a larger number of editors and reporters from newspapers and media companies that included the Columbia Broadcasting System, *The Washington Post, Time*, and Scripps Howard. A smattering of labor leaders and university presidents also made the guest list. In his short remarks, Truman argued that the United States could alleviate global problems, but more importantly had the responsibility to do so.

Truman said at the outset of this speech that because of its economic power, the nation was "charged today with a heavy responsibility," and then using the word "responsibility" again, added that the "responsibility for the survival of the world economy … falls directly on the United States." Addressing the skeptics, he concluded, "[it] would be a great mistake, I think, to consider our world responsibilities as crushing burdens that we assume gloomily and carry only because the alternative is so frightful." It was an opportunity to make the world better. Channeling Alexander Hamilton's writings on the power of government, he then explained, "This great country of ours has within its power to lead the world in the years ahead to peace and plenty such as never before have been known. Modern science, accompanied by safeguards for the freedom and dignity of mankind, could transform the world if applied wisely and linked up properly with capital and statesmanship."[48] Marshall, in his follow-up speech, made the anti-communist argument. The Soviet Union had been exploiting European economic chaos to lay the groundwork for its eventual expansion, and that strategy was working. They might seize Western Europe and be cheered by the people as saviors. If the United States did nothing, the Soviets could gain control, country by country. The alternative, the Marshall Plan, was buying "an option for the future" and helping Europe rebuild itself.[49]

The administration also created a private entity, the Citizen's Committee for the Marshall Plan, to build public support in a way that government officials could not. While technically an independent body and in name chaired by Henry Stimson, the former Secretary of State and Secretary of War, it operated as an administration marketing and organizational front.[50] One aspect of its operation, led by former Undersecretary of State and future Secretary of State Dean Acheson, was organizing testimony from business and industry leaders for congressional committees. This included recruiting speakers, getting them in front of the committees, and helping them prepare their testimony.[51] Another part of its strategy was building grassroots support by creating regional subcommittees and a "Women's Division" led by Edith Willkie, Wendell Willkie's widow. These subcommittees were encouraged to organize local events with pro-Marshall Plan speakers, distribute petitions, write letters to the editor, and ask radio stations to read pro-Marshall Plan scripts. The committee also produced a weekly fact sheet that it sent to newspapers and columnists and members of Congress, and it published stand-alone booklets such as "The Marshall Plan is Up to You," "Twenty Questions on the Marshall Plan," and "What About the Marshall Plan." In its few months of operations, it distributed more than 1.25 million items.[52]

Its most popular publication, by far, was the Munro Leaf illustrated pamphlet, "Who is the Man Against the Marshall Plan?" Leaf was a well-known author, and most famous for writing the 1936 children's book, *The Story of Ferdinand.* Directed toward a wide audience, the text addressed a range of objections to the Marshall Plan, explaining that although they initially sounded logical they did not "bear up" to scrutiny. The pamphlet explained that the "man" against the plan was "well-meaning and patriotic" and believed "certain things to be true," but he "doesn't bother to find out WHY he believes them, but he believes them nonetheless and says so … all over the country; in barbershops, railroad cars, at parties, clambakes and his own dinner table." With simple drawings, the pamphlet explored ten simple "arguments" against the Marshall Plan, including "we can't afford it!," "they are lazy!," "it's a Wall Street plot!," and "let 'em go bust!" The pamphlet's responses used similar folksy language. To the argument "we can't afford it!," for example, the pamphlet explained that if the man against the Marshall Plan was told exactly "what we spend a year on movies, chewing gum, soft-drinks, and cigarettes" and wanted to take that money and send it to Europe, "he may accuse you of trying to lower our standard of living." But the Marshall Plan was not asking for that; it was asking something like what "we bet on the horses last year alone ($6 billion) plus only a part of what our girls spent in the same time on lipstick, powder and other cosmetics." The argument, obviously, was that this was frivolous spending by women and gamblers, and people who mattered could do without betting and cosmetics. To the argument, "it's a Wall Street plot!," the reply was simpler. The pamphlet explained there was not "a shred of proof in the world but it sounds good and gives them an easy out." They could just as easily blame "'Organized Labor' or 'Volunteer Firemen' – anything to have an excuse for hiding their heads in the sandpiles of their own selfishness."[53]

The committee also placed advertisements in leading newspapers. Under the banner "STOP STALIN NOW," one ad argued that "World War III was not inevitable. Only a disastrous blunder of American policy which would permit the Russian totalitarian state to overrun the free nations of western Europe would

FIGURE 2.1 The cover of "Who is the Man Against the Marshall Plan…"

make such a war inevitable." The problem, the ad copy acknowledged, was opposition from the "extreme right and extreme left" to the Marshall Plan. On the left, opponents "representing the 'Give-Russia-A-Free-Hand-In-Europe' school advocate no aid except through wholly international channels." More seriously, the ad campaign suggested that a bigger threat came from the right, from "the 'Whittle-It-Down, We're-For-The-Marshall-Plan-But' senators and congressmen. They would like a plan but a cheap one," with the expectation that the United States could have a "strong and free Europe" without having to pay for it. That was an "illusion." The Committee urged readers to write or

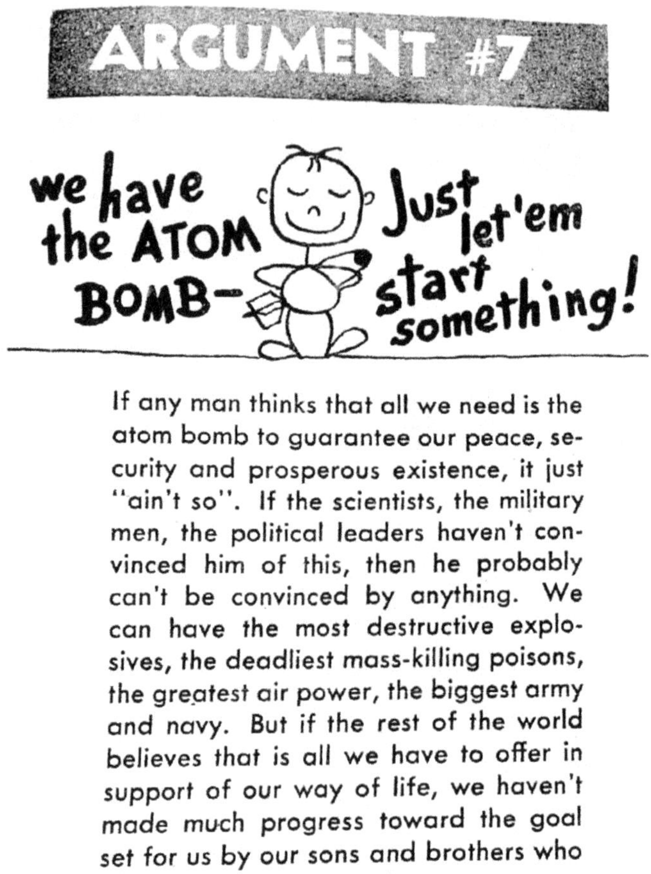
ARGUMENT #7

we have the ATOM BOMB— Just let'em start something!

If any man thinks that all we need is the atom bomb to guarantee our peace, security and prosperous existence, it just "ain't so". If the scientists, the military men, the political leaders haven't convinced him of this, then he probably can't be convinced by anything. We can have the most destructive explosives, the deadliest mass-killing poisons, the greatest air power, the biggest army and navy. But if the rest of the world believes that is all we have to offer in support of our way of life, we haven't made much progress toward the goal set for us by our sons and brothers who died in battle. When free men are so outnumbered that only atom bombs can save them from slavery, then none of us will be free much longer.

FIGURE 2.2 One of the "Arguments" from "Who is the Man Against the Marshall Plan…"

telephone their representatives as the "overwhelming voice" of the people could "move Congress to action."[54]

According to national polling data collected by Gallup, as Table 2.1 shows, this work was successful in building awareness about and support for the Marshall Plan. Yet the data also suggest opposition grew. Many, and perhaps as many as half the people who learned about the plan in late 1947 and early 1948, told pollsters they disapproved. The overall trend was that those aware of the plan and supportive of the plan rose significantly, but they never passed 50 percent in the surveys.

TABLE 2.1 Polling on the Marshall Plan (in percent)[55]

		July 25–30, 1947	*August 8–13, 1947*	*August 29–September 3, 1947*	*October 3–8, 1947*	*October 24–29, 1947*	*November 7–12, 1947*	*January 2–7, 1948*	*January 23–28, 1948*	*February 6–11, 1948*
Responding "Yes" to the question, "Have you heard or read about the Marshall Plan?"		60	51	59	68	61	64	79	71	79
Responses from those who claimed they were aware	Approve/ Favorable	43	51	54	51	47	56	47	52	57
	Disapprove/ Unfavorable	10	10	14	11	15	17	19	21	18
	No opinion/ Don't know	47	39	32	38	38	27	33	28	25
Total of those both aware of the Marshall Plan and expressing clear approval or a favorable opinion		26	26	32	35	39	36	37	37	49

Congressional Debates About the Marshall Plan: Do They Deserve It?

All of this campaigning and lobbying built to congressional debates on the plan, which had been transformed from a broad idea into a detailed piece of legislation by executive branch committees. Standard for any legislation, the bill (technically the European Recovery Program) went first to congressional committees and then to the Senate and House of Representatives. These offered a new platform for critics and skeptics, who in some cases rehashed earlier criticisms of aid spending and in other respects expanded the discussion.

One thread that ran throughout the hearings and floor debates was how much the Europeans deserved help. Were they poor enough that there were humanitarian responsibilities? Could US aid make a difference in ensuring that beneficiaries would grow into reliable allies, or would the spending fail to improve material conditions and fail to promote US geopolitical interests? Editors of the British magazine, *The Economist*, explained this was an inevitable "tragic element" in the debates over funding the Marshall Plan. They wrote that the people of the United States were being asked to organize themselves as if they were at war, while at peace, and they had a government structured purposefully by the Constitution to "prevent action" and "favour the laggards and the 'do-nothings' and to frustrate the responsible few." Given this, they continued, "It is inevitable that all the discussion in America should be about whether the European nations deserve help, or will turn to the best advantage whatever help is given them."[56]

In some cases, debates about the broad questions concerning interests and responsibilities were narrowed into specific conversations about how much different countries should get, as legislators and aid advocates emphasized that not all recipients were equal and not all deserved assistance. One early case addressed aid to Germany. James Sheldon, a board member from the Society for Prevention of World War III, testifying before the Senate Foreign Relations Committee in late January 1948, argued that it would be "indefensible and unsound" to reinvigorate Germany and allow it, once again, to threaten world peace. Sheldon's organization had roots in the Writers' War Board, a technically private organization led by author Rex Stout, a detective fiction writer, dedicated to building public support for World War II. As the war was ending, Stoudt developed this second organization to push for an unforgiving and severe peace settlement, suggesting that any German reindustrialization would likely threaten European stability once again. His instincts were similar to those that inspired the Morgenthau Plan, a proposal offered by US Treasury Secretary Henry Morgenthau, Jr., in 1944 to stop Germany from rebuilding its industrial capacity.

Sheldon testified that aid would "become an instrument for the revival of those predatory forces in Germany which have always looked with scorn upon democracy" and play into the hands of "Germany Firsters," which will lead to "the enormous growth of extremists and totalitarian ideologies of the very kind we want to prevent." He reminded the senators that "the Germans of 1948 were the very same Germans who heiled Hitler during those terrible years when most of Europe was trampled underfoot by the German boot." Given their historical unmatched propensity for "duplicity," it made no sense to trust them again.[57] This argument found little traction as Germany faced the most severe humanitarian crises and was on the front line of the emergent Cold War. Few people worried that it represented a threat in the late 1940s; the real danger, Marshall had said, was that failing to help might lead to the chaos that precipitated World War II.[58]

There were other, very different, country-specific objections for aid to nations that had not been involved in the fighting, which struck many legislators as inexplicable. Missouri representative Marion Bennett (R) attacked the inclusion of Ireland, saying that it had neither participated in the war nor suffered as a result. He noted there was also funding in the bills for Iceland (where the United States had built airports during the war), which did not need any rebuilding. Representative Robert Rich of Pennsylvania (R) colorfully said, "$797,000,000 to Ireland. Jiminy crickets, did you ever think that they would get Communism in Ireland? St. Patrick would never allow it." He continued, rhetorically, "What did we do for Iceland? We went over there and built them the greatest airports in the world. We asked them to let us use those airports. They turned us down. They told us to go home. Now you want to go back over there and give them $38,000,000. What for? To gain the good will? Of whom?" If the point was postwar reconstruction, this made no sense. California representative Chester Holifield (D) attacked the decision to send money to Spain, which also was not a party to World War II, and made a case that would become significant in debates about foreign aid much later. He said helping Spain, ruled by the dictatorial fascist government of Generalissimo Francisco Franco, completely undermined the argument that Marshall Plan's goal was advancing democracy and US values. New York representative Leo Isacson (D) made a similar case, saying it would disturbingly legitimize all the help Spain gave Hitler.[59]

However, the amounts for these countries were small, and criticism of aid to non-World War II belligerents was a minor issue. There were much larger country-specific attacks on aid to Great Britain, however, that focused on its government and its international record. Addressing the British prime minister Clement Attlee's Labour Party's policies, Illinois representative Ralph Church (R) made the popular and widely repeated argument that the British were using US money to construct a socialist government, which he said violated basic US values. Attacking Truman, the New Deal, and the Marshall Plan all at once, he said that Truman was trying to use the Marshall Plan to internationalize the socialist-like New Deal by subsidizing "socialism in England, communism and other-isms other than Americanism." But it was not only a mistake that "tax-payers were indirectly underwriting the socialistic schemes of the administration in power in Great Britain," there would be real harm as a result. "Instead of pursuing policies that would lead to increased production," he said the British Government had "pursued policies which represented an additional burden on their national economy and, by their very nature, retarded economic recovery." Representative Daniel Reed (R) of New York put it more simply, saying, "we are pouring billions into Great Britain to support a form of government which we are supposed to be fighting."[60] For the many legislators who equated any form of social welfare spending as putting the government on the slippery slope toward communism, this was a powerful attack.

There was a second issue about funding to Great Britain, raised only briefly during the debates on authorizing Marshall Plan funding but discussed more significantly in June 1948 during conversations about the follow-up aid appropriation bill. Several representatives, mostly from urban areas with substantial Jewish populations, attacked aid to Great Britain because of its anti-Jewish policies in the Middle East. New York representative Emanuel Celler (D) explained that toward the end of British control of Palestine, which had recently become the State of Israel,

> Britain piously stated she would maintain law and order. She fomented disorder. She pontifically stated that she would remain neutral during the mandate, but she encouraged Arab attacks against the Jews. She supplied the Arabs with implements of war. Her idea of neutrality was aiding the attackers and disarming the attacked and depriving the Jews of the means of defense. Then Bevin [the British Foreign Secretary] sabotaged the partition decision. He refused to abide by the United Nations' decision that a seaport and the hinterland be vacated for Jewish immigration by February 1. He closed the port of Haifa and sealed off all immigration. He refused to permit the Palestine Commission of the United Nations to enter … . Bevin then started

> a large-scale war against the Jews through his stooges like Abdullah, Feisel, and Faruk. He waged a squalid war by proxy against the Jews.[61]

Celler then proposed an amendment to the bill saying that because Great Britain had acted irresponsibly and maliciously, it should not receive any Marshall Plan money. Fellow New York Representative Arthur Klein (D) claimed more pointedly, "We should remember also that if we give them this money we are just helping them to turn over large amounts of money to the Arabs who have embarked on the present war of annihilation in Palestine."[62] Celler's amendment unsurprisingly failed, as a Marshall Plan without Great Britain at its core would have been illogical, but it was indicative of the ways that specific regional foreign policy interests would impact debates about foreign aid in the future.

The Larger Congressional Challenges

More broadly than legislators who objected to specific countries, Wallace's allies, led by Idaho senator Glen Taylor, also attacked the Marshall Plan. Here, and with Taft's supporters as well, the extensive public debate conditioned the legislative discussion.

In a monumental speech, so lengthy that Taylor agreed to stop speaking on the night of March 9, 1948, and continue again on the morning of March 10, he argued that the Marshall Plan would lead to increased conflict and violence. He explained the plan would not "accomplish the desired object of those who sponsor it, namely, buying the friendship of western European nations with a view to their becoming our allies in an expected war against Soviet Russia. Friends cannot be bought, and we do not make allies of nations by interfering in their internal affairs."[63] Taylor's critique expanded beyond the Marshall Plan, however, to a fuller attack on US postwar politics. Noting that with Vandenberg's support, the Marshall Plan was becoming the core of the "bipartisan foreign policy." This closed down national dialogue about the US role in the world. "In the matter of foreign affairs" he continued, "there is no longer a two-party system in America. We have a one-party system just as certainly as Hitler did, and it is beginning to appear that the only difference between the old parties in domestic policies is a matter of talk and messages on the State of the Union." Taylor, who, as noted earlier, would join Wallace's ticket as his vice-presidential running mate, continued,

> Now the bipartisan Wall Street military clique knew that their scheme was full of holes and wide open to criticism. They knew it would be bad if the American people got wise to their schemes. So what did they do … . They just took a page from Adolf Hitler's book and started a Red hunt. Anybody who disagreed was a Communist. They were in an excellent position to make it stick because they had most of the press … . [I]n the last two years the names of the liberal

> commentators who have disappeared from the radio, those who might have criticized and exposed this nefarious plot against the peace, but who have been booted off the radio for one excuse or another, are legion.[64]

Vito Marcantonio of New York, a member of the independent American Labor Party, echoed Taylor's point in the House. He explained that in fighting against the Marshall Plan, he would not "be deterred by any vituperation that may come from any tobacco patriot or from any cotton king or any corn and corny orator or from any arrogant Jim Crow flag-waver who brazenly talks of democracy here, but personally refuses to apply it in the communities he represents." The Marshall Plan, he asserted, was "a bill for imperialism and monopoly capitalists," and by fighting against it, he and his supporters were "not attacking America – we are defending America because the enemy of America today, the enemy of the world today, is Wall Street monopoly capital."[65]

Taylor in the Senate, and Marcantonio in the House of Representatives, had few allies. Taylor had presented a replacement aid bill, modeled on Wallace's argument that the United Nations, rather than the United States, should manage aid to Europe. This proposal failed in the Senate 74 to 3, with only William Langer (R-ND) and Claude Pepper (D-FL) joining Taylor. Langer was one of the most vehement critics of the Marshall Plan, and seemed to believe that Taylor's idea would have sabotaged the bill from moving forward. Claude Pepper was Taylor's only real supporter in the Senate; he shared the view that confrontation with the Soviet Union was counterproductive to European peace.[66]

Taft's allies, however, mostly in the Republican Party, launched a stronger and more sustained attack, though they obviously also failed to stop the bill.[67] Missouri senator James Kem (R) was among the most vocal critics, explaining that the Senate had been asked to "continue a policy of extending governmental grants and so-called loans to European countries in the hope that a more prosperous and peaceful world will result." But, he explained, the United States "pursued this policy almost without remission since the end of the First World War, at a tremendous cost to ourselves" and without meaningful results. Recent experience with UNRRA demonstrated the problem, as half of its spending had ended up in communist nations. As bad, throughout Europe, corrupt officials took advantage of UNRRA and "made the most of their opportunity to profiteer, and large quantities of foodstuffs made their way into the black market." Now he said, the UNRRA "was a thing rejected, scorned, and unsung."[68]

Minnesota senator Joseph Ball (R) built on the points about waste and poor results. His understanding was that the "latest reports from Greece indicate that all we have succeeded in doing is holding the line against a few thousand communist guerrillas. We have no way of knowing how much this particular pressure has cost Russia, but I would guess that it is probably less than $300,000." He continued, doing the hypothetical math, that "by spending $1, Russia can force the United States in carrying out this containment policy to spend a thousand dollars … that appears to me to be a hopeless, suicidal policy which can have only one end result, the economic bankruptcy of the United States." He asserted he could not "support a foreign policy whose sole answer to every succeeding international crisis seems to be the expenditure of more and more of American resources all over the world."[69]

Critical senators suggested that instead of the Marshall Plan, money should go in one of two directions. Nevada senator George Malone (R) argued that if the United States was serious about fighting communism, it should spend on preparations for actual fighting. Instead of relying on Europeans to help in some future war with the Soviets, and using aid as a roundabout way to obtain their help, the United States should just use its dollars on a massive military build-up. He explained, "We backed into two world wars in our generation unprepared and denying that we would fight. Let us try it once prepared to fight, and telling the world and our own people frankly that we will fight."[70] Others, including Kem, said that all this spending would be better at home. He argued that the war had been costly and there was a need to rebuild the United States economy. He speculated that if instead of all the postwar foreign aid, which he termed "operation rat hole," the United States had spent that money domestically, "we could have limed, fertilized, and terraced every acre of good farm land in the United States, paid for the Pick-Sloan Mississippi Valley flood-control plan, and still would have had ample funds to gravel every dirt road in the United States and build 7,000 miles of two-laned concrete highways." It made little sense to spend money on European development, he insisted, when there were things to fix at home.[71]

Senator Charles Brooks of Illinois (R) similarly advanced this point in breaking down the cost of the Marshall Plan for each of his constituents. He noted the United States had already spent $24.1 billion on foreign assistance from 1945 to 1947, which amounted to $183 per Illinois resident. The Marshall Plan would be another $17 billion, and another $129 per resident. Added up, it would be more than $1 billion for the people of Chicago. Given that the median family income in 1948 was $3,120, it was a powerful way to make the case that this spending represented a real sacrifice to Illinois families.[72] Texas senator W. Lee O'Daniel (D) built on Brooks' point. He said, thinking about actual taxpayers, that "I will, as a private citizen, go down into my own pocket and take as much of my personal money as I can afford to contribute to charity. I will give to whomsoever I may choose in any nation on earth, regardless of race, religion, color, or political belief, if such people are hungry or sick and unable to sustain themselves." Yet, he argued that as a senator he could not "go into the pockets of other citizens … to give it as charity to foreigners." It was not a power that existed under the Constitution, and not ethical.[73] O'Daniel seemed to be suggesting something similar to the argument made by the prominent Protestant theologian Reinhold Niebuhr in *Moral Man and Immoral Society*. Niebuhr argued in 1932 that while individuals had a responsibility to be moral, and by extension give charity when possible, states had no such obligation because they had responsibilities to the taxpayers to use funds wisely and responsibly. Arguing that aid was charity instead of a foreign policy investment, as O'Daniel did, undermined its whole logic.[74]

There was a geographic connection to Marshall Plan opposition that helps explain some of its basis. Most of the leading Marshall Plan opponents came from Midwestern states, broadly construed, where prewar isolationism had also been most powerful.[75] One continuity for these Midwesterners was economic. Trade patterns, and perceptions of them, were less internationalized in the Midwest than in other parts of the country. As voters looked at their economic activity and found few foreign connections, it would have been far easier to suggest that what happened abroad did not matter, and worrying about Hitler's threat or spending money on the Marshall Plan would be harder to justify. Some opposition was also political. Republicans had long presented themselves as a party of small business and a counter to Democratic-dominated big-city political machines. Democrats were more active in pushing for global engagement and global responsibility, first under Wilson, then with Roosevelt and Truman.[76]

Like prewar isolationists, Marshall Plan opponents also understood they were in a minority, that bills would be passed, and that the United States' international position was changing, but they held to their view that these changes were a mistake, and that the United States risked weakening itself, or even losing its economic strength if it recklessly embraced internationalism. They were outsiders, claiming they were fighting for the nation in the face of leaders who hoped to put the interests of foreigners ahead of loyal citizens. Ultimately, of course, they lost, and Congress passed the Marshall Plan; on March 14, 1948 the Senate voted 69 to 17 in favor, and two weeks later the House followed up with a 329 to 74 vote.[77]

Fighting Point Four

Less than a year after Congress passed the Marshall Plan authorizing legislation, Truman called for the creation of the Point Four program in his 1949 inaugural address. This was a second step toward making foreign aid a permanent fixture in US foreign policy. He argued in the speech that the United States needed to move beyond the Marshall Plan and Europe to advance "peace and freedom" throughout the world, and suggested four courses of action his administration would prioritize. The first three were (1) working with the United Nations to strengthen all democratic governments, (2) reducing trade barriers and encouraging economic growth everywhere, and (3) signing mutual defense treaties and providing military assistance to nations whose leaders understood global threats as US leaders did. The fourth, indicated by the name Point Four, was embarking "on a bold new program for making the benefits of our scientific advances and industrial progress available for the improvement and growth of underdeveloped areas."[78] Point Four built on Truman's policy in Europe and suggested similar approaches should be applied to other parts of the world also struggling with poverty. A key difference was that Point Four would need to become essentially permanent. It was reasonable to assume that Europe could be rebuilt and returned to its prewar developed and modern condition, but transforming parts of the world that had always been traditional and materially poor would require a far longer and more substantial effort.

It was also a much larger step in suggesting that the United States government should be globally engaged, and that Africa, the Middle East, Latin America, and Asia were all strategically important. Even more than the Marshall Plan, Point Four was a rejection of isolationist sentiments as it imagined that the United States had global responsibilities. Whereas the Marshall Plan was a program for reconstruction, Point Four's goal was development, moving backward peoples up a civilizational ladder from poverty and traditionalism to wealth and modernity; it was a secular extension of missionary ideas.

In the moment it was also less intuitively necessary. The Marshall Plan built on Truman's policies in Greece and Turkey and reflected a sense of panic about European instability and communist expansionism. Europeans, white and civilized, were facing chaos, and they needed help. Non-Europeans, less civilized and poor, had always been less civilized and poor, and the chaos of their existence seemed to be a historical constant. Certainly communists might eventually take advantage of poverty and chaos outside Europe, but there was no immediate threat, and thus no immediate need for action.

The way Point Four was included in the speech demonstrates this point. Flush with confidence following his 1948 presidential election victory, Truman wanted to do something dramatic and exciting in his inaugural address. He told State Department officials that he wanted a "democratic manifesto addressed to the peoples of the world, not just to the American people." His answer, Point Four, came from a memo that a relatively junior staffer in the State Department, Benjamin Hardy, had written a month before. Hardy, who had served in Brazil and was inspired by the Marshall Plan, thought that other parts of the world also needed help. He argued that instability beyond Europe and East Asia threatened long-term US power because people in materially poorer societies watched the progress of wealthier countries and would not be satisfied with the comparison; unless they saw change, they would become revolutionaries, and the United States would face a global communist threat.[79] Hardy's memo made it to Truman, who liked the ambitious idea and thought it fit his goals for the speech perfectly.[80]

Progress getting money for the program was slow. In late June 1949, Truman sent Congress a request to enact two legislative proposals. He wanted $45 million to launch Point Four, and approval for the Export-Import Bank to encourage US investment in materially poorer societies. Truman administration officials, anticipating opposition, contradictorily suggested that these represented the start of a "bold new" program but that they were also "modest."[81]

Senate and House committees held hearings in September and October 1949 on both Truman requests, but neither body took up the legislation. The chair of the Senate Foreign Relations Committee, Tom Connally (D-TX), did not believe the plan made sense, nor that it would make it through Congress.

Vandenberg, who had lost his position as the committee chair when the Democrats retook control of the Senate, was the senior Republican, and he agreed with Connally. Without Vandenberg and Connally, or at least one of them, Point Four did not have a chance. In the House, there was similarly no enthusiasm. The Republican minority leader, Joseph W. Martin (R-MA), argued that the United States needed to focus on its internal security, rather than Truman's international plan, and kept the bill from moving forward. He said he was concerned about the Soviet Union's testing of an atomic device, and added that Congress "should suspend new spending until we find out what we need for defense against the atom." Security, he suggested, was more important than "charitable and benevolent deeds."[82]

Pennsylvania Representative James G. Fulton (R) captured the varied congressional objections during the House Foreign Affairs Committee hearings. Cataloging potential problems, he said there was no built-in limit on where aid might go, or how it might be used. He said that aid could end up in the hands of Soviet-leaning governments like those in Yugoslavia, or be sent to dictatorships like the one in Argentina. He also made a fiscally conservative argument, saying that Point Four would also take money from poorer people in the United States. Yet the biggest problem was the lack of a termination date, with the likelihood that foreign aid might become a perpetual feature of US foreign policy. Fulton accused Truman officials of having no idea how long Point Four could last, and suggested they wanted spending to last to "infinity." His colleague, Ohio Republican John Vorys, one of the most active Representatives on international relations questions, backed Fulton. He said he did not understand how it would work and how US aid could transform the world. It was, he said, the "craziest thing I ever saw," and added that "Rube Goldberg must have been your consultant" in thinking through the plan's operation.[83]

In addition to the unenthusiastic reception, there was also a legislative scheduling problem. Even if there had been support for Point Four, there was not enough time to pass anything in 1949. Despite proposing the plan in January and asking for a specific figure in July, Truman only sent Congress a complete bill in late September, which was too close to the end of the congressional session to have time on the legislative calendar. So despite Truman's push for what was supposed to be a signature program, it went nowhere in 1949.[84]

Truman tried again with Point Four in 1950 calling it "must have legislation," as he still thought of it as a major initiative that would demonstrate the transformative power of government. He explained in a speech to the American Society of Civil Engineers that he hoped the program could harness "all the engineers of this great United States of ours, and all the other great technical men – the architects, the physicians – everybody who has a special skill for the welfare of humanity" to "make the other fellow as contented as we can be, by helping him develop his resources for his own welfare and benefit." He also suggested the program would help US industry, saying that if the plan could raise global living standards by 2 percent, the "other fellow" would "need so many things that we can produce to give to him, that we never will catch up with the demand."[85] But despite this push, few people were paying attention, especially compared with the Marshall Plan. In an April 1950 poll, only 24 percent of those asked said they had heard or read anything about Point Four; in November 1950 that had changed little, as only 26 percent responded they knew about it.[86]

Public pressure might have made a difference, but without it, congressional leaders had little reason to fight for Point Four. Truman said it was necessary, but few legislators, even ones that strongly backed him, seemed to agree. Another problem was that Truman was making this new funding request just as there was a growing chorus to cut Marshall Plan spending. By 1950 most observers in Washington felt that Europe seemed to be recovering, and the panic of 1947 and 1948 was no longer warranted. Multiple surveys indicated that Europeans were producing about as much as they had before the war, if not more, and that recovery had happened. Truman agreed, and cut his January 1950 budget request for Europe by 20 percent, and made similar reductions in aid to occupied areas in Asia. Nevertheless, he again asked for $45 million for Point Four to be included in a $3.3 billion foreign aid bill.[87]

In the House, there was resistance and little enthusiasm for Point Four. Only the maneuverings of Representative Christian Herter (R-MA), who had been instrumental in 1947 in building support for the Marshall Plan and would later serve as President Eisenhower's Secretary of State, really pushed it along. Herter, who claimed to support Point Four, proposed an amendment to the overall aid authorization bill to cut the proposed funding from $45 million to $25 million. This passed 117 to 78. Herter claimed that the cut was the only way to save the plan in the face of attacks from its most vocal opponents such as John Jennings (R-TN) and Arthur Miller (R-NB). Jennings said that his constituents wanted expenditures and taxes cut, and that he did not trust the Truman administration to handle the money effectively given that its diplomatic policy was a "shambles" and "the most ghastly debacle that all history records." Miller said it was a mistake that "we as a country will be sticking our noses into the business of other people all over the world." He said (prophetically) that although the request was only $45 million now, it would soon be in the billions.[88]

Truman had tried to fight back against the cut. In a note to Speaker of the House Sam Rayburn (D-TX), Truman argued that in "countries where the choice between Communist totalitarianism and the free way of life is in the balance, this program can tip the scales toward the way of freedom." He said if the cuts remained, it would "largely destroy the program's effectiveness. More than that, it will be regarded throughout the world as evidence that this country cannot be depended upon to help millions of people in the underdeveloped areas of the world in bettering their lot." He added the attempt to save money "will do more for the Communists in their attack on the free world than hundreds of millions of dollars of their own propaganda."[89] Truman, of course, had created this problem himself. He had asked Congress to fund an aid program, and then claimed that failure to fund it would be a boon to communists, neglecting to mention that if he had not introduced the program in the first place, there would have been no geopolitical issue with a lack of funding.

The Senate passage of the legislation was more complicated, but also reflected a lack of interest. There were some efforts to just push it off. Senators Leverett Saltonstall (R-MA) and Eugene Milikin (R-CO) argued that consideration of Point Four be postponed for another year, and that the Senate should launch a bipartisan investigation into its potential. If that investigation indicated the program's necessity and practicality, then it made sense to approve funding, but only after all Marshall Plan money had been spent, which would have been at least two additional years.[90] Many senators seemed skeptical about Truman's larger aid plan, and sensing an opportunity, Taft introduced an amendment to cut $500 million from the $3.3 billion aid request, which lost in a 40 to 40 tie. Capitalizing on this, Saltonstall and Milikin said there were just too many questions about the bill, and there was certainly no urgency to pass Point Four. This led them, and others, to try to amend the funding request to cut Point Four. The most notable and aggressive was Texan Tom Connally's proposal to remove it from the bill altogether, which lost in a 37 to 36 vote. The tightness of this vote demonstrated the lack of enthusiasm for Point Four, and how close it came to getting killed. The slim majority willing to back Truman was then able to keep the full $45 million Truman had requested in the bill.[91]

Just as he had been in the early phases of the fight against the Marshall Plan, Taft was among the strongest Point Four opponents. He rejected the idea that state power should be involved in societal uplift, arguing it was best left to the charitable and capitalist private sector. He explained, "If projects are sound, there are plenty of big American firms prepared to send their experts" to help make development happen. Instead, Point Four was a "welfare service" that would create a "kind of wide-open distribution of all kinds of aid to all kinds of people anywhere in the world the President might desire to help." It was "simply an idea summoned out of someone's mind of some other way the Government money can be spent, of some other way the United States can go around the world and assume to interfere with the affairs of other people and try to improve the standards of living of other people." This touched on the view that helping people fight poverty outside the United States was not the job of the US government, and that the United States did not have the power to make such change happen. He argued, "this nation is wholly incapable of improving the standards of living of the peoples of India and China. That is beyond our capacity … Why on earth should we undertake to enter upon this brand new program? It seems to me to be inconsistent with practically everything the best in the United States has advocated."[92]

Following passage of the spending bill in both chambers, House and Senate members met in a conference committee to prepare a final bill. Given the House had only authorized $25 million for Point Four and the Senate's bill had approved $45 million, the obvious compromise was $35 million, and the bill returned to both houses for a final vote. Under normal circumstances, votes taken after a conference committee report were pro forma. Legislators usually agreed to accept limited modifications in any bill that did not distort its meaning. Yet, on its return to the Senate on May 23, 1950, Taft once again tried to kill Point Four. He argued, clearly as a way of reopening the debate, that the conference bill did not take the will of the Senate into account.

Taft repeated his point that the bill represented a new and dangerous departure for the United States because it did not have "an anti-Communist connotation or a connotation of a program by which we are aiding countries which are supposed to be fighting Communism." Instead, he explained, "this program is wide open to the entire world."[93] Taft contended that the conference report allowed the president to make unlimited commitments, which violated the spirit of the Senate bill. The Senate, he claimed, had only authorized a bill "to aid the efforts of the people of economically underdeveloped areas to develop their resources and improve their working and living conditions by encouraging the exchange of technical knowledge and skills." But the conference bill added a phrase that aid should "contribute to raising standards of living, creating new sources of wealth, increasing productivity, and expanding purchasing power." Taft said this was too ambitious, and a major divergence.

Taft wanted to fight so strongly because the country was already over-committed to foreign aid "far beyond the financial capacity of the United States." He argued that with the Marshall Plan and aid spending in Asia it was not the time to take on even more. The budget deficit, he said, would be more than $6 billion. Point Four was just too much. Congress was "committing ourselves to a great program to help every nation throughout the world." And while "this is only a small program at this time … we are committing ourselves" to a project that could not achieve its goals. The United States could help "a little, but our help is not going to make any great, fundamental change in the condition of the people, because one people cannot do that for another." In the end, both Taft and Truman lost. Taft was unable to stop the bill, and Truman had little choice but to accept the reduced $35 million figure.[94]

The fight in 1950 against Point Four was not the end of challenges to Truman's foreign aid initiatives. It was rather the start of a much longer story. This discussion, in introducing those challenges, suggests a perspective absent in the scholarship about Truman's foreign policy and his interest in using foreign aid in Greece and Turkey, via the Marshall Plan and through Point Four. On one hand, it explains that on the whole, Truman was able to gain support from Congress despite the consistent and logical fear that aid's opponents could torpedo his plans. On the other hand, it demonstrates that Truman's Cold War vision and his belief in foreign aid was not a consensus position, and there was substantial opposition to his assumptions about US power and the role of government. In the case of Point Four, the opposition limited the amount of money he could ask for and what he could spend. These challenges did not go away, and each subsequent year in the Truman administration they were renewed by the same opponents making the same arguments, which set the tone for the Eisenhower administration to develop, at least initially, a different approach to aid programming that reflected this anti-aid chorus.

Notes

1 Gilbert Bailey, "Report from Rushville, Indiana," *NYT*, August 27, 1947. The citizens of Rushville were not unique. The *New York Herald Tribune* sent a reporter across the United States to gauge opinion about global events. He found people were "too busy with their own crowded lives and the country's internal problems" to worry about Europe. John O'Reilly, "How Strong is America: Americans Found Too Busy with Own Active Lives," *New York Herald Tribune*, September 24, 1947.
2 "Indiana Discovered by New York," *Chicago Tribune*, September 4, 1947.
3 George C. Marshall, "Speech to Harvard University Alumni, June 5, 1947," George C. Marshall Foundation, www.marshallfoundation.org/marshall/the-marshall-plan/marshall-plan-speech (accessed October 15, 2020).
4 Ibid.
5 Marshall had been critical of the "flamboyant anti-communism" in President Truman's address to Congress on the Greek crisis on March 12, 1947. Charles E. Bohlen, *Witness to History* (New York, 1973), 261; Ferald J. Bryan, "George C. Marshall at Harvard: A Study of the Origins and Construction of the 'Marshall Plan' Speech," *Presidential Studies Quarterly* 21, 3 (Summer 1991), 489–502; Ben Steil, *The Marshall Plan: Dawn of the Cold War* (New York, 2018); Will Moreland, *The Marshall Plan and the Shaping of American Strategy* (Washington, 2017); Michael Hogan, *The Marshall Plan, America, Britain, and the Reconstruction of Europe* (New York, 1987).
6 Marshall, "Speech to Harvard Alumni."
7 George Guess, *The Politics of United States Foreign Aid* (London, 1987), 30; David Ekbladh, *The Great American Mission* (Princeton, 2009), 86–89; Andrew Williams, "'Reconstruction' before the Marshall Plan," *Review of International Studies* 31, 2 (July 2005), 550–553; Michael Schaller, "Securing the Great Crescent: Occupied Japan and the Origins of Containment in Southeast Asia," *The Journal of American History* 69, 2 (September 1982), 392–414; James I. Matray, "Development Delayed: US Economic Policy in Occupied Korea, 1945–1948," *Journal of American-East Asian Relations* 10, 1–2 (January 2001), 29–52; Nicholas Balabkins, *Germany Under Direct Controls: Economic Aspects of Industrial Disarmament 1945–1948* (New Brunswick, NJ, 1964), 101.
8 Robert A. Pollard, *Economic Security and the Origins of the Cold War 1945–1950* (New York, 1985), 66–81; Ruth Logue, *History of US Foreign Aid Since the Second World War* (Washington, 1961), 6.
9 Amikam Nachmani, "Civil War and Foreign Intervention in Greece, 1946–1949," *Journal of Contemporary History* 25, 4 (October 1990), 489–522; Dean Acheson to Truman, "Memorandum: Proposed Agreement on Aid to Greece," August 7, 1946 (www.trumanlibrary.gov/library/online-collections/truman-doctrine); "British Embassy to the Department of State," Document 24, *Foreign Relations of the United States, 1947, The Near East and Africa, Volume V* (Washington, 1971).
10 Harry S. Truman, "Special Message to the Congress on Greece and Turkey," Gerhard Peters and John T. Woolley, eds, APP, www.presidency.ucsb.edu/node/232818 (accessed September 2, 2020); Harry S. Truman, "The President's News Conference," March 26, 1947, Gerhard Peters and John T. Woolley, eds, APP, www.presidency.ucsb.edu/node/232843 (accessed September 24, 2020); Felix Belair, "New Policy Set Up," *NYT*, March 13, 1947; Dennis Merrill, "The Truman Doctrine: Containing Communism and Modernity," *Presidential Studies Quarterly* 36, 1 (March 2006), 27–37;

Robert Frazier, "Kennan, 'Universalism,' and the Truman Doctrine," *Journal of Cold War Studies* 11, 2 (Spring 2009), 3–34.

11 *Calendars of the United States House of Representative and History of Legislation, Eightieth Congress* (Washington, 1949), 323; *CR*, April 22, 1947, 3793; *CR*, May 9, 1947, 4975.

12 *CR*, April 22, 1947, 3760, 3762, 3767.

13 Francis Case to Truman, May 10, 1947, Greece & Turkey – 1947, Box 1426, Official File 426, Papers of Harry S. Truman, Harry S. Truman Library, Independence, MO (hereafter HSTL).

14 *CR*, May 9, 1947, 4955.

15 *Calendars of the United States House of Representative and History of Legislation, Eightieth Congress* (Washington, 1949), 324.

16 Joseph Starobin, "Should Americans Back the Marshall Plan," Marshall Plan, Box 72, Pamphlet Collection PE043, Reference Center for Marxist Studies, Tamiment Library, New York University, New York.

17 William Z. Foster, *Labor and the Marshall Plan* (New Century Publishers, 1948), 2, 7, 11.

18 Foster, *Labor and the Marshall Plan*, 2, 7, 11; Starobin, "Should Americans Back the Marshall Plan."

19 J. Samuel Walker, *Henry A. Wallace and American Foreign Policy* (Westport, CT, 1976), 84; Graham White and John Maze, *Henry A. Wallace: His Search for a New World Order* (Chapel Hill, 1995), 193–201.

20 John W. Partin, "Roosevelt, Byrnes, and the 1944 Vice-Presidential Nomination," *The Historian* 42, 1 (November 1979), 85–100; Alonzo Hamby, "Henry Wallace, the Liberals, and Soviet-American Relations," *The Review of Politics* 30, 2 (April 1968), 153–169; White and Maze, *Henry A. Wallace*, 199–209.

21 Henry Wallace, "Peaceful Economic Abundance," December 4, 1945, in Mayako Shimamoto, *Henry A. Wallace's Criticism of America's Atomic Monopoly, 1945–1948* (Newcastle upon Tyne, UK, 2016), 105; Walker, *Henry A. Wallace*, 123; White and Maze, *Henry A. Wallace*, 219–224.

22 Henry Wallace, "The Way to Peace, September 12, 1946," *Washington Post*, September 13, 1946; Alonzo Hamby, "Henry Wallace, the Liberals, and Soviet-American Relations," 153–169.

23 Wallace to Truman, July 23, 1946, Wallace, Clifford Papers, Subject File, Box 19, Clark M. Clifford Papers, HSTL.

24 Walker, *Henry A. Wallace and American Foreign Policy*, 149–163.

25 Wallace to Secretary Marshall, January 13, 1947, 1947 January, Box 34, Series III, Correspondence, Papers of Henry Agard Wallace, University of Iowa, Iowa City, Iowa (hereafter HAWP); Walker, *Henry A. Wallace*, 167–179.

26 Henry Wallace, "The Way to Help Greece," *The New Republic*, March 17, 1947; Henry Wallace, "Response to Truman's Speech on Greece and Turkey," March 13, 1947, reprinted by the *Gazette and Daily*, York, PA, March 14, 1947, collected in March 14, Box 34, Series III, Correspondence, HAWP.

27 Henry Wallace, "Bevin Muddies the Waters," *The New Republic*, June 30, 1947; Henry Wallace, "What We Must Do Now," *The New Republic*, July 14, 1947.

28 William Walton, "Men Around Marshall," *The New Republic*, September 22, 1947; Thomas Divine, *Henry Wallace's 1948 Presidential Campaign and the Future of Postwar Liberalism* (Chapel Hill, 2013).

29 Schlesinger, Stephen. "FDR's Five Policemen: Creating the United Nations," *World Policy Journal* 11, 3 (1994), 88–93.

30 Richard Walton, *Henry Wallace, Harry Truman, and the Cold War* (New York, 1976), 118–180.

31 Walton, *Henry Wallace, Harry Truman and the Cold War*, 155–158.

32 "Memo Re. Wallace Situation," Wallace, Clifford Papers, Subject File, Box 19, Clark M. Clifford Papers, HSTL.

33 "Robert W. Kenny keynote remarks at the Democrats for Wallace conference, Fresno, California, July 19, 1947," 1947 May-September, Box 35, Series III, Correspondence, HAWP.
34 "Wallace Warns of Wall St. Rule," *NYT*, September 12, 1947.
35 Walton, *Henry Wallace, Harry Truman and the Cold War*, 182.
36 "The Wallace Plan vs. the Marshall Plan," Campaign Literature R-Z, Box 1, Series IV, Campaigns, Elections, and Inaugurations, HAWP; "Let's Get Out the Vote," *Songs for Wallace*, Mementos, Box 1, Series IV, Campaigns, Elections, and Inaugurations, HAWP.
37 Walton, *Henry Wallace, Harry Truman and the Cold War*, 231.
38 Thomas Devine, *Henry Wallace's 1948 Presidential Campaign and the Future of Postwar Liberalism* (Chapel Hill, 2013), 286–292.
39 "Text of Senator Taft's Tacoma Address, September 29, 1947," *NYT*, September 30, 1947.
40 "Text of Senator Taft's Tacoma Address, September 29, 1947"; "Taft Outlines His Views on Foreign Policy," *New York Herald Tribune*, September 29, 1947; "U.S. Foreign Policy Failure, Says Taft; Offers Substitute," *NYT*, September 29, 1947.
41 "Text of Taft Speech Listing Objections to Scale of Marshall Plan for Aid to Europe" *NYT*, November 11, 1947; Thomas L. Stokes, "Taft Trying to Scare the Voters?," *Atlanta Constitution*, November 15, 1947.
42 *CR*, November 28, 1947, 10929; Thomas L. Stokes, "Senator Taft Turns to Foreign Policy," *The Atlanta Constitution*, February 16, 1948.
43 Quoted in Hank Meijer, "Arthur Vandenberg and the Fight for Neutrality, 1939," *Michigan Historical Review* 16, 2 (Fall 1990), 1–21; Lawrence S. Kaplan, *The Conversion of Senator Arthur S. Vandenberg: From Isolationist to International Engagement* (Lexington, KY, 2015), 66, 82–85.
44 Kaplan, 194–196; Lawrence Haas, *Harry and Arthur: Truman, Vandenberg, and the Partnership that Created the Free World* (Lincoln, NB, 2016), 193–195; Marquis Childs, "Washington Calling: Vandenberg vs. Ball," *Washington Post*, March 5, 1948; "Bipartisan Sell Out," *Chicago Tribune*, June 16, 1947; "The Twenty Senators," *New York Herald Tribune*, January 15, 1948; Richard L. Strout, "There's Always Senator Vandenberg," *The Christian Science Monitor* April 15, 1948.
45 Arthur Krock, "What Was Probably a Blessing in Disguise," *NYT*, October 31, 1947; "Isolationism Learns the Facts," *Christian Science Monitor*, October 22, 1947; "Congressional Travel Helped Break Down Wall of Isolationism," *The Austin Statesman*, December 16, 1947; Cabell Phillips, "Congressional Tours Big Aid to Marshall Plan," *NYT*, October 19, 1947.
46 "Congress Group Sets Special Lindon Study," *NYT*, September 2, 1947; "US Group to Visit Two Eastern Nations," *NYT*, September 5, 1947; Mallory Browne, "Herter Sub-Group for Aid to Britain," *NYT*, October 1, 1947; C. P. Trussel, "Herter Group, Back, Finds Europe Too Hopeful on Aid," *NYT*, October 10, 1947.
47 Jack Raymond, "Taber Opposes Aid to Europe at Once," *NYT*, October 4, 1947; "GOP to Demand 'Facts' Before Aiding Europe: Truman Spending Policy Called Confused," *Chicago Tribune*, October 24, 1947; Arthur Krock, "What Was Probably a Blessing in Disguise," *NYT*, October 31, 1947.
48 "Remarks by the President to the Group Meeting at the White House, October 27, 1947," Meeting of October 27, 1947, Box 1427, OF 426, Official File, Papers of HST, HSTL.
49 "Indian Summer in Washington, Leo Barnett Memo, November 3, 1947" Meeting of October 27, 1947, Box 1427, OF 426, Official File, Papers of HST, HSTL.
50 Robert Patterson to Vandenberg, "Committee for the Marshall Plan letter about testimony to Congress," February 16, 1948, OF 426, Box 1420, Official File, Papers of HST, HSTL.

51 "Report on the Activities of the Committee for the Marshall Plan," Committee for the Marshall Plan 1947–1948 [3 of 3], Box 4, Political and Governmental File, Dean G. Acheson Papers, HSTL; "Positions of American National Organizations, February 19, 1948" Committee for the Marshall Plan 1947–1948 [2 of 3], Box 4, Political and Governmental File, Dean G. Acheson Papers, HSTL; "Notes on cultivation of Senators, January 29, 1958" Committee for the Marshall Plan 1947–1948 [2 of 3], Box 4, Political and Governmental File, Dean G. Acheson Papers, HSTL; Henry Parkman to Dean Acheson, March 17, 1948; Committee for the Marshall Plan 1947–1948 [2 of 3], Box 4, Political and Governmental File, Dean G. Acheson Papers, HSTL.

52 "Report on the Activities of the Committee for the Marshall Plan," Committee for the Marshall Plan 1947–1948 [3 of 3], Box 4, Political and Governmental File, Dean G. Acheson Papers, HSTL.

53 Munro Leaf and the Committee for the Marshall Plan to Aid European Recovery, "Who is the Man Against the Marshall Plan," Who is the Man Against the Marshall Plan, Box 6, Dean G. Acheson Papers, HSTL; Michael Wala, "Selling the Marshall Plan at Home: The Committee for the Marshall Plan to Aid European Recovery," *Diplomatic History* 10, 3 (July 1986), 247–265.

54 "Committee for the Marshall Plan Advertisement" Committee for the Marshall Plan 1947–1948 [2 of 3], Box 4, Dean G. Acheson Papers, HSTL.

55 Conducted by Gallup, datasets USGALLUP.47–401, USGALLUP.47–402, USGALL UP.47–403, USGALLUP.47–405, USGALLUP.110247, USGALLUP.120747, USGA LLUP.410, USGALLUP.48–411, and USGALLUP.48–412, collected by the Roper Center for Public Opinion Research, ropercenter.cornell.edu (accessed February 14, 2018). Note that answers in the "No opinion/Don't know" category also include those who did not answer or who gave qualified answers indicating neither complete support nor opposition, that in some cases poll questions gave respondents the opportunity to indicate level of support or opposition and this has been simplified here into approval or disapproval. There were minor variations in the wording of questions (i.e. "Have you heard or read about the Marshall Plan for helping Europe?," "Have you heard or read about the Marshall Plan?," or "Have you heard or read anything about the Marshall Plan for aiding European recovery?"). Total in final row determined by multiplying percent of those aware of the Marshall Plan by those expressing clear approval or a favorable opinion, then rounding to nearest percentage.

56 "Crisis of Leadership," *The Economist*, October 11, 1947.

57 "Statement of James H. Shelton, Member of the Advisory Council of the Society for Prevention of World War III," US Senate, *Hearings Before the Committee on Foreign Relations on United States Assistance to European Recovery*, Part 3 (Washington, 1948), 1049–1054; Steven Casey, "The Campaign to Sell a Harsh Peace for Germany to the American Public, 1944–1948," *History* 90, 297 (January 2005), 62–92.

58 Gar Alperovitz and Kai Bird, "A Theory of Cold War Dynamics: U.S. Policy, Germany, and the Bomb," *The History Teacher* 29, 3 (May 1996), 281–300.

59 *CR*, March 9, 1948, 2387; *CR*, March 29, 1948, 3625; *CR*, March 30, 1948, 3711; *CR*, March 31, 1948, 3830.

60 *CR*, March 25, 1948, 3562; *CR*, March 30, 1948, 3722; *CR*, March 31, 1948, 3821.

61 *CR*, March 25, 1948, 3522; *CR*, March 31, 1948, 382; *CR*, June 4, 1948, 7163, 7179.

62 *CR*, June 4, 1948, 7183.

63 *CR*, March 9, 1948, 2385–2386.

64 *CR*, March 9, 1948, 2389.

65 *CR*, March 31, 1948, 3873.

66 "Press Release, November 25, 1947" and "Draft Resolution," European Recovery Programs, International Relations, Box 51, Vito Marcantonio Papers, New York Public Library, New York; *CR*, March 10, 1948, 2460. Pepper, like Taylor, counseled

a Wallace-like openness toward working with the Soviet Union. He did not back Wallace in the 1948 election, but was publically tepid about Truman.

67 Taft was absent when the actual voting happened in the early morning of March 14, 1948, so he was recorded as "not voting," but he did pair his vote with Nebraska Senator Hugh Butler, which allowed him to indicate that had he been present, he would have voted for the bill. *CR*, March 13, 1948, 2793.

68 *CR*, March 12, 1948, 2618.

69 *CR*, March 13, 1948, 2778.

70 *CR*, March 5, 1948, 2215.

71 *CR*, March 12, 1948, 2618, 2619, 2629.

72 *CR*, March 13, 1948, 2760.

73 *CR*, March 10, 1948, 2643.

74 Reinhold Niebuhr, *Moral Man and Immoral Society: A Study in Ethics and Politics* (New York, 1932).

75 Peter G. Boyle, "The Roots of Isolationism," *Journal of American Studies* 6, 1 (April 1972), 41–50; Richard F. Grimmett, "Who Were the Senate Isolationists?" *Pacific Historical Review* 42, 4 (November 1973), 479–498; James Reston, "The European Aid Debate," *Los Angeles Times*, January 6, 1948.

76 Bernard Fensterwald, "The Anatomy of American Isolationism and Expansionism," Parts I and II, *Journal of Conflict Resolution* 2, 2 and 4 (June 1958 and December 1958), 111–140, 280–310; Ralph H. Smuckler, "The Region of Isolationism," *The American Political Science Review* 47, 2 (June 1953), 386–401.

77 *CR*, March 13, 1948, 2793; *CR*, March 31, 1948, 3874–3875; Jay Walz, "Policy of US Seen in Senate ERP Vote," *NYT*, March 15, 1948; Felix Belair, "All Curbs Beaten," *NYT*, April 1,1948.

78 Harry S. Truman, "Inaugural Address," Gerhard Peters and John T. Woolley, eds, APP, www.presidency.ucsb.edu/node/229929 (accessed September 10, 2020).

79 Vernon Ruttan, *United States Development Assistance Policy: The Domestic Politics of Foreign Aid* (Baltimore, 1996), 50; Clark Clifford with Richard Holbrooke, *Counsel to the President* (New York, 1991), 248–253; Harry S. Truman, *Memoirs: Volume 2, 1946–1952, Years of Trial and Hope* (New York, 1956), 223–239.

80 Betty Snead, "Point IV: How Ben Hardy's Idea Became an Historic Speech", *War on Hunger; A Report from The Agency for International Development* 7, 5 (May 1973), 7; "Acheson Press Conference," January 26, 1949, Document 297, *Foreign Relations of the United States 1949, National Security Affairs, Foreign Economic Policy, Volume I* (Washington, 1976).

81 Harold B. Hinton, "Point Four Plans Attract Support," *NYT*, June 25, 1949; Walter W. Waggoner, "Point Four Plans Complete," *NYT*, September 25, 1949; "Bold New Aid Plan Ready this Session," *NYT*, May 19, 1949.

82 James Reston, "Point Four's Cost Set at $48,000,000,000," *NYT*, June 15, 1949; "Truman's Point Four Meets Hostility at House Hearing," *NYT*, September 28, 1949; James Reston, "Truman Message Asks $45,000,000 for Point-4 Fund," *NYT*, June 22, 1949.

83 US House of Representatives, *Hearings Before the Committee on Foreign Affairs, House of Representatives, Eighty-First Congress, First Session H.R. 5615, September 27, 1949* (Washington, 1950), 31–33; "Truman's Point Four Meets Hostility at House Hearing," *NYT*, September 28, 1949.

84 C. P. Trussel, "Close Harmonious," *NYT*, October 20, 1949.

85 Harry S. Truman, "Remarks to the American Society of Civil Engineers," Gerhard Peters and John T. Woolley, eds, APP, www.presidency.ucsb.edu/node/230307 (accessed October 16, 2020).

86 Conducted by the National Opinion Research Center, University of Chicago, Datasets USNORC1950–0292, USNORC1950–0280, collected by the Roper Center for Public Opinion Research, ropercenter.cornell.edu (accessed February 14, 2018).

87 William White, "Point Four Slated for 'Must' Status," *NYT*, December 16, 1949; C.P. Russel, "Senate Unit Votes Point 4, Limits Aid to Technical Skill," *NYT*, April 5, 1949; "Foreign Economic Assistance Act," CQ *Almanac 1950* (Washington, 1951), 204–218; Felix Belair, "20% Less of Funds Requested for All Our Foreign Relations," *NYT*, January 10, 1950; Felix Belair, "Senate Unit Votes $3,300,000,000 in Aid for Foreign Lands," *NYT*, March 22, 1950.
88 *CR*, March 31, 1950, 4538, 4537; Harold Hinton, "Point Four Program Meets Wide Opposition," *NYT*, April 16, 1950.
89 Truman to Rayburn, August 25, 1950, Point Four Program, Box 115, President's Secretary Files (PSF), Truman Papers, Truman Library.
90 *CR*, May 4, 1950, 6373; Felix Belair, "Senate Will Vote on Aid Bill Today," *NYT*, April 29, 1950.
91 *CR*, May 5, 1950, 6478–6479, 6481; *CR*, May 6, 1950, 6446; Felix Belair, "$3,122,450,000 Voted by Senate for Foreign Aid," *NYT*, May 6, 1950.
92 *CR*, May 5, 1950, 6478.
93 *CR*, May 24, 1950, 7593.
94 *CR*, May 24, 1950, 7593; C. P. Trussell, "Aid Bill Blocked in Senate by GOP Attack on Point 4," *NYT*, May 24, 1950; C. P. Trussell, "Foreign Aid Voted by Senate," *NYT*, May 26, 1950.

3

AID OPPOSITION AND THE PUBLIC IN THE 1950S

Congressional leaders in the 1950s, especially fiscally conservative ones, continued to fight against aid programming. President Dwight D. Eisenhower (R), who succeeded Truman in 1953, also worried about too much aid spending. His doubt led to a less government-driven approach at the start of his presidency. Over time, however, he shifted and became increasingly convinced that the United States needed a bigger and more energetic aid program. There was also a spirited public debate in this period outside Washington, in which activists and writers tried to influence the policy process. Like opponents in Congress, critics in the public sphere approached economic aid from multiple directions, but in each case they challenged ideologies about development. Some, like the authors of the novel *The Ugly American*, William Lederer and Eugene Burdick, they reached a wide audience. Others, like the Citizen's Foreign Aid Committee and its better-known companion, the John Birch Society, never had a mainstream impact, but they did develop relationships with elected officials. This forced the Eisenhower administration to fight back and defend aid, and explain why it was money well spent.

Eisenhower and Foreign Aid

Eisenhower was instinctually skeptical about US foreign aid when he took office. He accepted the notion that poorer societies could be improved by external application of aid and expertise, and believed this type of transformation should be a US foreign policy goal. He also worried, like Truman administration officials had, that poverty might spur social conflict, which would help communists gain power. However, Eisenhower rejected the idea (at least at the outset) that government money should drive the process. Instead, he believed private capital was a better and more appropriate way to promote growth. This was consistent with views of other Republican fiscal conservatives, like Taft, who hoped to see a smaller and less activist government. It also connected to a longer history of the party's opposition to government-led economic development in the New Deal, and to Republican self-identification as the party of business.[1]

Hesitancy about an activist state reflected Eisenhower's personal beliefs. He thought he needed to be a mediating and stabilizing force in a country facing the Cold War and rapid technological advancement, and that rather than actively press for change (which might be divisive), he should use his influence to encourage national cooperation. This would be difficult, he believed, because of unchecked concentrations of power in society. He explained this fear in a 1949 address to the American Bar Association as he spoke about "the unbearable selfishness of vested interest" and "the blindness of those who, protesting devotion to the public welfare, falsely declare that only government can bring us happiness, security and opportunity."[2] His goal, he explained, was to instead bring all sectors of society together in sober mutual collaboration to find a "middle way" between political parties, regional interests, and labor and private capital. In seeking this middle way, he argued the pendulum had swung too far away from capital, as government leaders in previous Democratic administrations had used their power to remake society. He wanted that to end and for the pendulum to swing back to the middle. This principle would also be applied to foreign aid, as he wanted government to have a smaller role in remaking other societies, and hoped business would do that work.[3]

Eisenhower expressed these ideas in an October 1952 campaign speech largely dedicated to economic aid. He said that improving global economic conditions was "one of the indispensable requirements of peace …" and argued that poverty "must be relieved if economic difficulty is not to be transformed into political catastrophe." In a nod to Truman and the Marshall Plan, he added that US economic aid had been essential in the postwar world, and it was still needed. In the case of technical assistance to poorer countries (Point Four), he claimed it was in the United States' "own enlightened self-interest" to intensify that aid. The larger point he tried to make, though, was that the United States needed to shift its strategy and limit government's role in creating growth. He noted that following "World War II, our foreign economic program, not including any military expenditures, has cost us $33,000,000,000." He continued, "This huge outlay has not succeeded in producing a minimum basis for the free-world nations to stand on their own feet without our continuing support … something has been wrong with our thinking." It was imperative to "find a substitute for the purely temporary business of bolstering the free nations through annual handouts … [which] gets neither permanent results nor real friends."[4]

Eisenhower said he wanted to "tell the American story … [to] show what spirit, incentive and reward" had done to create the US economy, and to export American capitalist ideas internationally. Some of this could be done through people-to-people programs that would teach foreign business and labor leaders about the US system, but more substantively it had to be done through a coordinated foreign policy approach that would integrate global markets and generate trade and investment.[5] US private investment had to be the core of this approach and do the meaningful work of driving growth. The job of government would be encouraging "other nations to create conditions that invite an invigorating flow abroad of American private capital investment." Eisenhower hoped to "summon the best minds we have" to "build a new economic alliance of free nations" to advance prosperity via market solutions, and in so doing, help win the Cold War.[6]

There was no inconsistency in Eisenhower's logic that government could create conditions that would help private industry spur foreign growth. It was moving to a centrist position that placed government in a coordinating role, and swinging the pendulum away from government control. A further advantage, Eisenhower explained, was that helping US businesses export would build the domestic economy by obtaining access to the "raw materials needed for our own economy," and by helping "hold or expand markets for American agricultural and industrial exports." This view was consistent with what Marshall Plan organizers had suggested; a goal in both cases was promoting US economic growth in the long term.[7]

The question for Eisenhower was how to implement these ideas in a practical way. In his May 1953 message to Congress requesting funds for 1954, Eisenhower asked for $5.8 billion in foreign aid, a $1.8 billion reduction from what the Truman administration had signaled would be appropriate moving forward. The key shift, other than the cut, was in the substantial sum requested for military assistance ($5.25 billion), and the far smaller amount ($550 million) requested for economic development assistance. This reflected Eisenhower's general sense that, unlike economic aid, military aid would be vital for winning the Cold War. He explained, "The devotion of so large a portion of this request to military purposes is a measure of the peril in which free nations continue to live." Economic aid, he said, was not unimportant, and would demonstrate a US interest in strengthening the "foundations of opportunity and freedom" and countering the "conditions exploited by subversive forces," but it was secondary.[8]

The shift in spending priorities was only part of a reassessment, and did not answer questions about how best to implement structural changes to economic aid programs. To that end, Eisenhower commissioned a series of studies, first by the International Development Advisory Board, an external committee chaired by Eric Johnston, a former president of the US Chamber of Commerce, and then a second study from an ad hoc commission led by steel industry executive Clarence Randall.

Johnston's report, published in December 1953, made a case for a substantial US effort in global technical assistance, using the argument that the United States had the capability to help other nations transform themselves. The committee, which included business and labor leaders, and medical professionals and journalists, explained that they believed the United States had "particular qualifications" and "alone of the major countries of the Free World combines recent experience in self-development as an underdeveloped country with modern technology, education, and hygiene." But the report's authors made it clear that they were not talking about money, only about expertise. This was consistent with Eisenhower's position, and also the philosophy behind Point Four. The US aim, they said, should be to "lay foundations for self-improvement through work on the elimination of debilitating diseases and the control of conditions endangering health and life, through dissemination of knowledge regarding better farm methods, through the improvement of education, [and] through providing technical assistance on matters of transportation to enable people to bring the product of their toil to market." The United States could fix the broken world, they believed, but they rejected the notion that spending money would achieve that. The way forward was promotion of US-style capitalism built with US know-how.[9]

The Randall Report, released the next month, was broader and addressed all phases of US foreign economic policy. The section on foreign aid made clear the commission's view that past aid, given in the immediate postwar period (the Marshall Plan) had been successful, but that this phase of aid programming should cease. They wrote, "as the need for economic aid for postwar recovery disappears, demands are increasing for general economic aid unconnected with recovery from war or preparation for defense. Underdeveloped areas are claiming a right to economic aid from the United States … . We recognize no such right." While low-cost technical assistance programs might be important for economic development, they "need not and should not become a 'big money' program and should not involve capital investments." Buffeting Eisenhower's argument, the Randall Report suggested that increased US investment abroad would help both the US economy and the economies of other countries by aiding "the development abroad of primary resources to meet the ever-increasing civilian and defense needs of the United States and the free world." Even more directly, the report's authors argued,

> The United States Government should make clear that primary reliance must be placed on private investment to undertake the job of assisting in economic development abroad. It should point out that United States resources for public loans are limited and inadequate in relation to total investment needs, and that public lending or other forms of public financing will not be a substitute for private investment.[10]

Aid as a Cold War Tool

Within a year, however, Eisenhower seemed to be changing his mind about the role of foreign aid and the necessity of a greater US commitment, albeit slowly. During a National Security Council meeting in February 1955, he explained he was starting to see more clearly that economic aid should be part "of an over-all world program to strengthen the forces of freedom against Communist advances." He still wanted to emphasize technical cooperation, but worried that foreign countries did not have the capability to use this kind of support without substantially greater US government involvement. More directly, he also started to wonder if the United States had been offering enough aid to fight the Cold War effectively.[11]

Eisenhower believed that the United States needed to spend more to keep up with Soviet foreign aid spending, which had increased significantly following Joseph Stalin's death in 1953. The new Soviet leaders were much more aggressive in using aid to back nationalist and anti-imperialist movements in Africa, Asia, the Middle East, and to a lesser extent Latin America. This was a new kind of Cold War competition. One example of this came in the educational field. As historian Constantin Katsakioris explained, from the mid-1950s on, the Soviets began offering hundreds of scholarships to students, mostly from Arab countries, to study in Russian universities. They also helped fund the construction of educational institutions throughout the Middle East.[12] In other parts of the world, they were similarly spending freely, offering a $30 million credit to Argentina in 1953 for the purchase of oil drilling equipment, and funding national development projects in Afghanistan in 1954 and India and Burma (now Myanmar) in 1955.[13] This was a key issue in a National Security Council meeting in November 1955, as Eisenhower, Secretary of State John Foster Dulles, Vice President Richard Nixon, and Treasury Secretary George M. Humphrey contemplated the need to increase budget requests for aid. From one perspective it did not matter if aid worked; this was about buying popularity. Certainly it would have been good if aid could help create economic growth and stability in materially poorer parts of the world, but that did not really matter if the Soviets were making aid-granting a competition. If it was a competition, the United States needed to match Soviet efforts, and ideally stay ahead by doing more, no matter the cost or aid's efficacy.[14]

Not all members of Eisenhower's inner circle agreed. In multiple meetings, Humphrey and Secretary of Defense Charles Wilson argued against changing course. Humphrey, a stickler for Republican ideas about private industry, and with a reflexive antipathy to government spending, insisted the United States needed to stick to stimulating private industry. He argued that aid was anti-capitalistic and would not create economic growth. Eisenhower countered that he was not so sure he still agreed with Humphrey's position, and admitted that in the Cold War scheme of things he was not particularly worried that foreign aid had to go hand in hand with expanded capitalism if the real goal was winning friends. Denmark, Norway, and Sweden, he noted, were steady allies and socialistic.[15] Supporting activist government, and even socialist governments, with an eye toward winning the Cold War, seemed strategically wise.

This push for greater foreign aid occurred, even as Eisenhower administration officials faced evidence that aid programs were not creating development, and at the minimum, that they were beset by substantial problems. In a wide-ranging conversation about aid in December 1955, representatives from the International Cooperation Administration (ICA), the agency then managing foreign aid, gave a presentation to the National Security Council. John B. Ohly, an ICA official, explained that the United States was "making no progress whatsoever in getting the load off its own back and directing Korea in the path of future stability and self-support." In India, there was far more poverty, and US aid could never meet local needs; its government required billions of dollars to fund its second five-year development plan, and the United States was proposing only a relatively minuscule $81 million in economic aid. The lack of a sufficiently tangible commitment in India worried Eisenhower, who wanted it to remain neutral in the Cold War, or better, "neutral on our side."[16]

Audits of aid programs published by the US Comptroller General in 1955 and 1956 showed problems and demonstrated that aid programs were badly constructed and administered, which further complicated decisions about how to proceed. An audit of the program for Lebanon was especially disturbing. The United States had made $21.3 million available to Lebanon between 1952 and 1955, but $5 million was never sent because the Lebanese Parliament failed to ratify one of the loan agreements. There was no planning agency in Lebanon, making it impossible to manage joint operations or coordinate between US officials and those from other donor countries or private foundations. This led to duplication of efforts and bungled operations. In one example, expensive equipment for a public health laboratory had been paid for and shipped, but it waited in storage because the Lebanese government had not completed the building where it could be set up. Not all problems could be laid at the feet of the Lebanese. Farm equipment ordered in the fall of 1954 took more than a year to be shipped because US officials in Lebanon and Washington could not agree about what was needed. Another problem was that the staff at the US embassy in Beirut did not get definitive and timely budget information, and they spent $218,000 more than they had been allotted.[17]

The situation in Lebanon was not unique. A 1955 audit of US programming in Pakistan found similar problems that included delays, ineffective procurement operations, and in this case underspending. The auditors said that even if all the money had been spent, there would have been serious problems because of Pakistan's inability to absorb and utilize funds and US inability to administer multiple programs at once.[18] They found the same issues in Iran, leading to delays in the construction of vital projects like the Keraj Dam and a water treatment plant in Tehran. The 1955 audit for Iran also highlighted that three years after committing to fund a cotton mill, its equipment had not yet been delivered. Similarly, two sugar mills were behind schedule, and while a cement plant had been completed, it was not in service because access roads had not been constructed.[19]

Secretary Humphrey tried to highlight these failures in NSC meetings. During a conversation about Spain in May 1956, he railed against a lack of organization in aid programming. There was "sloppy thinking" all over the US government, and they were drifting toward what the Truman administration had done. Defense Secretary Wilson argued more strongly, saying that they should stop accepting "losers" as allies. Framing his objections strategically, he suggested that countries like Spain, South Korea, and Taiwan were costing the United States more than they were worth. The people of the United States, he claimed, were suffering "colonialism in reverse," in that they were being exploited for the benefit of other nations. Humphrey agreed, and added he would rather have two or three good allies than 45 worthless ones.

Eisenhower disagreed. On a tactical point, he conceded that having "allies" might be overrated, but he insisted it was important to encourage nations to stay neutral, and a world of neutral countries was better than a world of communist ones.[20] The goal of foreign aid, to Eisenhower, was winning the Cold War. He said that the United States was probably offering too much foreign aid, and similarly accepted the idea that aid had not been having a positive impact, but it was political, and cutting it, or failing to sustain it, could lead to disastrous results. Thinking about aid as assistance was a mistake. The United States was engaged in a global war, and assistance was a way to help win that war; it was merely a tool, nothing more and nothing less. While it would have been better to rely on private industry to lead the way, it was not clear how to do that. Given the urgency of the global situation, there was no time to wait for private capital.[21]

Eisenhower's position was unique in that he backed aid even though he did not seem to believe that government action could alter and improve economic conditions in other countries. He clearly thought that other parts of the world were important to the United States, and that his government needed to compete with the Soviet Union's more aggressive economic foreign aid spending. He was well aware that in 1957 the Soviets had offered Ceylon (now Sri Lanka) almost $15.75 million to develop its rubber industry, and spent $22.4 million on aid to Cambodia and $12.6 million in Nepal. This was all in addition to an estimated $367 billion for North Korea and $100 billion for North Vietnam. The United States had to stay ahead.[22]

This changing view was reflected in comments Eisenhower made in May 1957 defending increased aid spending proposals. He said the core of US security came from its military, which operated as "a policeman on the corner to keep the robber out of our house and out of our neighborhood." But that was not enough, because the Soviets were "doing their best to take advantage of poverty and need in the developing nations," and they were turning people into communist supporters. The United States needed to be more aggressive. It would not "always go well," he said, and "weaknesses there are bound to be – troubles and disappointments as well," but that was not a reason to stop. The United States needed to engage a dynamic world and help nationalists who hoped to build their countries. Foreign aid would be an investment in these countries (and thus not really aid) to "wage peace," and it would be expensive. "The plain truth," he said, "was that the price of peace is high," which is why "taxes are high" and the "sacrifices demanded of each of us are great." But this was less costly than waging war. It was better than sacrificing "our sons, our families, our homes and our cities to our own shortsightedness."[23] His budget message for 1958 made the same case:

> we simply cannot afford to blight the hopes of the newly independent peoples who turn to the free world for help in their struggle for economic survival. Should we do so, these peoples will perforce be driven toward Communist or other totalitarian solutions to their problems. I know of no precise relation between economic well-being and responsible political development. Yet continued poverty and despair are conditions that will foredoom moderate political life in these countries. If the best that these free governments can offer their peoples is endless hopelessness and grinding poverty, then these governments will surely fall. Certain it is that our peace, our political freedom, and our prosperity would not long survive the sweep of Communist despotism over these new nations. Failure to provide adequate funds to help these struggling nations move forward could well become tragically expensive to every citizen in our country. Our mutual security programs have become, during the past ten years, proven instruments of tremendous power for winning our struggle for peace.[24]

This position led Eisenhower to appoint another study committee in November 1958, this time chaired by William Draper, an investment banker with the Wall Street firm Dillon, Read & Co. Eisenhower told Draper to study the "relative emphasis which should be given to military and economic programs, particularly in the less developed areas." Reporting in late March 1959, Draper and his colleagues offered a passionate plea for greater foreign aid, both military and economic. There had been problems in implementation, they conceded, but the administration needed to have the "determination to continue it and the ability to administer it well." Overall, they said, "despite imperfections of the programs, we have seen greater strength come to free world nations with the help of our aid." The poor implementation was only one obstacle, as significant domestic opposition had launched "repeated and bitter attacks on the foreign assistance programs" and raised "the basic question as to whether these programs are more useful implements of national security policy than equivalent efforts and resources devoted to other uses." The Eisenhower administration had to fight them, and explain that the "only alternative" to an "interdependent allied free world, strengthened by our aid where needed, would be the Fortress America concept – taking our first stand in the last ditch."[25]

Opposition in the Press

In focusing on domestic aid opponents, the Draper Committee was addressing the annual legislative efforts to reduce or eliminate aid spending. However, the opposition in Washington, to be discussed in later chapters, was only one part of the challenge to aid spending. There was also a public component to aid debates, driven by critics from various antagonistic perspectives.

Among the most strident public attacks on US aid came from publisher Robert R. McCormick's *Chicago Tribune* and its smaller affiliated papers. Through the first half of the twentieth century, the *Tribune* had consistently supported Republican politicians, but there was a shift towards vitriol and contempt for Democrats in the 1930s as McCormick decided that Roosevelt's New Deal was destroying the country. This led his writers to adopt a hostile anti-government agenda, and turned the paper from a respected news source into an advocacy platform for his views. The paper's editor, Joseph Medill, backing McCormick, argued that the role of a newspaper was "to inform and lead public opinion, and to furnish that check upon government which no constitution has ever been able to provide."[26] The animus toward Roosevelt led *Tribune* writers to adopt an uncompromising isolationist antiwar stance in the 1930s and early 1940s, and to continue attacking Roosevelt after Pearl Harbor. Its rival paper, the Chicago *Sun*, semi-humorously tracked this position, noting in the first part of September 1944 the *Tribune* had made 45 "hateful" comments about Roosevelt, five about Churchill and five about Stalin, but only one mildly negative comment about Hitler and the Nazis, and had said nothing negative about Hirohito and the Japanese.[27]

In the immediate postwar era, McCormick and the *Tribune* remained unrepentantly isolationist and consistently reiterated a position that entering World War II had been a mistake and a function of Roosevelt's deceitful machinations. One typical editorial argued that the "European War was none of our affair, and the contention that England was saving us from invasion was preposterous on its face." It added, "the administration provoked the attack on the fleet and base" at Pearl Harbor. This line of reasoning led to criticism of Secretary of State Marshall and the plan for European recovery, as he had been part of the "conspiracies which brought war upon America." *Tribune* editors explained that Marshall and the "State Department cabal," could not be, and should not be trusted to lead anything, including a massive relief effort.[28]

Secretary Marshall was one of many problems according to *Tribune* writers. Echoing what Charles Lindbergh had said in his 1941 Des Moines speech, they wrote that the British were self-centered and not true allies, holding on to the last vestiges of their international power and only backed by disloyal elites in Washington. It followed then, if it was an error to send financial aid to Great Britain, it would be worse to fund other Europeans in societies ripe with even more appalling moral and civilizational decay. In country after country, Europeans were creating socialist economic systems, the *Tribune* editors explained, and they appeared "to be losing, if they have not already lost, their political savvy and their economic energy."[29] By the early 1950s, as US aid spending in Europe started to wind down, the paper changed its tack, minimizing World War II conspiracies and ad hominem attacks on European culture, and adopting more straightforward fiscally conservative positions that aid spending was wasteful and unnecessary. Condemning Truman in early 1952, the editors wrote his "idea of economy" was to "underwrite military expansion in Europe, give economic aid to European countries which are rearming, increase 'Point Four' aid to underdeveloped countries, maintain all existing welfare programs with some increases in benefits, and embark on new welfare programs. No wonder Uncle Sam is regarded all over the world as Uncle Sucker."[30]

With Eisenhower in the White House, and a shift in aid policy, the *Tribune* was still aggressive, albeit slightly less so, and alert to backsliding. In a 1953 piece about Latin American and Filipino aid requests, the editors worried that foreign leaders suffered from a "hallucination that America's wealth is inexhaustible," and that US leaders were not being courageous enough to say that "there is such a thing as killing the goose that lays the golden eggs, and that the bird is already languishing from past demands on her."[31] A few days later, after explaining that the United States had made a mistake in entering both world wars, the editors complained that US leaders still felt "it is their particular duty to go on forever with the impossible job of trying to redeem every stupidity associated" with the interventions and fix European problems, even though socialists, who were actually communists in allied countries, were not particularly good allies. Unsurprisingly, as the Eisenhower administration became more enthusiastic about aid programming, the paper's editors became more antagonistic. They noted that Eisenhower had promised in 1952 to cut spending and taxation while limiting government's role in the economy. Yet, "the endless drain of foreign aid has been continued on the same scale with no more wisdom than ever."[32]

An editorial in 1954, entitled "Annual Giveaway," condemned aid bills as full of "sugar coating" that appealed to the selfish interests of exporters, and complained that billions of dollars were spent on a program that only "a small minority of the people" supported.[33] A few days later this attack continued as the editors explained that "A dollar gone from an Illinois taxpayer is a dollar he and his family won't see again. A dollar gone from Illinois is a dollar that won't come back."[34] By 1958 they were writing that, through foreign aid, Eisenhower was "fighting Communism according to the basic prescription of Karl Marx." Eisenhower had said that the United States, as the world's wealthiest and most powerful nation, needed to be more active than other nations in supplying aid. *Tribune* editors said this was just applying the communist concept, "from each according to his abilities, to each according to his need."[35]

This attack did not make much sense, but it seemed not to matter to *Tribune* editors, who consistently made specious assaults. In another difficult-to-follow argument, regarding funding for Jordan in 1958, they wrote that Eisenhower said Arabs were angry about their societies and demanded change, which might lead to communism. The editors pointed out that the United States had already spent $56 million in the country, though. They asked, why the United States should spend more money on people who might soon embrace the Soviet Union, purposefully misinterpreting Eisenhower's intent.[36]

FIGURE 3.1 *Who Wants to be an Understudy to a Comical Mule?* This *Chicago Tribune* cartoon chastises Republicans for following along with the "New Deal Global Buffoonery" of the Marshall Plan.

Source: ©1947 Chicago Tribune. All Rights Reserved. Distributed by Tribune Content Agency.

With its position as a leading regional paper, and ownership and partnerships with smaller papers across the country, the *Tribune* had a powerful voice in ensuring that these anti-aid narratives remained part of the national discourse, but its emotional and knee-jerk anti-aid platform was only one element in the wider public fight against aid spending.

Henry Hazlitt and Aid

Far more intellectual than the *Tribune*'s editors, Henry Hazlitt presented a more cogent and consistent public argument against foreign aid. He had been a newspaper reporter, writing about economic issues for most of the major New York newspapers (*Wall Street Journal, New York Evening Mail, New York Herald,* and the *New York Times*), and for *Newsweek* magazine. In 1946, he published *Economics in One Lesson*, a general textbook targeted to a non-academic audience that advanced ideas later to be associated with the Austrian economists, Ludwig von Mises and Freidrich Hayek; he sold more than one million copies. Incisively and engagingly, Hazlitt argued the "one lesson" his readers needed to know was that economic thought was riddled by "fallacies" caused by economists failing to appreciate the total impact of a policy. Boiled down to one sentence, he wrote, "The art of economics consists in looking not merely at the immediate but the longer effects of any act or policy; it consists in tracing the consequences of that policy not merely for one group but for all groups." Though not particularly incisive in itself, it opened up an Adam Smith-like critique of government involvement in the economy and a hunt for inefficient results of those actions. When governments intervened in markets, he argued, it might lead to improved conditions for some people, but it would also have an unseen cost in taxes paid by all citizens who financed that improvement. It was not growth, only the transfer of money. Even worse, government intervention would have a negative overall impact on profits in the private sector by hurting businesses that might have filled market needs instead. Businesses, in turn, would then pay fewer taxes, leading to a weaker society. That was the opposite of government's obvious goal. Hazlitt, perhaps unsurprisingly, was a close friend of the writer Ayn Rand, who expressed similar ideas in her popular 1943 book, *The Fountainhead*. Both rejected the idea that businesses needed to be regulated to serve the common good, and neither believed that government spending could improve society. Private spending would create growth, but government spending would stymie it.[37]

In his 1957 follow up to *Economics in One Lesson*, Hazlitt published *Will Dollars Save the World*? In this text, addressed to the same audience as his earlier book, he argued that economic aid would fail to achieve its aims because it relied on the principle that government could make wholesale economic changes occur. Addressing the Marshall Plan directly, he contended the largest obstacle to recovery was not lack of capital, but the existence of overvalued currencies that limited European export possibilities and promoted a flood of imports. Adjusting currency exchange rates in Europe, more than anything else, he insisted, would spur production by encouraging import substitution and export growth. He conceded there was postwar destruction and a need to rebuild, but the right path forward was not economic aid; rather it should have been a reevaluation of the Bretton Woods agreements that had created official exchange rates and hindered natural trade (and exchange rates that would float as supply and demand changed).

Following the argument that foreign aid would disrupt the functions of a market system, Hazlitt claimed that aid would most likely increase economic inefficiencies in recipient countries, rather than alleviate them. He wrote, "help from outside to any country goes eventually to relieve the LEAST urgent needs which the government of that country then decides to meet."[38] Using Yugoslavia as an example, he suggested that aid would allow its government to keep a large standing army, but without that aid, the government would have to cut the size of the military establishment and use national resources to produce food. Its soldiers would have to be released to work on farms. That would have been a more efficient way to solve the problem aid hoped to fix. More simply, Hazlitt said that interventions in an economy were always counterproductive because they promoted inefficient economic activity.

Hazlitt was also sensitive to the argument that aid might be a form of imperialism, and argued aid would just as likely cause anger as to lead aid recipients to look kindly at the United States. Conditions attached to aid were fundamentally necessary, he explained, otherwise aid-granting nations would have no guarantee that their assistance would be used as intended. Yet these conditions, stemming from the "mere fact that they are conditions, will be considered humiliating" and "an infringement of sovereignty and independence." To make this point he quoted an *Economist* article that explained,

> American opinion should be warned that over here, in Great Britain, one has the feeling of being driven into a corner by a complex of American actions and insistencies which, in combination, are quite intolerable. Not many people in this country believe the Communist thesis that it is the deliberate and conscious aim of American policy to ruin Britain … . But the evidence can certainly be read that way.[39]

Hazlitt also questioned the Marshall Plan by noting that the cause and effect relationship between granting aid and stopping communism was unproven. He explained that Marshall Plan authors assumed aid would stop communism, but they did not explain how that would work in practice. There was no evidence, he argued, that loans would create growth or keep people from accepting revolutionary ideologies. More to the point, if revolutionary ideologies were the problem, the United States should instead wage a propaganda war to explain "the merits of our free enterprise system and to contrast them with the hunger, terror and slavery under Communism."[40]

Hazlitt argued that aid essentially helped construct socialist systems in Europe and allowed socialist governments to make decisions about economic development. This was a problem because socialism, despite the protestations of its adherents who "talk of preserving the methods of democracy and the liberty of the individual," was as bad as communism in that it did not and could not permit economic liberty, which was the rock on which other liberties rested. If the United States' essence was wrapped up in the preservation of liberty, aid was fundamentally anti-American because it limited liberty abroad. Hazlitt's solution for European reconstruction, much as Eisenhower initially argued, was encouraging private capital flows through non-governmental loans. If Europeans relied on private loans, he said, they would take necessary steps toward reforming their economies and establishing an open market on their own.[41] This would be more economically efficient and politically just. In this argument, Hazlitt asserted the broader argument that government should not be engaged in the economy. That was the central point of *Economics in One Lesson*; in exploring aid spending, *Will Dollars Save the World?* took that position to its natural conclusion.

The Ugly American

Eschewing conversations about economic theory, other writers, such as Eugene W. Castle in his 1955 book, *Billions, Blunders, and Baloney: The Fantastic Story of How Uncle Sam is Squandering Your Money Overseas*, and William J. Lederer and Eugene Burdick in their 1958 novel *The Ugly American*, used examples culled from their own observations to explain aid's failures.[42] Castle, an innovator in producing and marketing films for home viewing, wrote engagingly and creatively about the failures of US-sponsored propaganda to get people around the world to like the United States. He argued that the United States had been spending extraordinary sums, but had little to show for its efforts because US diplomats saw themselves as elites and targeted their propaganda at the upper classes instead of toward poorer people. The Soviet Union, by contrast, had been much savvier, and with far fewer dollars made more friends. Speaking about his travel abroad, Castle tried to explain that the Cold War was not going well, and that aid's failures were caused by a lack of understanding of local conditions. This ensured that rather than helping win the Cold War, aid was creating resentment. Castle wrote colorfully:

> The flow of American money abroad since 1945 has been a reckless and unregulated river. The astronomical sums to which these spendings have mounted stagger the imagination. Uncle Sam has been the great international "Easy Touch" to whom the whole non-Communist world has come in urgent parade for its share of the pickings. All this has been done in the name of winning friendship for America. The price has been colossal, but still we have not won the friends. Like the proverbial parvenu we have tried heavy-handedly to buy our way into world leadership. We have not succeeded, but we have piled up a legacy of ill-will throughout the world … .[43]

This book, and a similar follow-up in 1957, *The Great Giveaway: The Realities of Foreign Aid*, set the stage for the most powerful anti-aid book of the 1950s (and really the most powerful of any era), Lederer and Burdick's *The Ugly American*.

Set in Sarkhan, a fictional Southeast Asian country, Lederer and Burdick told the story of a cast of characters engaged in foreign aid efforts. The book's central argument was that US overseas personnel were, with few exceptions, morally and intellectually woefully unprepared for their assignments. The United States government had no real effective language or cultural training for its diplomats who were mostly interested in foreign service as a cushy and respectable career, and who spent most of their time hobnobbing with local elites. They did not have the will or ability to advance US interests. The first ambassador to Sarkhan in the story, Louis Sears, demonstrated this point. He did not know anything meaningful about the country, and could not discern how local officials were using him for their own gain, which included lobbying for foreign aid that would line their own pockets but not have any impact on local development. Officials in Washington did not know about this problem. When they came to Sarkhan to investigate government corruption and the inefficiency of aid spending, the embassy staff tightly controlled their itineraries and presented a flattering image of US efforts, which in turn guaranteed that the gravy train of economic aid continued. The ineptitude of US officials, they wrote, helped improve the status of the Soviet Union, who had bothered to train its diplomats in local languages. Unlike US officials, the Soviets worked with all social and economic classes, and were stunningly effective in spreading their communist messages.

Here, Lederer and Burdick's concern was similar to the argument that pushed Eisenhower to reassess his views; the Soviets were doing it, and if the Soviets were doing it, the United States had to do it better or risk losing the Cold War. The book was not all criticism, though, and they further suggested there were better ways to offer aid. The heroes of the text, characters like the engineer Homer Atkins, described as an ugly man (the central character), shunned life in Asian capitals and hoped to work on small-scale community projects. He was more sensitive to the basic needs of ordinary people and able to fashion common-sense solutions to address their needs. In one key vignette, he noticed that it required a substantial effort to move water from one rice field to the next. He then worked with a local mechanic to develop a pump that used readily available equipment to solve the problem. This was not just a local success, though, as Atkins helped set up a sales operation that allowed the mechanic to distribute and service pumps throughout the country. The mechanic got wealthy, and rice yields improved. Lederer and Burdick applauded this sort of small-scale project, imagining it could improve the quality of life in Sarkhan and get people to understand that the United States was good. Atkins' wife Emma similarly helped the locals by introducing longer broom handles so that housewives did not have to stoop over as they swept their floors. They could finally stand up straight with confidence. External know-how, and a willingness to learn about ordinary people before trying to solve their problems, could make all the difference in improving the world.[44]

The Ugly American was a popular success, spending 78 weeks on the *New York Times* best-seller list from late 1958 through early 1960.[45] It forced the Eisenhower administration, through the ICA, to publish a point-by-point refutation of its attacks. The ICA noted, for example, that in the second chapter there was a story about bags of rice sent as US aid being relabeled by dockworkers as a gift from Russia. The government countered this was pure fiction. There had been a report of relabeling of tractors in Pakistan, which Lederer and Burdick seemed to have used as inspiration, but the ICA said it had never happened. The report also pushed back against the characterizations that Soviet personnel were better linguists and that press coverage in places like Burma (a close match for Sarkhan) was awful. It insisted that US aid mostly funded the kind of work Homer Atkins promoted.[46] ICA also reprinted an essay by historian Joseph Buttinger, published in *Dissent* magazine, that argued, "There is no truth in the book's message to the American public that the vast majority of our officials in Southeast Asia are still untrained and inexperienced." Buttinger said that this had been the case in the past, but it was no longer true. US officials were not "unwilling to learn, uninterested in their work, prejudiced against the local people, concerned chiefly with personal comfort, opposed to working outside the big cities, disinclined to read books, and keen only to get to their frequent gatherings for the consumption of hard liquor."[47]

The book became an issue in then Senator John F. Kennedy's 1960 presidential run. In January 1959, Kennedy joined California senator Clair Engle (D) in sending a copy of *The Ugly American* to every other US senator. They wrote to their colleagues that "The book is written in the form of fiction – a device by which the authors have reached a very large popular audience – but it is based squarely on fact."[48] During his campaign the following year, Kennedy cited Lederer and Burdick's work and argued the United States needed to compete more effectively on aid programming with the Soviet Union; they had sent out skilled diplomats, teachers, doctors, and technicians to "under-developed nations … to advance the cause of world Communism," and were making progress. The United States had not. As a result, he argued, the United States was losing the Cold War. It needed to emphasize language training for embassy staffs and do a better job of appointing qualified ambassadors. Alongside these aims, Kennedy proposed the creation of a volunteer Peace Corps, a group of inspired young men and women who could work overseas as "ambassadors of peace," operating as Homer Adkins had in providing "know-how" to peoples around the world.[49] Kennedy seemed to miss one major point, however. In imagining Peace Corps volunteers as young and enthusiastic, he was not addressing Lederer and Burdick's belief that the most effective personnel had extensive real-world experience and skills. Do-gooders without that experience, they had written, would be ineffectual.

Though highly critical of US aid efforts, Lederer and Burdick believed that US aid could be, and indeed needed to be, transformative in developing other societies. They believed that modern outsiders could use their technological skill, and perhaps racial superiority, to make people's primitive lives better. The example of Atkins' wife and the longer broom handle is the most glaring and absurd in this respect. She saw a problem that had existed for centuries, cut some wood, and fixed it in an afternoon. Concurrently, and in a contradictory way, Lederer and Burdick pushed for non-judgmental learning about other societies and a respect for local tradition and its power structures. This led them to argue that aid should always be small and respectful, and that grandiose aid projects would consistently fail. These smaller projects, they insisted, were a way to fulfill a responsibility to take up a white man's burden and serve the poor of the world.

The John Birch Society and Aid

The influential writings of the *Chicago Tribune*, Hazlitt, and Lederer and Burdick all advanced different variants of aid skepticism in the media, but there were other ways critics tried to build and mobilize public opposition. The most notable was through a lobbying organization, the Citizen's Foreign Aid Committee, that prepared its own independent studies, advertised in mass-market publications, and tried to engage legislators. The Citizen's Committee is noteworthy, in part, because of its advocacy and the commitment of its leaders to fighting aid spending, but also because it was part of the early history of the institutionalization of the modern conservative movement.

The Citizen's Committee began as an offshoot of another organization, For America, that the *Chicago Tribune* editor, Robert R. McCormick, had created in 1954 to respond to Eisenhower's centrism and moderation. McCormick hoped that For America could become a new political party, serving voters alienated by the internationalists in both parties who hoped to see more vigorous anti-communism at home and limited engagement abroad. For America would combat "super-internationalism and interventionism," and "restore the independence of the United States" by eradicating socialism.[50]

To lead For America, McCormick recruited Robert E. Wood, a former general and a leader of the America First Movement, and more significantly, Clarence Manion, the enterprising former dean of the Notre Dame Law School. Manion had been active within the America First Committee in the prewar era, and in 1950 published a small book, *The Key to Peace*, that emphasized the need to revert to the "real Americanism" of the past, which he saw as reverence for God and freedom from government control. This led to a speaking tour, and eventually to a relationship with Taft, who found Manion's writing compelling, and who was then looking to build momentum for a 1952 presidential campaign.

Eisenhower won the Republican nomination, instead of Taft, and then the election. Eisenhower hoped to unite the party by offering key Taft supporters administration jobs, and Manion became the chair of the Commission on Intergovernmental Relations. Manion was a poor fit for this role, though, and publically challenged the president's positions, which unsurprisingly led Eisenhower to force him to resign in 1954. Freed from government work, and angry about the country's direction, he became more active in political organizing, which included signing on to lead For America. He also launched a syndicated radio show, the *Manion Forum of Opinion*, initially carried on 29 stations across the United States, dedicated to explaining his views about national problems. From this position, as historian Nicole Hemmer has explained, Manion became the central figure in the construction of conservative media efforts and a pioneer in political talk-radio shows.[51]

The internal structure of For America never really functioned effectively, and following the establishment of the Citizen's Foreign Aid Committee in 1958 it became inactive (though still extant in name). To lead the committee, Manion recruited Walter Harnischfeger, a wealthy Wisconsin-based businessman who owned a company that built industrial construction equipment, and who had previously donated to Manion's radio show. He also encouraged a similarly inclined anti-foreign engagement former general, Bonner Fellers, to help organize day-to-day operations. Beyond Manion and McCormick, the Citizen's Committee had an important link to the John Birch Society. Understanding this connection is necessary to explain the organization's philosophy and aims more fully.[52]

Robert H. W. Welch, a candy manufacturer, had founded the John Birch Society in 1958, and it quickly became the most influential group, promoting a more frenetic and undoubtedly fringe conspiratorial and paranoid conservatism. Welch claimed that communists had infiltrated the United States government and proposed that the John Birch Society's job was to uncover and fight this treason. He claimed in *The Politician*, a manuscript distributed to members but never published, that President Eisenhower was a Soviet agent, and that his path to the presidency had begun when George C. Marshall, also a Soviet agent, appointed him as the commanding general in Europe. Welch wrote that Marshall's purpose in helping Eisenhower and fighting World War II "was not to save his country, but to carry forward Communist plans which would ultimately deliver it to Communism."[53] As President, Eisenhower then selected other communists to help him advance this agenda, including Secretary of State John Foster Dulles and his Supreme Court appointees, Earl Warren and William Brennan.[54]

Welch had named his society in memory of Captain John Birch, a US Army intelligence officer who had been serving in China at the end of World War II. On August 25, 1944, ten days after Japan had surrendered, Birch had been killed in an altercation with a Chinese Communist unit. Welch found this story compelling for two reasons: first, Birch represented the first casualty of a World War III between Communists and non-Communists that he believed had already begun, and second, his story was unknown to the wider public, suggesting that vigilance was necessary to uncover communist aggression and conspiracies.[55] In building the society, Welch used contacts from his work as director of the National Association of Manufacturers, and that organization's past presidents, William J. Greede, Robert W. Stoddard, and Ernest Swigert, all joined as founders. Other founders included oil industry executive Fred C. Koch and T. Coleman Andrews, the former commissioner of the Internal Revenue Service (who was both a John Birch Society founder and member of the Citizen's Foreign Aid Committee). These wealthy industrialists, like Welch, had been appalled at Eisenhower's moderation and thought he should have been even more aggressive in backing business against labor and in challenging the Soviet Union; they thought Welch understood what had gone wrong in Washington.[56]

By the end of the 1950s, the John Birch Society had become relatively well known and influential, in part because of Welch's organizational skills and relationships with wealthy patrons, and in part because most reporters saw his views as extreme, dangerous, and far-fetched. They sensed a good story, and that led politicians to wonder what the group was trying to do, which gave Welch a platform to air his views and recruit new members. Historian D. J. Mulloy offers a caveat about the members, and argues most did not necessarily accept Welch's conspiracy theories; they served as a kind of a "rhetorical shorthand" for the ills in society, he wrote, which included collectivism, the rise of big government, civil rights legislation, and high taxation. It did not matter, exactly, if Eisenhower (and later Kennedy) were deep-cover communists, only that they were destroying US society and government, and that they needed to be fought by authentic patriots.[57]

Though Welch framed his attack on the whole US government, he viewed aid as symptomatic of omnipresent pro-communist treason. In *The Politician* he focused on two examples, aid to Poland and Yugoslavia.[58] In October 1956, Eisenhower had offered Poland economic assistance as its communist leaders were increasingly critical of the Soviet Union following Stalin's death. The possibility existed, from Eisenhower's perspective, that Poland might assert its independence. To Welch, this was "just a means to help Communists in their worldwide plans." Eisenhower also offered aid to Josip Tito's Yugoslavia to try to keep that country non-aligned in the Cold War. Welch said that Tito was a Soviet ally, and "a murderous Communist tyrant of an enslaved people … who stood shoulder to shoulder for various causes dearest to the Kremlin's heart … ." Thus, Welch wrote it only made sense that Eisenhower, again, himself a communist, insisted on sending Tito military aid, especially jet planes, to "help the Communists in their plans for world conquest."[59]

Welch addressed foreign aid again in a May 1959 editorial letter in the John Birch Society Journal, *American Opinion*. Here, once more, Welch attacked aid to Poland, and also aid to Laos, as direct aid to communists, but he also made the more complex case that aid to governments helped them promote the "poisonous atmosphere in which Communism thrives." Using Bolivia as an example, he argued that aid had funded the nationalization of the tin mines and an agrarian reform program. The nationalizations, which were communist-like socialist efforts, "produced such chaos, suffering, and regimentation by force as to have made the present slight Communist grip on the country almost inevitable." As disturbingly, he said that in both Iran and Indonesia, the United States sent aid to known anti-American leaders. Welch's critique was unique in that he went beyond suggesting that this was "misguided idealism," "faulty strategy," or "innocent stupidity," as many others had argued, it was "willful treason."[60]

Welch outlined his larger plans to fight back in *The Blue Book of the John Birch Society*, which came out of a two-day presentation he gave in 1958 to his initial backers. One of his ideas was developing "fronts" to advocate for specific causes that would be independent of the John Birch Society yet advance its agendas.

Using front organizations was a communist tactic, he explained, and effective because they might appeal to an audience alienated by association with the John Birch Society.[61] Some of these, he noted, had already existed, including the Committee of One Million, formed to keep communist China from joining the United Nations, in which early John Birch Society members were leaders. Another was the Committee of Endorsers, which called for basing US "foreign policy solidly on moral law, patriotism, enlightened nationalism, and the teachings of Christ." This committee reformed itself as the Citizen's Foreign Relations Committee in 1957, with Welch and Manion both on its board.[62]

Welch and the John Birch Society constructed the new front organizations – the Committee Against Summit Entanglements, to oppose meetings between US and Soviet Leaders, and the Committee for the Monroe Doctrine, organized to push for an aggressive stance against Castro's government in Cuba.[63] The Citizen's Foreign Aid Committee, as a spin-off of For America, predated Welch's call for fronts, but like the others, its overlapping membership and similar ideological bent puts it in the category of John Birch Society-associated and aligned organizations.

The Citizen's Foreign Aid Committee

To be effective as a front, the Citizen's Foreign Aid Committee mostly avoided hyperbolic and conspiratorial language. Its leaders hoped to influence policy debates, and thus they presented themselves as part of a sober public-interest educational organization, giving testimony to Congress and publishing a newsletter that relatively solemnly followed and critiqued foreign aid legislation. Another point of separation was that Harnischfeger, despite his extensive connections to leading members, appears not to have been a John Birch Society member. Still, it is easy to see that Welch's rhetoric lay just below their arguments.[64]

In 1959 the Committee published its first major report, "Foreign Aid and You," which advanced mainstream fiscal conservative criticisms, arguing that aid was supporting socialist development abroad and that the program was riddled with mismanagement and waste. The report also offered more complex arguments about the ethics of foreign aid. Harnischfeger and the Committee said that US Christian leaders had often supported aid programs from an ethical perspective, claiming it was moral and just to help less fortunate people. The Committee challenged this idea, saying this was a communist notion, not a Christian one. The gospels, they wrote, explained that the way to help people was by changing their hearts, from within. Karl Marx's writings had called for changes from outside. They quoted Marx's collaborator, Friedrich Engels, as writing "the ultimate causes of all social changes and political revolutions are to be sought not in the heads of men, not in their better insight into external truth and justice, but in the changes in the methods of production and exchange; they are to be sought not in the philosophy, but in the economics of a particular epoch." Thus, foreign aid, by aiming to change other societies from an external position, rather than from an internal one, was communist. Here, in line with John Birch Society thinking, their argument rested on view that Christ's prophesy was dependent on the free market.

A less difficult suggestion was that aid was imperialistic, which would become a major objection in the 1960s and 1970s. The committee insisted, as Lederer and Burdick had, that aid was a means to "superimpose our modern, highly industrialized, fast-moving system upon underdeveloped countries with less complex living standard, slower tempo, and different cultures." The report continued, "it has taken us 175 years to reach our present standard of living. Foreign aid seeks to lift underdeveloped countries to a parity with us in a decade or two." This was "most unrealistic" and reflected a "patronizing attitude toward foreign peoples." It imagined that the United States could "buy" the backing of poorer people, which suggested that their support "is presumed to be for sale."

Functionally, and more conventionally, the Committee claimed that US policy had failed in its purpose of strengthening aid recipients. Aid to Britain had allowed that country to nationalize key industries and establish a socialized healthcare system, all of which represented a "long stride toward total socialism." Similarly, US aid had assisted industry nationalizations in Norway, Austria, France, Italy, Turkey, Pakistan, India, and Indonesia. These nationalization efforts had helped "destroy" true capitalist markets, raised taxes, and created "government systems and institutions hostile to those which have been derived from our Declaration of Independence and our Constitution." The Committee explained that in India, despite receiving substantial aid through the 1950s, the communists built the second largest national party. The Committee also repeated claims of long-time aid opponents, and critics like Burdick and Lederer, that aid administrators were often corrupt and mostly inefficient.

Finally, the Committee attacked US spending for Western European defense, especially through NATO, suggesting that the United States was "carrying far more than our share," and that Western Europeans were not paying enough. The Committee suggested that US military spending had allowed other countries to underspend on defense, which gave them more money, and was thus also a form of economic aid. US forces, they counseled, should withdraw and be replaced with ballistic missiles that would deter a Soviet attack. The Committee suggested that in the case of war, Western Europeans would likely proclaim neutrality in the face of probable and unpreventable Soviet bombings of their cities anyway; NATO and military aid were pointless, and the United States (with Canada) would be forced to face the Soviet Union alone.[65]

Its base among business leaders like Harnischfeger also gave the Committee opportunities to make compelling arguments about the costs of aid. One powerful example was the testimony offered to the Senate Appropriations Committee in 1960 by Conrad Kohler as it considered that year's foreign aid bill. A member of the Citizen's Foreign Aid Committee national leadership, Kohler was president of the Kohler-Joa corporation, a manufacturer of heavy machinery and equipment for the wood products industry. He claimed that foreign aid had led to the closure of five hardwood plywood manufacturing companies in Wisconsin, decimating local communities and hurting his business badly as he had supplied them with new machinery. The problem, Kohler suggested, was foreign aid for international plywood production. He pointed to the Philippines, where the United States spent $5 million to help build 21 new plywood plants that in 1959 exported over 213 million square feet of plywood back to the United States. He claimed that in 1951, only 7.7 percent of all plywood used in the US domestic market was imported, but in 1959 it was 73.5 percent.[66]

Kohler argued that all this hurt the US economy. He spoke about a letter he received from a Wisconsin labor leader, Robert Strenger, who agreed the industry was in decline. Strenger wrote that "the smaller plants in Wisconsin have been shut down, throwing people out of jobs, mostly because of this cheap plywood imported from Japan and elsewhere." Strenger continued, "we can appreciate assisting the foreign countries in raising their economic standards, but when it affects the wage earners of our own nation who are paying a good share of the assistance through taxes, we believe some study and action should be given to the domestic side of the issue." Kohler opined that the long-term global success of US business had come from its ability to reduce the costs of production as labor costs increased. Foreign aid destroyed that model as it allowed foreign competitors access to capital to buy machinery, yet they could still pay their workers a fraction of what US manufacturers paid. US companies, therefore, had little choice but to set up manufacturing facilities abroad to remain competitive. While Kohler could not demonstrate a causal link between aid and this problem, his argument was powerful. For years, foreign countries had exported little plywood to the United States, then these foreign countries received substantial aid programs to help develop their economies so their plywood exports to the United States grew substantially; in the end, US workers and industry suffered.[67]

Regardless, the Committee members were anxious to point out that they believed in global engagement; "Foreign Aid and You," the Committee's first report, prominently noted the disclaimer that, "Members of this committee are not Isolationists," though they defined this in entirely private and commercial terms. The report stated that members "believe in the principle that commercial intercourse is of great importance to stabilize the world," and that they also "subscribe to a reasonable expansion of sound foreign investments and loans at the business level." This was an unsurprising position in that many Committee members were involved in international business. Yet beyond commercial connections, the depth of anti-communist (and anti-Soviet Union) sensibilities also forced the Committee toward supporting a form of global engagement. They consistently argued that foreign aid weakened the United States' ability to challenge the Soviets, and that money should be spent on domestic defenses instead of aid. They also agreed that the United States could not completely stand by itself against the Soviets, and thus it made sense to offer military assistance to "countries we are morally obligated to defend and which are directly threatened with Red aggression."[68]

In part because of these kinds of economic appeals, the Citizen's Foreign Aid Committee was successful in developing relationships with politicians, though it is not clear if they changed anyone's mind or were just successful with legislators already skeptical about aid. Louisiana representative Otto Passman, the most important aid opponent in Congress in the late 1950s and early 1960s, and a central subject of the next chapter, routinely invited Harnischfeger and other Citizen's Foreign Aid Committee leaders to testify before Congress; other representatives talked about its publications on the Senate and House floors. It not entirely clear that Passman, or the other opponents, needed the Committee, however. As the following chapter will demonstrate, they developed their opinions on their own. They were in contact and coordinated with the Citizen's Foreign Aid Committee and occasionally received small campaign donations, but it would be hard to argue that they offered logistical, organizational, or policy advice, or that they could coordinate any substantial grass-roots mobilization. Like the aid supporters they critiqued, they too were part of an elite of wealthy business leaders.[69]

FIGURE 3.2 *Must This Continue?* This cartoon was part of a Citizen's Foreign Aid Committee advertisement, placed in small newspapers around the country. The text of the advertisement was an open letter to members of Congress that began, "Since the end of World War II Congress has voted 85.8 BILLION American tax dollars down a rat hole called foreign aid in a stupid attempt to buy friends and to stop the advance of Communism." It concluded by asking members of Congress if their decision would be protection of their sacred oath, or "BETRAYAL by international eggheads."

Source: "An Open Letter, May 3, 1961" Citizen's Foreign Aid Committee, Group Research Files, Box 78, Columbia University Rare Book and Manuscript Library, New York.

FIGURE 3.3 *Under Two Flags?* This editorial cartoon from the *New York Journal American* suggested that elite internationalists, who controlled educational systems, wanted a world government; internationalism would destroy national sovereignty.

Source: *New York Journal American*, October 26, 1960.

At times the Committee's measured tone did not prevail, and its members presented, or perhaps reverted to, John Birch Society-type language. In July 1962 Fellers went on Manion's syndicated radio show and mostly focused on the reasonable argument that foreign aid was partially responsible for the US trade deficit.[70] At the end of this interview though, Fellers moved past the economic case to suggest aid was part of a grander conspiracy. He claimed that

> The Presidency is surrounded by intellectual elite advisers. Foreign aid is the keystone of their program. On this they are unyielding. The elite dream contemplates a welfare state at home and lavish aid abroad. To effect this entails enormous expenditures which result in deficit spending. Through foreign aid, international socialism is already becoming a reality. The elite will readily sacrifice United States sovereignty to a world order … .[71]

Similarly, at the close of testimony to the House Appropriations Subcommittee on Foreign Operations (the Passman Committee), Harnischfeger completed an extended survey of aid's global failures and then explained the grave stakes involved in continuing to offer aid. He claimed that "Foreign aid is transferring the destiny of our country from ourselves to foreign hands. Foreign aid planners are actually liquidating our country as fast as they can." He concluded, using John Birch Society-like rhetoric, "If we go down, the rest of the world goes down with us, and our children will no longer be able to exercise the rights of free men. They will face the possibility of living in concentration camps."[72]

The Results of the Fights in the 1950s

Within the Eisenhower administration, aid officials fought these opponents on multiple fronts, making the case for aid's importance to Congress and the public. Sometimes, as with the response to *The Ugly American*, this meant attempting to refute facts and arguments, and sometimes it was more general defense.

Challenging the Citizen's Foreign Aid Committee 1959 report, *Foreign Aid and You*, officials in the State, Treasury, and Defense departments, with the staff at the ICA, published a response to highlight the report's mistakes. To the claim that the United States spent $41 billion between 1948 and 1958, and that there were 12,000 people directing aid programs, the Eisenhower administration suggested the actual number was $24.2 billion, though there were 12,844 people on the ICA payroll. The Citizen's Committee also claimed, more vaguely and with an accusation of collusion, that "in the last three presidential elections, candidates of both major parties carefully avoided making foreign aid an issue," and the public had "never had an opportunity to express themselves on foreign aid at the polls." The simple official response was that it was not an election issue because both parties, and their candidates, recognized aid's importance to national security and prosperity. This was not entirely accurate, as subgroups within both parties were aid skeptics, but it was an effective way of arguing that there was enough political support that dishonest politicking was unnecessary.[73]

ICA officials also published their own reports, preemptively trying to justify aid spending and undermine fiscal conservatives' claims. One powerful document was a 1957 study that argued while aid spending was expensive, the costs of doing nothing and allowing the Soviet Union free rein would be far greater. The study also claimed that aid spending had helped US businesses by providing recipient nations with US dollars and then requiring them to use that money to buy US products. Between the calendar years 1951 and 1955, aid funded an average of 30 percent of all US exports, which in 1955 meant, for example, $47.5 million in paper products, $72.2 million in tractor sales, and $512.1 million in aircraft engines and parts. It also amounted to $355 million in agricultural commodity sales and $50 million to US ocean shipping companies. All told, ICA estimated that 598,000 workers owed their jobs to aid spending. The direct impacts were only part of the story. Repeating what Truman had said about Point Four, as aid helped countries grow, they would become better customers. US firms exported $52 per capita in goods to the Netherlands in 1956. That figure was only $1.68 for Indonesia and $3.85 for Iran. ICA promised that as global wealth increased, US wealth would too.[74]

Despite ICA's reports, and even with public criticism, it is not entirely clear that public opinion shifted in a meaningful way throughout the decade. Pollsters had asked in March 1958, "In general, how do you feel about foreign aid, are you for it or against it?" 51 percent of respondents said they were for it, and 33 percent said they were against it.[75] But as with all polls, the phrasing of questions, such as in Table 3.1, could have a substantial impact on results.

This would suggest most people backed aid, at least to allies, but when the question included more complex political questions, as in Table 3.2, the pro-aid responses were less strong.

Questions that had wording about the costs of aid programs consistently led to polls indicating far less support. When asked in April 1957 if Eisenhower was asking for too much, not enough, or about the right amount of foreign aid (both military and economic), 37 percent said it was too much, as opposed to only 2 percent who thought it was not enough, with 48 percent saying it was about right. In January 1958, a more pointed question about the limits of support, whether the respondent would be willing to have their taxes raised "to meet Soviet economic competition and Soviet promises of economic aid to countries in Asia and Africa," 54 percent responded no, and only 32 percent replied they would.[78]

Another poll in August 1959 also showed hesitancy when respondents were asked, "Under present circumstances, do you think the amount of money the

TABLE 3.1 Approval Rate for Aid to Allies (in percent)[76]

As you may know, the United States has been sending economic aid – like machinery and supplies – to countries that have agreed to stand with us against communist aggression. Do you think we should continue to send economic aid to these countries, or not?

	January 55	*January 56*	*September 56*	*April 57*
Should	78	80	86	81
Should not	17	14	11	16
Don't know	6	6	3	3

TABLE 3.2 Approval Rate for Aid to Non-Allies (in percent)[77]

We have also sent economic aid to some countries like India, which have not joined us as allies against the communists. Do you think we should deny aid to such countries, or should we continue to send them economic aid?

	January 55	*January 56*	*September 56*	*April 57*
Continue to send	47	40	50	54
Deny aid	41	53	43	40
Don't know	12	7	8	6

United States is now devoting to foreign aid should be increased, reduced, or kept at about the present level?" Only 6 percent responded it should be increased, while a full 39 percent replied it should be decreased, and 36 percent said it should stay the same.[79] Reflecting change over time, this could be compared to a 1952 poll that asked a similar question, "The United States will be asked to spend about $8 billion next year for military and economic aid. Do you think this amount is too much, about right, or not enough to spend for this purpose?" Just over half replied that it was too much, 29 percent said it was about right and only 1 percent of respondents indicated it was not enough.[80] Compared to the 1959 poll, respondents appeared more supportive of aid programming than in 1952. In 1959 only 39 percent said aid should be reduced, while in 1952, 56 percent said it should be cut. However, the difference in wording and the specific inclusion of a dollar figure may have led to the dissimilar results.

TABLE 3.3 Views about Aid's Utility (in percent)[81]

	Do you think the aid we're sending to various foreign countries really helps the United States in any way, or doesn't it help at all?	*Do you think that all the aid we're sending to various foreign countries really helps the prosperity and security of the United States, or doesn't it help us very much at all?*
	March 1949	*December 1956*
Helps the United States	55	63
Hurts the United States	32	29
Don't know	13	8

Perhaps the most useful poll questions came out of surveys done in March 1949 and December 1956 in which relatively similar questions were asked (Table 3.3). While not worded identically, they still allow for a comparison suggesting, perhaps, a slight improvement in sentiments about foreign aid, but still the conclusion that roughly one-third of the people in the United States found aid problematic for one reason or another. Here, it is entirely possible that the added phrase in the December 1956 version, reminding respondents that aid might help US "prosperity and security," is accountable for the difference in the results.

These polls do not explain the specific reasons respondents might have thought aid hurt the United States. Some may have embraced John Birch Society views about communist infiltration in the government. Others likely worried about fiscal responsibility and opposed government largesse and handouts, and another set may have found the concerns described in *The Ugly American* enough to see aid as a waste. Nevertheless, they were all responding to something larger than economic aid. They were all sharing opinions about how the United States should engage the world and about the appropriate role for government.

Notes

1 Thomas V. DiBacco, "American Business and Foreign Aid: The Eisenhower Years," *The Business History Review* 41, 1 (Spring 1967), 21–35.
2 "Speech to the American Bar Association, September 5, 1949," quoted in Robert Griffith, "Dwight D. Eisenhower and the Corporate Commonwealth," *American Historical Review* 87, 1 (February 1982), 87–122, 90.
3 James Ledbetter, Unwarranted Influence: Dwight D. Eisenhower and the Military-Industrial Complex (New Haven, 2011), 56–57; Griffith "Eisenhower and the Corporate Commonwealth," 87–122.
4 "Eisenhower to the Herald-Tribune Forum," *NYT*, October 22, 1952.
5 Ibid.; Matt Loayza, "A Curative and Creative Force: The Exchange of Persons Program and Eisenhower's Inter-American Policies, 1953–1961," *Diplomatic History* 37, 5 (November 2013), 946–970.
6 Ibid.
7 "Eisenhower to the Herald-Tribune Forum, October 21, 1952," *NYT*, October 22, 1952; Donald K. David, "Address before the Business Advisory Council, October 17, 1958," Addresses 1957–1958 (4), Box 4, James Hopkins Smith Jr. Papers 1932–1980, Dwight D. Eisenhower Library, Abilene, KS (hereafter DDEL).
8 Dwight D. Eisenhower, "Special Message to the Congress on the Mutual Security Program," Peters and Wooley, eds, APP, www.presidency.ucsb.edu/node/231715 (accessed October 19, 2020); Felix Belair, "Aid Bill Approved as Democrats Save Measure in House," *NYT*, June 20, 1953.
9 "Conclusions and Recommendations of the International Development Advisory Board," 1953 Dec, Box 1, Papers of Albert H. Huntington, Jr. 1948–1990, DDEL.
10 Commission on Foreign Economic Policy, "Report to the President and the Congress, January 23, 1954" (Washington, 1954), 9, 12, 16.
11 Meeting notes, 235th meeting of the NSC, February 3, 1955, Box 6, NSC Series, Dwight D. Eisenhower: Papers of the President 1953–1961 (Ann Whitman File), DDEL.
12 Constantin Katsakioris, "Soviet Lessons for Arab Modernization Soviet Educational Aid to Arab Countries after 1956," *Journal of Modern European History* 8, 1 (2010), 85–106; Taffet, *Foreign Aid as Foreign Policy: The Alliance for Progress in Latin America* (Routledge, 2007), 14.
13 Branko M. Pešelj, "Communist Economic Offensive: Soviet Foreign Aid – Means and Effects," *Law and Contemporary Problems* 29, 4 (Autumn 1964), 983–999; Paul Mosely, *Foreign Aid: Its Defense and Reform* (Lexington, KY, 1987), 24.
14 Meeting notes, 267th meeting of the NSC, November 21, 1955, Box 7, NSC Series, Dwight D. Eisenhower: Papers of the President 1953–1961 (Ann Whitman File), DDEL.
15 Ibid.
16 Ibid.
17 "Audit Report to the Congress of the United States, United States Assistance Program for Lebanon, June 30, 1955," International Cooperation Administration (7), Box 143, White House Central Files, Official Files 1953–1961, OF 8-Q International Cooperation Administration (4), DDEL.
18 "Audit Report to the Congress of the United States, United States Assistance Program for Pakistan," International Cooperation Administration (2), Box 142, White House Central Files, Official Files 1953–1961, OF 8-Q International Cooperation Administration (4), DDEL. The report is undated, but an accompanying memo has the date December 27, 1955, which may be from significantly after the initial publication of the audit.
19 "Audit Report to the Congress of the United States, United States Assistance Program for Iran, June 30, 1955," International Cooperation Administration (2), Box 142,

White House Central Files, Official Files 1953–1961, OF 8-Q International Cooperation Administration (4), DDEL.

20 Meeting notes, 283th meeting of the NSC, May 4, 1956, Box 7, NSC Series, Dwight D. Eisenhower: Papers of the President 1953–1961 (Ann Whitman File), DDEL.

21 Meeting notes, 301st meeting of the NSC, October 26, 1956, Box 7, NSC Series, Dwight D. Eisenhower: Papers of the President 1953–1961 (Ann Whitman File), DDEL.

22 J. H. Smith to Richard Russell, December 12, 1957, International Cooperation Administration (13), Box 143, White House Central Files, Official Files 1953–1961, OF 8-Q International Cooperation Administration (4), DDEL.

23 Meeting notes, May 9, 1957, L-38 (1), Box 4, Legislative Meeting Series, Office of the Staff Secretary Records 1952–1961, DDEL; Dwight D. Eisenhower, "Radio and Television Report to the American People on the Cost of Their Government." Peters and Wooley, eds, APP www.presidency.ucsb.edu/node/233286 (accessed October 17, 2020); William S. White, "Eisenhower Sets 3.8 Billion Floor for Foreign Aid," *NYT*, May 10, 1957.

24 Dwight D. Eisenhower, "Special Message to the Congress on the Mutual Security Programs, May 21, 1957," Peters and Wooley, eds, APP, www.presidency.ucsb.edu/node/233299 (accessed October 17, 2020).

25 "Composite Report of the President's Committee to Study the United States Military Assistance Program," Washington, 1959; "To the Aid of Aid," *Time Magazine*, March 30, 1959.

26 "Battle of the Century – The Chicago Tribune Against the Enemies of Freedom and Truth," *Chicago Tribune*; June 10, 1947.

27 Elmer Gertz, "Chicago's Adult Delinquent," *Public Opinion Quarterly* 8, 3 (Autumn 1944), 416–424.

28 "A Foreign Policy Fed on Falsehood," *Chicago Tribune*, July 17, 1947; "No Good Can Result," *Chicago Tribune*, June 7, 1947.

29 "A Foreign Policy Fed on Falsehood," *Chicago Tribune*, July 1947; "Civilization on the Skids," *Chicago Tribune*, September 9, 1947.

30 "The Budget and You," *Chicago Tribune*, January 23, 1952; William Moore, "I Help Myself, So Can Europe," *Chicago Tribune*, February 17, 1948.

31 "Brother, Can You Spare a Billion," *Chicago Tribune*, November 30, 1953.

32 "Eisenhower's Thesis," *Chicago Tribune*, December 5, 1953; "Somebody Please Tell Him," *Chicago Tribune*, November 7, 1958.

33 "The Annual Giveaway," *Chicago Tribune*, July 1, 1954.

34 "What it Costs You," *Chicago Tribune*, July 20, 1954.

35 "Eisenhower's Marxian Prescription," *Chicago Tribune*, July 3, 1958.

36 "Guess Who Pays," *Chicago Tribune*, August 12, 1958.

37 Henry Hazlitt, *Economics in One Lesson* (New York, 1946), 5–6; Chris Matthew Sciabarra and Larry J. Sechrest, "Ayn Rand Among the Austrians," *The Journal of Ayn Rand Studies*, 6, 2 (Spring 2005), 241–250.

38 Hazlitt, *Will Dollars Save the World*? (New York, 1957), 26–27.

39 Ibid., 34.

40 Ibid., 58–59.

41 Ibid., 61–62, 75–76.

42 William J. Lederer and Eugene Burdick, *The Ugly American* (New York, 1958); Eugene Castle, *Billions, Blunders, and Baloney: The Fantastic Story of how Uncle Sam is Squandering Your Money Overseas* (New York, 1955). Castle also produced a second anti-aid book, *The Great Giveaway: The Realities of Foreign Aid* (New York, 1957).

43 Castle, *Billions, Blunders, and Baloney*, 49.

44 Daniel Immerwahr, *Thinking Small: The United States and the Lure of Community Development* (Cambridge, MA, 2015), 1–15.

45 Lewis Nichols, "In and Out of Books," *NYT*, April 17, 1960; Rupert Wilkinson "Connections with Toughness: The Novels of Eugene Burdick," *Journal of American Studies* 11, 2 (August 1977), 223–239. In 1963, writer and director George Englund turned the *Ugly American* into a motion picture starring Marlin Brando.
46 "Reply to Criticism in the Ugly American," International Cooperation Administration (no date), RG 286 Agency for International Development, Box 9, Entry P173, Congressional Committee and Miscellaneous Files, 1953–1962, USAID/Congressional Liaison Staff, Folder: The Ugly American, National Archives College Park, MD.
47 Joseph Buttinger, Fact of Fiction on Foreign Aid, *Dissent* 6, 3 (Summer 1959), 317–369, quote on 326.
48 "The Best-Selling Novel that Has Become an Affair of State," *NYT*, January 23, 1959.
49 "Excerpts from Kennedy's Speech Urging US 'Peace Corps'," *NYT*, November 3, 1960.
50 "Facts About: Citizen's Foreign Aid Committee," Citizen's Foreign Aid Committee, Box 78, Group Research Archives, Columbia University Rare Book and Manuscript Library, New York.
51 Nicole Hemmer, *Messengers of the Right: Conservative Media and the Transformation of American Politics* (Philadelphia, 2016), 22–24, 46; Justus D. Doenecke, "General Robert E. Wood: The Evolution of a Conservative," *Journal of the Illinois State Historical Society* 71, 3 (August 1978), 174.
52 Hemmer, *Messengers of the Right*, 133; "Facts About: Citizen's Foreign Aid Committee," Citizen's Foreign Aid Committee, Box 78, Group Research Archives, Columbia University Rare Book and Manuscript Library, New York.
53 Robert H. W. Welch, *The Politician* (Belmont, MA, 1957); Welch later backed off, slightly, on his accusations that Eisenhower was a Communist, stating in a television interview and in other venues that he had never called Eisenhower a "card-carrying Communist" and that his views were not official John Birch Society views. He did not challenge the statement, "the chances are very strong that Milton Eisenhower is actually Dwight Eisenhower's superior in within the Communist Party." Gene Grove, *Inside the John Birch Society* (Greenwich, CT, 1961), 12–13.
54 Welch, *The Politician*, 239–210.
55 D. J. Mulloy, *The World of the John Birch Society: Conspiracy, Conservatism, and the Cold War* (Nashville, 2014), 7–8.
56 Ibid., 8–9. Koch was the father of political financiers Charles and David Koch.
57 Ibid., 11.
58 Welch, *The Politician*, 244.
59 Krzysztof Persak, "The Polish-Soviet Confrontation in 1956 and the Attempted Soviet Military Intervention in Poland," *Europe-Asia Studies* 58, 8 (December 2006), 1285–1310; Dwight D. Eisenhower, "Radio and Television Report to the American People on the Developments in Eastern Europe and the Middle East," Peters and Wooley, eds, APP, www.presidency.ucsb.edu/node/233787 (accessed October 18, 2020); "US Aid Silence Worries Poland," *NYT*, December 4, 1956; Welch, *The Politician*, 244–248.
60 "Some Questions about Foreign Aid," *American Opinion*, May 1959, 25–28.
61 Welch, The Blue Book of the John Birch Society (self-published, 10th printing, 1961), 86–94.
62 "Announcement of the Formation of the Citizen's Foreign Relations Committee, February 11, 1957," Folder: Citizen's Foreign Relations Committee, Group Research Archives, Box 17, Columbia University Book and Manuscript Library, New York.
63 "Committee Against Summit Entanglements, June 17, 1959," Reprinted in *American Opinion*, July-August 1959; "Committee for the Monroe Doctrine introduction letter, January 3, 1963," Folder: Monroe Doctrine, Box 5, Patrick Knight Papers, Robert F. Wagner Labor Archives, New York University, New York.

64 "Double Trouble," Washington Observer Newsletter, February 1, 1969, No. 73 in Box 78, Group Research Archives, Columbia University Rare Book and Manuscript Library, New York; Harnischfeger may certainly have been a member of the John Birch Society, and he definitely had multiple personal connections to members, but research has not uncovered any membership details.
65 "Foreign Aid and You: A First Report by the Citizen's Foreign Aid Committee," Citizen's Foreign Aid Committee, 1959, reprinted as "Report on the Mutual Security Program by the Citizen's Foreign Aid Committee," Committee on Foreign Affairs, United States House of Representatives, April 27, 1959 (Washington, 1959), 10.
66 Conrad Kohler testimony, US Senate, *Hearings Before the Committee on Appropriations, 86th Congress, on H.R. 12619* (Washington, 1960), 708–712.
67 Ibid.
68 "Foreign Aid and You," 12–13.
69 One particularly good example is the insertion by Robert Dole (R-KS, future vice-presidential and presidential candidate) of a letter penned by Howard Buffet. Buffet had been a member of the House of Representatives and is the father of investor Warren Buffet, he was also a leading member of Citizen's Foreign Aid Committee. *CR,* August 28, 1961, A6742-A6743.
70 Barry Eichengreen, *Exorbitant Privilege: The Rise and Fall of the Dollar and the Future of the International Monetary System* (New York, 2001), 97–120; Ronald I. McKinnon, *The Unloved Dollar Standard: From Bretton Woods to the Rise of China* (New York, 2013), 30–47; Robert Leeson, *Ideology and the International Economy: The Decline and Fall of Bretton Woods* (New York, 2003).
71 Statement of Walter Harnischfeger before the House Appropriations Subcommittee on Foreign Operations, August 19, 1961, Citizen's Foreign Aid Committee (Studies & Testimony of), Box 78, Group Research Archives, Columbia University Rare Book and Manuscript Library, New York.
72 Ibid.
73 "Executive Branch Comments, Report on the Mutual Security Program," April 17, 1959, Committee on Foreign Affairs, House of Representatives, 86th Congress, 1st Session (Washington, 1959).
74 "Effects of the Mutual Security Program on the United States Economy," Office of Statistics and Reports, International Cooperation Administration, May 14, 1957, Subject Files: 1957–1962, USAID/Congressional Relations, Box 15, RG 286, National Archives II, College Park, MD (Hereafter NARA).
75 Conducted by Gallup, Dataset USAIPO1958–0596, collected by the Roper Center for Public Opinion Research, ropercenter.cornell.edu (accessed February 14, 2018).
76 Conducted by National Opinion Research Center, University of Chicago, Datasets USNO RC1955–0366, USNORC1956–0382, USNORC1956–0393, and USNORC1956–0399, collected by the Roper Center for Public Opinion Research, ropercenter.cornell.edu (accessed February 14, 2018).
77 Conducted by National Opinion Research Center, University of Chicago, Datasets USNORC1955–0366, USNORC1956–0382, USNORC1956–0393, and USNORC1 956–0399, collected by the Roper Center for Public Opinion Research, ropercenter.cor nell.edu (accessed February 14, 2018).
78 Conducted by National Opinion Research Center, University of Chicago, Dataset USNORC1957–0404, collected by the Roper Center for Public Opinion Research, ropercenter.cornell.edu (accessed February 14, 2018); Conducted by Gallup Organization, Dataset USAIPO1958–0593, collected by the Roper Center for Public Opinion Research, ropercenter.cornell.edu (accessed February 14, 2018).
79 Conducted by Institute for International Social Research/Gallup, Dataset USIISR1959–12, collected by the Roper Center for Public Opinion Research, ropercenter.cornell.edu (accessed February 14, 2018).

80 Caldwell to Hollister, February 17, 1959, Polls, Box 14, USAID/Congressional Liaison Staff, RG 286, NARA. This figure represented the available funds, not authorized or appropriated funds, and not how much would be spent. It was an approximation of all the appropriated funds and all the unexpended funds from prior years.

81 Conducted by National Opinion Research Center, University of Chicago, Datasets USNORC1949–0164, USNORC1956–0401, collected by the Roper Center for Public Opinion Research, ropercenter.cornell.edu (accessed February 14, 2018).

4

OTTO PASSMAN AND THE FIGHT AGAINST MODERNIZATION THEORY

While Eisenhower slowly warmed to backing aid, Kennedy believed from the start of his presidency that a vigorous and expansive aid program could transform the world. The United States, he thought, could begin to eliminate poverty and create global prosperity, and in so doing, ensure US victory in the Cold War. He was certainly aware of past US failings; in 1959 he had encouraged his colleagues in the Senate to read Lederer and Burdick's *The Ugly American*, but he was optimistic about the power of government spending and believed problems could be fixed. The United States had not fully committed itself to foreign aid, and not committed itself to doing it right. Kennedy wanted to do more and do it better.

To that end, Kennedy introduced new initiatives. He called for the reorganization of US aid programs and the creation of a new bureaucracy, the Agency for International Development (USAID), that would only handle non-military aid. This would highlight the centrality of economic aid to US foreign policy and help recipient nations understand Kennedy's priorities. He also asked for significantly more money from Congress than Eisenhower had and for the authority to make multiyear loans. Finally, he pushed for the creation of the Peace Corps, a people-to-people program inspired by *The Ugly American*, and for the Alliance for Progress, a massive aid effort in Latin America dedicated to eliminating the conditions that drove Castro's successful revolution in Cuba.[1]

A cursory review of these efforts suggests Kennedy was successful in integrating aid spending into larger US foreign policy and in building programs that demonstrated his vision. This reorientation, and some of his concrete successes, were a high-water mark in a national commitment to foreign economic aid. Yet, a closer examination suggests Kennedy's victories were incomplete, and that opponents to his programs (and to aid more generally) limited his ability to create the kinds of change he had wanted.

Kennedy argued that foreign aid needed to be a top US foreign policy priority, that the program needed to be reformed, and that he needed more money and flexibility to achieve success. Unsurprisingly the same aid opponents who fought Eisenhower's spending disagreed. They broadly argued that Kennedy's approach increased funding for a program that was fundamentally flawed; it would waste money and weaken the country. Said differently, if foreign aid was a mistake, giving Kennedy more power and more money would just make that mistake worse. Louisiana representative, Otto Passman (D), the chair of the subcommittee within the Appropriations Committee that dealt with foreign aid spending, was the most important leader in these efforts and Kennedy's most significant foe. Passman had been critical of Eisenhower's aid programs and worked to limit spending in the 1950s. Facing Kennedy's larger requests, he became an even more formidable adversary, and was ultimately responsible for cutting billions of dollars from aid budgets.

Passman's successes came, in part, from his energy and enthusiasm for fighting aid. He worked diligently to learn about the minutia of legislation, and usually knew more than administration officials about aid budgets. Because he could point to specific poorly constructed programs and waste, he could make the larger case that all economic aid programs needed spending cuts. Passman was also effective because enough of his colleagues agreed with him; they agreed with his assessment that Kennedy was asking for too much money and that taxpayers should not be footing the bill for this exuberance. These disputes were most obviously about spending decisions, but they were also about conflicting perceptions of state power and the nation's role in the world.

Kennedy's Vision

From the first moments of his presidency, Kennedy spoke about expanded a foreign aid program as a national priority. His inaugural address included the lofty and iconic sentiment, "Let every nation know, whether it wishes us well or ill, that we shall pay any price, bear any burden, meet any hardship, support any friend, oppose any foe to assure the survival and the success of liberty." This connected directly to his foreign aid pitch. He proclaimed,

> To those people in the huts and villages of half the globe struggling to break the bonds of mass misery, we pledge our best efforts to help them help themselves, for whatever period is required – not because the Communists may be doing it, not because we seek their votes, but because it is right. If a free society cannot help the many who are poor, it cannot save the few who are rich.[2]

A few weeks later, on March 1, 1961, Kennedy sent Congress a request to authorize the establishment of the Peace Corps, and just after that, on March 13, he invited diplomatic representatives from Latin American countries to the White House to introduce the Alliance for Progress.[3] Then, on March 22, he made the case to Congress for all this spending with a message outlining his goals and offering his policy justification. Giving aid, he said, was part of a moral national obligation for the United States as "a wise leader and a good neighbor in the interdependent community of nations." It was also an economic obligation for "the wealthiest people in a world of largely poor people," and a political obligation for "the single largest counter to the adversaries of freedom." Repeating the mantra Truman and Eisenhower had invoked, he explained failure to provide aid "would be disastrous" as "widespread poverty and chaos [would] lead to a collapse of existing political and social structures which would inevitably invite the advance of totalitarianism into every weak and unstable area." Addressing disorder and tyranny would be far more expensive than the sums he wanted.

Kennedy had been inspired by his exposure to a set of ideas called "Modernization Theory" that were developed by Walt W. Rostow and Max Millikan at the Center for International Studies at the Massachusetts Institute of Technology. They argued, as chapter 1 explained, that all societies could be divided into two categories, "modern" and "traditional." The modern states had complex economic structures that created surplus wealth, which led to cultural enlightenments and political freedoms. Traditional societies, by contrast, had simple economic structures, and within them, cultural and political systems had changed little over time. They were "backward" and "poor." Modern societies, the modernization theorists believed, were objectively better than traditional ones in that they offered the opportunity for people to advance, grow, and participate in a larger human community.[4]

In his celebrated 1960 book, *The Stages of Economic Growth: A Non-Communist Manifesto*, Rostow explained how societies might advance from traditional to modern. He argued that all societies had once been traditional, but in each case there been a "sharp stimulus" that rapidly propelled economic development and led to modernization. He further suggested there were many traditional places around the world ready for a rapid leap forward, or in his words, a "takeoff," and that foreign aid could be the sharp stimulus that would spur takeoff and could be a way to fight the Cold War. Rostow explained that the Soviet Union was a "modern" society, and argued that if the United States did not help the takeoffs occur, the communists might. This would lead to the construction of less effective, and less free modern societies, and also would represent a colossal defeat in the Cold War. On the other hand, if the United States could get takeoffs to happen, it would secure global allies and international trading partners.[5] Like Burdick and Lederder, they imagined that societies in other parts of the world were "fixable." With US know-how they could begin to transition from their "primitive" condition to a "modern" one, and he agreed with the premise that doing so was a fundamental requirement for winning the Cold War.

These ideas inspired Kennedy. They appealed to his basic understanding about the potential for government action and soothed his Cold War anxieties; they offered a new and more sophisticated way to engage the world. Eisenhower had focused on military power and had been reactive in responding to political conflicts in Africa, Asia, Latin America, and the Middle East. Kennedy wanted a proactive policy that understood that economic questions drove political and military ones. He thus invited Rostow, who he had sought out for advice in the late 1950s, to join his administration and help construct his new foreign aid programs.

The key to making aid work, Rostow reasoned to Kennedy, was that the United States needed to focus on long-term development planning. It had to have a consistent and well-thought-out strategy, and then the patience to implement it over many years. Rostow had critiqued Eisenhower administration officials for aid spending that was "almost wholly defensive in character" with "neither the resources, the administration, nor the criteria designed to move undeveloped countries toward sustained economic growth." As Rostow explained to Kennedy, the United States would have to construct a much larger and more consistent program to make takeoffs happen. The United States needed "a major and ruthless overhaul of existing programs … with a new emphasis on basic education; on bringing modern science to bear in the undeveloped areas; on technological training to complement economic programs; and the financing of projects aimed at modernizing social institutions."[6] But that would only be possible if Kennedy could get Congress to pass multiyear authorizations and appropriations that would allow long-term planning.

Going back to the Marshall Plan, each year the president asked for money for a single year's spending, which limited aid administrators' ability to work with recipient nations, make commitments, and plot development strategies. Kennedy wanted the ability instead to offer aid recipient nations a long-term commitment, and he could not do that if he had to keep asking for money. Aid had failed, he and Rostow believed, not so much because the theory behind aid spending was wrong, but in large part because it had been done badly. Because it was not long term it could not be systematic or strategic. Kennedy explained in his March 22 request to Congress that

> The lack of stability and continuity in the program – the necessity to accommodate all planning to a yearly deadline – when combined with a confusing multiplicity of American aid agencies within a single nation abroad – have reduced the effectiveness of our own assistance and made more difficult the task of setting realistic targets and sound standards. Piecemeal projects, hastily designed to match the rhythm of the fiscal year are no substitute for orderly long-term planning.[7]

Kennedy offered this pitch again in another message to Congress, this time delivered in person on May 25, 1961. He had initially called for $4 billion in March, but with a sense of optimism, added an extra $535 million to that request. This particular speech is well known because it included Kennedy's request for funding a national space program. He famously said he wanted money dedicated to landing "a man on the moon and returning him safely to earth," but that bid followed his aid appeal. Both the moon program and the foreign aid request shared the philosophic underpinning that government had the capacity to transform the world. They also represented the idea that it was necessary to fight the Cold War on a global (or universal) scale. Calling for more aid, Kennedy explained, "I do not see how anyone who is concerned – as we all are – about the growing threats to freedom around the globe – and who is asking what more we can do as a people – can weaken or oppose the single most important program available for building the frontiers of freedom."[8]

Two days later, at Kennedy's request, J. William Fulbright (D-AR) introduced the foreign aid bill in the Senate and then opened hearings in the Senate Foreign Relations Committee. To Fulbright's committee, Secretary of State Dean Rusk defined the stakes in grandiose terms. "Every age," he began, "historians remind us, is an age of transition. But some ages are surely more transitional than others. I cannot but feel that ours is pre-eminently such an age; and that here, just beyond the middle of the twentieth century, humanity stands, for better or for worse, on the threshold of a new historic epoch." He explained, "ahead of us stretches an unknown future which our own actions can endow with direction and content. What we decide now will determine whether the second half of the 20th century records a plunge into chaos or a steady ascent into more effective coherence and order." Rusk added that "President Kennedy has rightly called the economic measures here under consideration 'the single most important program available for building the frontiers of freedom.'"[9]

Kennedy's Limited Win

This lofty rhetoric, and the high hopes for transforming foreign aid, almost immediately ran into the reality of congressional opposition. In August 1961, following passage through the Senate Foreign Relations Committee, the full Senate began deliberations on Kennedy's proposed bill with the request for multiyear spending and substantially greater outlays. The predictable protestations came from fiscally conservative senators who claimed they were worried about spending priorities and costs. Olin Johnson, a Democrat from South Carolina, had one of the simplest arguments against the bill, suggesting that aid was nothing more than a "giant handout" that would do nothing to alter global conditions. He said that since the end of World War II the nation had "poured money out hand over fist to the four corners of the world to try to stop Communism and preserve the peace." He continued, there was no evidence of successes as "today we find ourselves in the same fix we would have been in if we had never spent one nickel on foreign aid … . We cannot buy freedom with money." Barry Goldwater (R-AZ), a well-known opponent of government spending (and the Republican presidential candidate in 1964), agreed. He said that he could not think of a single "country that has become our friend since 1950 through the giving by us of money. Instead, we have lost friends. But Communism has gained friends, although Communism has not been engaged in giving away the money of its people." Goldwater was wrong that the Soviet Union had not offered substantial economic aid; it had, but certainly far less than the United States.[10]

The Nebraskan Republican senator Roman Hruska built on Goldwater's idea, but in a more sophisticated way. Hruska shared Goldwater's skepticism about government power, but connected that cynicism with a broader opposition to US global engagement. He said that Kennedy's plan would fail because of an inherent flaw in appreciating how aid recipients would respond to the new aid program. Speaking specifically about Kennedy's proposal for aid to Latin America, the Alliance for Progress, Hruska applauded the theory in that particular plan of only giving aid to countries that had crafted comprehensive development blueprints, but he said it would not work. He correctly prophesied that Latin Americans would resent being told "We do not like your ways of doing business. We do not like your housing or your schools. We do not like your ways. We do not think your tax systems are fair, they should be changed and each of you should pay your share of taxes." This was essentially imperialism and would only antagonize the Latin Americans most likely to back US Cold War efforts.[11]

Hruska, Goldwater, and Olin Johnson all had long histories of opposing spending, but Kennedy ally and self-identified liberal Senator Patrick McNamara (D-MI) also raised questions about aid spending. He argued that, as much as he wanted to extol compassion and assistance for peoples around the world, it was necessary to offer support at home first. Throughout his two terms in the Senate, McNamara had concentrated on passing legislation to address poverty, improve education, and expand healthcare for the elderly. He believed foreign aid got in the way of these priorities. He explained to his colleagues, "It is often said that half the people in this world go to bed hungry every night. I sympathize with this situation, but I submit that too many of these hungry people live in the United States." The compassion and sympathy in the aid bill should therefore "be directed toward millions of unemployed workers and their families – the elderly who cannot afford medical care they so desperately need – the children who are being short-changed on education – all of whom are citizens and residents of the United States."[12] Goldwater, who had little in common with McNamara politically, expressed the same idea. Goldwater had said, "It is very easy to stand on the floor of the Senate and express a great humane feeling for the people of the Congo or for the people of southeast Asia, or for the people of undeveloped countries in South America and Latin America … . It is not easy for me to advocate cutting back or discontinuing foreign economic aid. However, I believe that we in America must first look to America." Goldwater was being somewhat disingenuous here, as he opposed both domestic and foreign assistance programs. Though to be fair, this debate was about a foreign aid bill, and "look to America" did not necessarily mean increased domestic spending.[13]

The major issue in the Senate, and the most divisive one, was Kennedy's request for multiyear spending. As noted, Kennedy and his advisors believed this provision was the best chance for fixing aid; it would allow them to make long-range plans and avoid the annual funding debates that highlighted aid's failure, rather than its successes. However, congressional leaders saw this idea as an attack on the fundamental nature of US democracy. George Aiken (R) of Vermont, who had historically supported aid programs, was among the most animated in his opposition. He argued that members of Congress were specifically elected by the people to control government spending and check the executive; allowing multiyear allocations would dilute Congress' power in both those respects, which by extension would reduce the power of voters. He conceded it would be more efficient to approve multiyear appropriations, but argued there was "no price high enough to warrant the unbalancing of our framework of government." Fundamentally, he insisted, "Control of the public purse through congressional appropriations is the only effective means Congress has of overseeing and insuring that legislative programs are carried out in accord with their original intentions." Aiken reminded his peers that John C. Calhoun, the nineteenth-century politician, had said that congressional control over spending was "the sinew of our strength." Aiken insisted that abandoning that concept was "an evil that cannot be tolerated."[14]

Aiken's objections, and the way they resonated in the Senate, led Harry Byrd (D-VA) to introduce an amendment to eliminate the five-year borrowing authority from the spending authorization bill. Byrd shared Goldwater's fiscal conservatism and had been a vocal aid skeptic in the 1950s. He echoed Goldwater's comments that it would be irresponsible to give more authority to aid administrators given their historic billion-dollar failures. Instead of allowing the president more flexibility on multiyear appropriations, there should be less. Aid bills needed Congress' "exceptional control and exceptional investigation." Support for Kennedy was too strong, however, and this amendment failed in a 39 to 56 vote. The "no" votes came from Democrats in Southern states like Byrd and from Republicans like Aiken, who expressed concerns about presidential power, and like Goldwater, who more generally opposed government spending. Following a cut to $4.076 billion (down from Kennedy's $4.535 billion request), the Senate passed the bill in a 66 to 24 vote.[15]

The bill had a tough time in the House for similar reasons. Similarly to Aiken, Representative Frances Bolton (R-OH) highlighted his "long loyalty to the foreign aid program" and efforts to "further the programs put forth by whatever administration was in power," but said the issue with multiyear authorizations and appropriations was "whether we are going to abrogate our rights and abandon our responsibilities and just turn it all over to the President, or not." R. Walter Riehlman (R-NY) also claimed to have supported past aid legislation, but said it was "perfectly obvious that the true interest of our foreign-aid planners lies in destroying effective congressional control over the operation." He agreed that the "wisdom of long-range planning is evident," but said the "long-range abdication of congressional responsibility is not so evident." Charles Gubser (R-CA) insisted he was "troubled" to take his first vote against foreign aid, but felt he had no choice. He did not have faith in "career State Department people with little or no experience in the workaday world they seek to establish for recipient nations." The Constitution gave Congress power because collectively they could make more "intelligent decisions" than the officials "in the State Department whose experience is narrow and limited."[16]

As Byrd did in the Senate, Dalip Saund (D-CA) offered an amendment to remove multiyear spending from Kennedy's aid bill. He explained that "efforts to promote democracy and build strong free societies in many of the under-developed countries of the world through massive expenditures of US funds have been, to say the least, not successful." Saund, who was the first Indian-American elected to Congress and generally enthusiastic about Kennedy's leadership, had taken a trip in 1957 to Vietnam, Indonesia, and the Philippines to observe aid programs, and reported he was disgusted by all the waste. With this in mind, he said, "it made no sense to give the planners more control" with less oversight. Unlike in the Senate, Saund's amendment passed 197 to 185, effectively killing the multiyear spending plan. This was a "teller" vote, meaning there was no roll call, which limits analysis of who voted and why.[17] Many Republicans, like Bolton, Reihlman, and Gubser, protested that party had nothing to do with their positions, but it is reasonable to imagine they might have been more amenable to this plan if introduced by a leader from their own party. Still, Saund, a Democrat from California who had been supportive of government spending in multiple other areas, introduced the amendment, and certainly many fiscally conservative Democrats from the South would have been backers as well.

President Kennedy immediately objected, sending a note to the House that, just as "Secretary Dillon is about to sign our long-range pledge to Latin America [for the Alliance for Progress], when Asia and Africa are poised between economic development and chaos, [and] when Mr. Khrushchev is probing the West for any sign that our resolve is weakening, I cannot believe that the bipartisan support always given this program is at this crucial moment to be abandoned." He urged the House to reconsider and "demonstrate that this nation is still united in its determination to meet its responsibilities and halt the spread of Communism and Castroism by every available means." But it was too late, and following passage of the larger bill in the House, its negotiators met with Senate leaders to craft a compromise bill that omitted the multiyear spending authority. On August 31 they agreed to authorize $4.253 billion in foreign aid spending.[18] The minor $282 million cut from the original request can be considered a Kennedy victory, but the loss on multiyear spending authority was a crushing defeat.

Passman as the Chief Antagonist

There were more defeats to come. Hearings in the Subcommittee on Foreign Operations Appropriations of the House Committee on Appropriations

(Passman's Committee) opened on June 29, 1961, well before either chamber had even begun deliberations on passing an aid spending authorization bill. This was the second part of foreign aid's journey through Congress. The authorization bill, discussed above, acted as a statement of intent to spend money, but it needed to be followed by an appropriation bill to support its payment. Passman's subcommittee's job was to review the authorization figures and present an appropriation request to the full Appropriations Committee, which would then be sent to the full House for approval (and eventually to deliberations with Senate negotiators over a compromise conference bill that would include the final appropriation figures. See Appendix D for a flowchart of the process).

Passman exercised substantial power over his subcommittee, which year after year advanced appropriation bills that had lower aid spending than the authorization bills. This work effectively cut hundreds of millions of dollars in spending from US aid programming, and easily made Passman the program's most effective foil. One key factor helping him get his way was that Clarence Cannon (D-MO), the chair of the full House Committee on Appropriations from 1941 to 1964 (except in 1947–1949 and 1953–1955 when Republicans held the majority), consistently backed him. Cannon shared Passman's sense that aid bills were too expensive, and was happy to let Passman fight the public battle and then quietly push his bills forward.[19] Passman also faced little opposition within his committee, in part because he and Cannon packed it with sympathetic aid-skeptical members, and in part because Passman operated in an era when junior representatives were far less likely to challenge senior ones. The accepted wisdom in Washington, in political scientist Samuel Huntington's words, was that "the way to get along was to get along."[20] This meant party leaders would only support the advancement of junior colleagues to better committee assignments if they did what their leadership wanted. Passman also had help from the Republicans on the committee. John Taber, a Republican from New York, served as the ranking minority member on the subcommittee in the 1950s and early 1960s and also the ranking Republican on the full appropriations committee (and chair of both when the Republicans had the majority). He shared Passman's aversion to foreign aid spending, and government spending more generally, which provided bipartisan support. There had been an opportunity to oust Passman from his position following the 1960 election, as he, along with other Democrats in Southern states refused to endorse the national Kennedy-Johnson ticket. Kennedy had encouraged House leaders to punish Passman, but Cannon and the rest of the House Democratic leadership balked, leaving him in place.[21]

Passman claimed his opposition to aid rested on his personal experiences as a "self-made" man who had never taken government handouts. His parents were poor Louisiana tenant farmers, and in his early teens he left home to work a number of odd jobs that included running errands at a grocery store. He was frugal and responsible enough, he said, that despite his meager wages he could both send money home to his parents and build up a savings account. While employed at the grocery store he completed high school, and then attended a small business college. Following graduation, he worked as a salesman and later opened a commercial kitchen supply company, becoming successful selling equipment to restaurants, hotels, and especially to schools (which were being built with government funds). In 1942, he joined the Navy as a lieutenant and served at an airbase in Florida doing supply operations; he later claimed the bureaucratic inefficiency he witnessed in the Navy led him to run for Congress in 1946.[22]

Despite his aversion to government spending, as a new representative, Passman made his initial priority obtaining money for flood protection and levee building, as his district in northeast Louisiana bordered the Mississippi River and contained numerous flood-prone rivers and bayous. He was successful in this effort, getting $40 million for his district in just his first five years in office. Before he arrived in Washington, Congress had passed bills for this work, but they had stalled in the Appropriations Committee. Passman's rather obvious solution was convincing the other, more senior members of the Louisiana delegation to back him for a seat on that powerful committee so he could push the legislation along. He later recalled that the more senior members of Louisiana's delegation were happy with their committee assignments, so they supported him, even though new representatives rarely got such plum positions.[23]

Once on the Appropriations Committee, Passman became close with Cannon, who liked him and saw him as a reliable like-minded supporter who wanted to limit spending. This led to Passman's appointment to the Executive Steering Committee of the Appropriations Committee. Even before this though, Passman had joined the chorus of anti-Marshall Plan voices in 1948, calling it a "give-away program" that was "squandering our children's and grandchildren's lives." As part of his work on the Appropriations Committee, he took trips in 1949, 1951, and 1952 to inspect aid programs in Europe and Asia. This travel reinforced his views about aid profligacy, though it is clear he did not undertake them with an open mind. He told a reporter shortly before one of his departures that he expected to be "more convinced of the folly of the program than ever."[24] In 1953 he intensified his attacks on foreign aid and began to assert himself as a leader on the issue in the House. He likely felt emboldened because most of the levee and flood control projects he had pushed for were either completed or fully funded. He had served his district effectively on this front and did not need to curry favor with administration officials to get projects moving anymore, and as importantly, the Republican victories in the 1953 elections freed him. Not only had Eisenhower won the presidential election, but Republicans took control of the House of Representatives. As a Democrat, facing a Republican president and a Republican majority in the House, it was easier to be critical. He and Cannon were outsiders (albeit only temporarily), and he used the moment to attempt to become the legislative leader fighting Eisenhower's foreign aid requests. Following the 1954 elections, in which the Democrats regained control of the House of Representatives, Cannon understandably appointed Passman chair of the Foreign

Affairs Subcommittee of the Appropriations Committee, a post he would hold until 1976. He later claimed Cannon gave him the position with the explicit instruction to cut Eisenhower's aid requests as deeply as possible.[25]

As Appendix A demonstrates, Passman did well at this job. In 1955, Eisenhower asked for $3.53 billion in foreign aid, the House and Senate knocked this down to $3.285 billion, but Passman's committee lopped off even more, proposing a $2.639 billion bill. The following year, his committee cut less, just over $300 million, which was still a substantial sum. At the start of the next budget cycle, in early 1957, Eisenhower decided to try a little flattery in an attempt to encourage Passman to be more cooperative, but it did not go well. Passman later recounted the story to a reporter. He said,

> They sent for me in a long, black Cadillac. I guess the first time I had ever been in one. I felt real important, which is not my usual way of feeling. When I got to the President's study in the White House, all the big shots were there, Admiral Radford and Secretary Dulles and the leaders of Congress. We had tea and little cakes, and they sat me right across from the President. They went around the room, asking for comments, one minute each. When they got to me, I said I would need more than one minute, maybe six or seven minutes, to tell them what was wrong with their program … . I gave the facts, and then the meeting broke up.

"The facts" were a staple of Passman's speeches. He worked hard to memorize details about aid spending legislation, which he argued was wasteful, which then allowed for blanket condemnations. According to one of Eisenhower's aides, the president had never heard anything like it, and after the meeting was over he turned to a staff member and said, "Remind me never to invite that fellow down here again."[26]

Passman's position on foreign aid was about more than government waste. It was a response based on his comprehensive understanding of the world. Just as Kennedy's approach reflected his sensibilities about state power, Passman also saw the nation in his own way, which was a philosophical position diametrically opposed to Kennedy's. With the exception of levee-building, he believed that not only was government unable to transform and improve society, its actions usually made things worse, because they were inefficient and insensitive to local conditions.

Throughout his career he emphasized that waste was an inevitable consequence of government spending. In his early speeches to constituents, before even getting heavily involved in foreign aid, he denounced out-of-control government budgets and other Representatives' limited interest in standing up to the president and his budget requests, when it was obvious that money was being misspent. He wanted to find the flaws, and highlight them as inescapable mismanagement that could only be limited with reduced spending.[27] But the sense

FIGURE 4.1 *The Foreign Octopus Consumes US Dollars.* This illustration accompanied an article by Eugene Castle in the *American Mercury* that quoted Passman as saying, "Our highest paid bureaucrats and their subordinates are working without letup to convince Members of Congress and the American People that the foreign aid program is indispensable and that ever more funds are required to support it."

Source: In Eugene Castle, "Foreign Spree for Our Superspenders," *American Mercury*, May 1957.

that resources were being wasted went beyond just money. In part because of his experience with the ways that intensive crop cultivation had led to soil runoff, he also worried about how citizens had wasted vital environmental resources, which he saw as a great national failure. In a passionate early speech, he explained that the "story of the waste of this country's riches is a sad story of greed and selfishness." It was a brutal national history of wildlife extermination; people felt free to hunt, shoot, and kill without thinking about conserving resources. The same had happened with land. People wanted crops, and their greed to do as much as possible as quickly as possible led to a "reckless stripping away of the vegetable cover of the soil" that "has driven out the animals and invited the forces of erosion." He said "the same wanton waste and disregard for the future is to be seen in the almost criminal waste of oil" and in deforestation where there was "never a thought of planting young trees, never a thought of preserving the timberland." Thus, stopping waste and conserving resources was a central part of his congressional responsibility, but it fell within a larger context of believing that actions dedicated to advancing progress often made things worse.[28]

This position was reflected in his view of the Civil Rights movement as an effort to use government power to transform society, and also his embrace of segregationism and "state's rights." He claimed, as many others did, that the 1954 Supreme

Court decision in the Brown vs. Topeka case that determined that segregated schools were unconstitutional was part of an "unceasing barrage of malicious and misleading propaganda, assaulting the integrity, character, customs and mores of the people of the Southern States." He declared in response, "I was born a segregationist and I will die one." He did not argue that segregation was just, only that it was part of the fabric of life, and that black and white people of the South supported it because it was a natural condition. Southern blacks, he said, knew that they were being "exploited by the radical and pink-fringed N.A.A.C.P., and its sister organizations and captive politicians, and they resent as deeply as their white neighbors these efforts to destroy the identity of their race." Still, he lamented that black voters rarely backed him, even though he insisted that "never in my life have I uttered derogatory statements about the colored man."[29]

Change, and perhaps even progress that might improve the lives of blacks, was possible though. He acknowledged there was a problem of "second-class citizenship" in the South (as well as in the North), but rejected the idea that government intervention might improve this situation. The only way change could work was if black citizens transformed their own communities, if they pulled themselves up from their subordinate position and made changes themselves. That was not happening though. Blacks, Passman said, "refuse or neglect to discharge the duties, responsibilities and obligations that must be given in return for the enjoyment of first-class citizenship," and they did not "observe the same moral standards as whites."[30] No external power could fix that. This obviously paralleled his belief about aid's inability to help people in other countries.

Activist government was thus the fundamental problem because it was trying to achieve something that could not be done. He grumbled about the "misconception on the part of many that government can create and sustain prosperity, and also that government can give something for nothing." It was the job of locals, he said, not outsiders, to determine how to preserve social order, which meant segregation. He explained that this was "part of the life of the people of many states – including of course, Louisiana – and confirmed by our habits, traditions, customs, and way of life." But getting back to his core idea, he argued his constituents needed to understand, that "excessive demands by the people for Federal financial aid" created "the predicament in which we find ourselves today" because with "Federal aid comes Federal controls."[31] Rather than being constructive to local communities, aid was destructive.

Passman's ideas about race and segregation in Louisiana informed his views about foreign aid programs. Historian Amanda Schlumpberger, one of the few scholars to closely interrogate Passman's record, argues that he was not alone in making this connection, and suggests it was also powerful for other white Southern leaders. She wrote that the most important segregationist leader of the era, George Wallace, the governor of Alabama from 1963 to 1967 and a presidential candidate in 1968, also explicitly connected foreign aid and domestic government power. For Wallace, Passman, and many other Southern whites, the Brown decision and subsequent federal government desegregation efforts were evidence that government was dedicated to destroying their Southern way of life. It was evidence that government was misguidedly and calamitously trying to fix the South, which was in essence what was happening with foreign aid. Notably, it was the same group of Northern elite leaders pushing both ideas. Opposition to aid, Schlumpberger aptly put it, was part of a "shared language of resentment, nationalism, anti-liberalism, and unilateralism" connecting Southern whites.[32] Voting records in Congress bear this out. In the 66 to 24 Senate vote on Kennedy's aid bill in 1961, all 13 Democrats who voted "no" came from Southern states.[33]

Here, Passman and the other anti-aid Southern Democrats who similarly fought against federal government involvement in the Civil Rights movement were expressing a fundamental challenge to modernization theory. Rostow and Kennedy had argued that "modern" societies were better than "traditional" ones. Yet these Southern whites rejected that notion and the supporting assumptions of the intellectuals that went with it. They argued that traditional societies were stable, orderly, beneficent, and blessed by scripture; they were better than modern ones. They needed to be preserved and protected against aggressive policies dedicated to destroying their values. Unsurprisingly, they were angry and resentful about the challenge to their way of life, and they tended to lump all types of pro-modernism "do-gooderism" in the same pile.

The attack on traditional culture was also, in part, an attack on traditional religion, and thus to Passman and many others, an attack on their foundational understanding of the nation. In an early speech, he argued that the "source of democracy is Christianity, and liberty comes from God." It was tragic, he said, "that the Constitution makes no reference to God," as God had been more central to the construction of society than the Constitution had been.[34] Here Passman's rhetoric overlapped with John Birch Society ideas, and also the widely syndicated 1950s and 1960s radio and television evangelist, Billy James Hargis, who preached a nationalistic, anti-government, segregationist Christian message. Communism, as an anti-God doctrine, was behind state intervention in all forms, and good Christians needed to fight proto-communism in US society. On these grounds, Hargis argued to his listeners across the country that foreign aid was "treasonous" because it was state intervention, and would strengthen global communism, rather than undermine it.[35] The state, as a secular intrusive entity, was threatening Christ's will and the national body of free souls, and the national body needed to fight back to defang the state.

Passman's worldview is not particularly surprising, and he likely emphasized it as part of his electoral calculus. As a white politician in a majority-white state, he could never have been elected without trumpeting his segregationist credentials, and they were certainly part of his overwhelming reelection victories in the 1950s and 1960s. At the same time, the language about race, coded as part of a conversation about traditionalism, or explicit when critiquing non-whites as incapable of self-rule or economic development, is rare in his extensive public and private writings about aid, though not entirely absent.

Passman consistently preferred to focus on the economics of aid and its tactical strategic defects, and emphasized waste as an example of government failure. This approach was his strength. Passman could not win an argument with legislators about foreign aid if he made explicitly racist arguments. He could win if he exposed the technical flaws in its operation, highlight corruption, and raise questions about the relationships between spending and foreign policy goals. As noted, his detailed knowledge of aid bills allowed him to dominate committee hearings. One reporter wrote, "he may bedevil a single witness for as much as a half a day about a shred of trivia, and give the rough and earthy edge of his tongue to any colleague who tries to interrupt."[36]

Passman clearly did use racist language in discussing foreign aid, but not on the record. One aid official who testified in front of his committee claimed that he would often go off the record and say things like, "those Indian bastards are never going to amount to anything," but then change his tone as official recordings and transcription resumed.[37] A colleague reported, even more disgracefully, that when a black messenger came into his hearing room, he shouted, "We're going to cut you up a piece of land out there in Africa, and we're going to make you a king; put you on a throne. Then you can qualify for foreign aid. How much do you want?" This was part of a long, four-day discussion specifically on problems with a small aid grant to Cameroon that seemed to be racially motivated. A member of his committee suggested this was something Passman liked to do because "the Cameroons and other African countries are not exactly popular down where Otto comes from."[38]

Passman and the Public

Passman was not shy about his search for allies and supporters. In the late 1950s he developed close relationships with leading anti-aid pundits such as Clarence Manion and others in the Citizen's Foreign Aid Committee, explored in the previous chapter. Passman also sent regular letters to incoming colleagues as part of his own internal lobbying efforts. He insisted in these letters that it was necessary to provide a counter to the "propaganda for fantastic amounts of foreign aid" that members would face. That propaganda and pressure, Passman claimed, would "equal all the pressures you will be subjected to on all other issues combined." As a result of his many efforts, as he was fighting Kennedy's enlarged foreign aid in the early 1960s, Passman was becoming a minor national figure. Signaling that arrival, in August 1961 he participated in a discussion about foreign aid with Arkansas senator Fulbright, the chair of the Senate Foreign Relations Committee, on NBC's "Meet the Press," where he repeated his detail-oriented critiques about waste, inefficiency, and government failure.[39]

This appearance, along with the greater attention, led hundreds, if not thousands, of ordinary voters across the country who were angry about aid and government overreach to contact him to express support. For example, one Harry

Nettles complained he was angry about "the infamous decisions of the Supreme Court … [and] people who take pleasure in striking at the South. Then there is the obnoxious Civil Rights Law, the massive give away to foreign country governments." All these were connected as elements of a single worldview of resentment toward the elites that Nettles understood to be running and destroying the country. Another supporter, John Daly, more directly wrote, "We're told that our schools, hospitals, roads, [and] farms LACK cash. Charity begins at home!" He added "A minority of 'do-gooders' still dominates both major parties. It's time for a change." For good measure, he stamped his stationery, "Our INCOME TAXES: of Marxists, by Marxists, and for Marxists!"[40]

For many correspondents, it was not a big leap from fretting about foreign aid do-gooders to believing that the do-gooders were part of a dangerous conspiracy. Mrs Robert Colin of Kenmore, NY, who called herself a "mother of five trying to feed a family on our sick American dollar," started her letter by explaining that she was concerned about fiscal issues. She complained that she was thirty years old and that long after her death "foreign aid would be rolling merrily along. It is too good a thing for too many politicians who like to get soft jobs in the government." But she was also a supporter of the John Birch Society-like Herbert Holdridge, a retired US general who she said was dedicated to unmasking the "puppets and outlaws in government who have betrayed our people, and … the sinister, invisible forces which pull the strings from behind the scenes." She wanted Passman to see Holdridge's broadside that explained how government worked. Holdridge claimed the State Department was composed of disloyal "puppets of 'Big Money,'" "black international Jesuits!," and "Georgetown School of Diplomatic Sedition" employees. Instead of following the constitution, they were beholden to NATO and were "satellites of the Vatican."[41]

While Holdridge and Mrs Colin worried about Jesuits, others focused on Jews. One anonymous admirer sent Passman a letter that explained, all in capital letters, that the United States was under threat by the "Zionist Communist Slave State of Russia" that had been carefully nurturing and carrying out a "master plan" for global domination. Part of the plan was orchestrated by the Supreme Court, notably justices "Felix Frankfurter, Austrian Born Zionist, Communist Sympathizer" and Earl Warren, who was "brainwashed by his Talmudic instruction." Foreign aid, the anonymous author said, was the "enemy's prize method for strangling our economy and killing us off with taxes." It was orchestrated by the "Zionist money changer Bernard Baruch." The infamous fabrication, *The Protocols of the Elders of Zion*, the author explained, would make all of these plans for Jewish world domination clear, including the construction of a "Negro Communist State" to be carved out of the US South.[42] Anger about foreign aid was only one element of this worldview, but it fit perfectly into conspiracy theories about elites, intellectuals, foreigners, and communists working to destroy the nation.

Not all of Passman's support came from the conspiratorially minded, though, or even those angry about race issues and the destruction of traditional society;

and, to be fair, all elected officials receive that kind of mail. More common were the dozens and dozens of letters from less paranoid citizens concerned about government spending. The manager of the Spokane Milk Producers Association, for example, complained about the wastefulness of a tramway being built in India, and a Veterans of Foreign Wars leader in Boise, Idaho, wrote that he hoped aid money would go to pensions for World War I veterans instead. Anna Marie Schiff of Evansville, Indiana, wrote that her husband just lost his job, and that they had paid $12,000 in income taxes in the previous five years. Even his last paycheck had money taken out for foreign aid; she asked, "What about aid to the U.S. people who are unemployed."[43]

Others wrote about their direct experience of aid's failures. Robert D. Wolcott told Passman that he had served in Vietnam in 1955 and 1956 and "saw, first hand, many cases of waste" that he hoped to explain to Passman in person. Arnold Krochmal, a professor at the University of Wyoming, had served as an advisor to a US agricultural aid program in Afghanistan. He resigned from the position because he was "nauseated" by "the servility of American representation, the bankruptcy of leadership and the pathetic eagerness to throw away money and advice on a government that makes no pretense of living up to its agreements with the American government." Similarly, John E. Owen, a UN official in Dacca (then part of Pakistan and now in Bangladesh), wrote he had watched for three years "how American aid has been wasted and how many of the Pakistanis have the idea that the US is a bottomless pit from which it is our obligation to give and give and give without ceasing." He wished that Passman might see how officials used aid to enrich themselves, and how little US aid was helping the needy. It was a "shameful story," he wrote, and added, "if the American tax-payers knew the half of it, they would demand that all aid to Pakistan be stopped immediately."[44] It did not require racism then, or irrational hysteria about domestic enemies, to believe aid was a mess and a mistake, and Passman stood tallest in pointing out these failures.

Passman and Kennedy's Initial Aid Request

Thus Passman, as he challenged Kennedy's aid program in 1961, had a well-developed sense of the justice of his cause, the substantial support of his constituents, and an understanding that people all over the country wanted him to succeed. His committee met from June 29 to August 19, 1961, to scrutinize the authorization bill at a granular level, to raise questions about the necessity of specific projects, and to explore how money had been spent in the prior year. It was obvious throughout that Passman would recommend a substantial spending cut. On August 29 he announced his committee would present an appropriation request of $3.357 billion for the fiscal year that had begun on July 1. This was $1.178 billion less than Kennedy had requested, and $896 million less than passed by the joint House and Senate authorization bill. Passman crowed, "It's a great day for the American taxpayer." In the next step, Clarence Cannon, the chair of the full House Appropriations Committee, refused to alter Passman's proposed figure and sent it directly to the full House. This refusal came despite a joint plea from both Secretary of State Dean Rusk and Secretary of Defense Robert McNamara. Both urged Cannon "to review with the utmost care the proposed reduction and to reinstate in full the amounts involved," They argued, "This nation finds itself in an atmosphere of mounting crisis in which the forces of international Communism stand poised to seize upon every opportunity to exploit any sign of weakness in the free world." Cannon needed to change his mind because his actions were "being watched by peoples everywhere."[45]

From his retirement in Gettysburg, Pennsylvania, Eisenhower issued a statement that the "slashes are incomprehensible to me, especially in light of present world tensions." He added that he was "sure" a "large majority of thinking American citizens, Democrats and Republicans alike, would join me in urging vigorous support of efforts to remedy the damage that would result from these committee recommendations." Kennedy, from his vacation home in Hyannis, Massachusetts, added, "I urge the Congress to appropriate foreign aid funds of a magnitude as close as possible to the original request – a request which in the opinion of both President Eisenhower and myself represented the minimum amount necessary to meet our basic commitments and responsibilities." More than that, he added, "The fight for freedom throughout the world is in a climactic hour … . We must not lose this battle." Passman was unsurprisingly the villain in the press. The widely syndicated columnist Drew Pearson captured the tenor of the response, and reflecting Kennedy and Eisenhower's comments, said Passman had been delighting leaders in the Kremlin who called him "Comrade Passman" and were happy "to see the chief peacetime weapon of the US government abroad cut to pieces."[46]

But Cannon held fast, and a few days later the House began considering the modified appropriation in a raucous session that began with a long Passman speech. Rusk, McNamara, Kennedy, and Eisenhower were overwrought, he said, as there was an additional $5.3 billion "in the aid pipeline" from funds that had been appropriated but not spent in prior years, and an additional $1.8 billion in foreign currency accumulated in payments made by previous aid beneficiaries that could also be used. With the $3.357 billion he was recommending for this bill, Kennedy would still have close to $11 billion to spend.[47] Passman also noted that even with his recommended cut, the bill would be significantly larger than any recent foreign aid appropriations (except for 1957).[48]

Passman told his colleagues, "Repeatedly I have been cast in the role of the man who would jeopardize the foreign aid program because I criticize the waste, the extravagance, the unnecessary disbursements, the excessive buildup of personnel, the foolish planning and programed needs, the uncompleted programs, the entrenched officialdom, as well as the perpetuation of their concepts." But he said he was doing his job in protecting the taxpayer, and more than that, ensuring that programs would actually succeed because they were well thought out and well administered. Poetically, he noted,

> Once again I am being called to play the part of Joshua, to blow down the illusionary fortress of aid, whereas my primary function, as is the duty of our subcommittee, is to cut and prune this ever-growing foreign aid plant of ours, so as to contain it, to train its branches aright and by this very process to insure that fruit will result. Sometimes our pruning knife may cut deep, but the purpose is to cut our wasteful growth and insure proper results commensurate to the purpose and nature of our planting. As any good husbandman knows, without this pruning, the best of plants runs wild, loses its vigor, and dies off.

He insisted that in this fight, he, rather than Kennedy, was the damaged party. He was under attack, but confident in victory because he had "facts" about waste and the actual amounts needed because of his committee's study and its hearings. He had to "fortify" himself to face the "unbelievable opposition … the pressure, the promises, the pleading, the propaganda, the persuasion, and the political plum pulling."[49]

Kennedy, like Eisenhower before him, obviously found Passman infuriating. Larry O'Brien, a Kennedy (and later Johnson) aide, told an interviewer that Passman "aggravated the President to no end … . He was downright impossible. I don't think there was a more difficult exercise in my years in the White House than the exercise that took place regarding foreign aid and Passman." O'Brien added, "If you asked me to select one member of Congress, House or Senate, that caused the President and the White House the most difficulty, interestingly enough I'd have to designate a Democrat … Passman."[50]

To fight back, Kennedy mobilized his supporters in the House to challenge Passman's reduced appropriation, focusing on the point that his cut followed so closely upon the much larger authorization bill. Representative John V. Lindsay from New York City, among the more outspoken pro-aid Republicans, captured this idea and explained, "In the Foreign Assistance Act of 1961, we enunciated a policy of support for the economic and social advancement of the less developed countries in strong terms … . What kind of an impression are we conveying of the unity, solidity, and purposefulness of this country if only a few days later we repudiate this fundamental decision?" He continued, referring to the $4.253 billion authorization passed on August 31, "Can those of us who voted the bill and the conference report now believe in good conscience that the amounts that seemed valid only a few days ago are no longer so?" This sentiment had an impact as multiple amendments added funds back into bill, yet most of Passman's cuts remained.[51]

Kennedy was more successful in the Senate, which voted 62 to 17 on September 15 for an appropriation of $4.196 billion, which was close to the $4.253 billion passed in the authorization (though still well short of the $4.535 billion

Kennedy had requested). From there, the authorization bill went to a conference committee to determine a final figure that could pass each chamber. Passman, part of the House negotiating committee, again pledged a fight, saying he would try to cut the Senate number "plenty."[52] Senator Javits (R-NY), who had supported Kennedy's higher budget requests and was a Senate conferee, vowed to push back. He remarked,

> We have had a very bad experience in conferences with the other body on foreign aid bills. Somehow or other, the representatives of the other body in these conferences have been far more determined than have ours, and almost invariably the bill has ended up very much more like what it was when it came over to the Senate from the House than what happened to it here in the Senate.

He asked, rhetorically, "Will we stand more firm than we have heretofore? Or will we again, as we have heretofore, see conferees come back after a relatively short time in the conference to say, we are sorry, but this is the best we can do?"[53]

Despite Javits' commitment to holding firm, almost immediately Senate negotiators agreed to cut their appropriation request to $4.033 billion to reach a deal, to which the House negotiators countered with $3.777 billion. Passman, leading the House team, insisted he would not budge much beyond that, saying the senators "seem to resent my position … . They have the attitude that we don't know what we are talking about. Well, we do." He postured that while he "might yield a little," he did not intend to back down. Hanging over the conference committee negotiation was the fact that both chambers had hoped to adjourn on Sunday, September 24. This gave the conference some urgency as the date approached, helping Passman, who put off meetings and forced both chambers to postpone their official adjournment. Senate leaders, led by Carl Hayden (D-AZ), insisted the bill needed to be at least $4 billion, which Passman rejected. In response, Hayden toyed with the idea of trying to force the House to vote on the Senate bill, though this carried a risk because many representatives had already left Washington, and it might have been impossible to get a quorum in the House. It was even possible that because so many representatives had left, Passman's backers might hold a majority and could do far more damage to the bill.[54]

Ultimately, senators had no choice but to agree to go below $4 billion, which had become a symbolic barrier, and concede to a $3.914 billion appropriation. Passman proudly called it an "administration defeat," a position that Kennedy administration officials confided to reporters was essentially accurate. The final appropriation was larger than any previous aid bill, and it was indicative of healthy support for Kennedy's ideas about aid, modernization, and their importance to the Cold War. At the same time, the bill's struggles, including the earlier loss of the multiyear authority and the substantial cut, showed that Kennedy could not fully recast US foreign policy through transforming and energizing aid programs. There were enough people in Congress who rejected the tenets of modernization theory and voted against him, which limited what he could do. Kennedy was frustrated, and he reportedly asked one of his allies in Congress, "What am I going to do about Otto Passman?" The humorous reply was, "You're surrounded by a lot of well-armed Secret Servicemen. Why don't you just tell one of them to shoot him – by accident of course. In fact, Mr. President, if you promise me immunity, I'll do it myself."[55]

It was in the context of this limited success that the celebrated political theorist Hans Morgenthau argued that debates about aid were not debates about helping the world, but much more narrow conversations about domestic politics. He objected to the political process that determined spending in writing:

> The public debate on foreign aid has contributed little to understanding. In the spring of every year the nation engages in such a debate, carried on almost exclusively in terms of the amount of money to be spent for purposes of foreign aid rather than of the substantive purposes which a policy of foreign aid is supposed to serve. The Administration tries, as it were, to sell a certain amount of foreign aid to Congress, and Congress refuses to buy that amount. Congress generally appropriates about ten percent less than what the Administration has requested, and the Administration spends what is appropriated as it sees fit within the general categories authorized.[56]

Morganthau missed something substantial in his pithy summary. He saw the debates as about money, and deplored the cynicism of aid budget bargaining. He did not appreciate that the bargaining was substantive and not sport; it was movement toward compromise from individuals approaching aid's philosophical underpinnings from opposite poles.

The Aid Fight in 1962 and 1963

The passage of the foreign aid bill the following year followed a similar course. For fiscal year 1963, Kennedy again requested a substantial increase in foreign aid spending. He argued that his proposed figure, $4.878 billion, was essential for advancing US interests abroad and helping win the Cold War.[57] As in the previous year, congressional leaders were mostly supportive in the initial stages. The Senate Foreign Relations Committee passed a $4.662 billion spending authorization bill on May 22, 1962, and the House passed a similar bill of $4.668 billion the following day. This led to a conference authorization bill of $4.672 billion which Kennedy signed on August 1, 1962.[58]

But as in the previous year the real fight had not begun. Passman at first said he hoped to cut the bill by $2.5 billion, but eventually pushed his committee for a $1.5 billion cut, which the full Appropriations Committee reduced to a $1.124 billion cut. House leaders opted to vote on that figure ($3.627 billion), fearing that an open debate might lead to an even lower number.[59] The Senate then passed its own $4.422 billion appropriation, which led to a conference committee negotiation. In a repeat of 1961, Passman once again played a powerful role in the conference, and as in the previous year he held up adjournment. In 1962, an election year, this was a much more significant issue. Passman's intransigence, and the desire of the other members of the committee to go home, once again allowed him to force the final authorization below $4 billion at $3.928 billion.[60] That is, Passman's efforts led Congress to pass a bill $949 million less than Kennedy had wanted, and $744 million less than they had agreed upon just a few months earlier. Passman did not get his $1.5 billion cut, but by any metric, lopping off $949 million, or 19 percent, from the initial request was a substantial accomplishment.

As with the Truman and Eisenhower administrations, Kennedy administration officials tried to fight back by educating the public about aid and its place in US foreign policy. David Bell, the director of the Agency for International Development, regularly spoke and published articles about aid's successes. In a speech in December 1962, for example, he pushed the idea that the United States needed to engage with the world, and that the government wanted to help others. He said people around the world merely wanted what people in the United States had. He claimed, "They too want to become independent and self-supporting and to achieve economic and social progress through free institutions." Beyond that, "We and they have a natural, combined, harmonized interest in the process by which their resources plus those that we contribute are applied to this common objective." He added that economic growth was a "mutual process," in which nations worked together, and thus, by "irrefutable logic, the United States' national interest in this field is something that depends not only on ourselves, but on what others do."[61]

Beyond the formal effort, Kennedy officials also hoped to counter the impact of groups like the Citizen's Foreign Aid Committee by creating the Citizen's Committee for International Development, a technically independent pro-foreign aid group, similar to the Citizen's Committee for the Marshall Plan that the Truman administration had sponsored. Though launched with great expectations, this committee never found its footing and did not last.[62] Kennedy also hoped, as Eisenhower had, that through the creation of a presidential study commission of experts and distinguished citizens, he could sell aid to a skeptical public and a reluctant Congress. The commission could recommend restructuring aid programs in ways Kennedy wanted, which would then build support for those changes. It could also explain to the public and Congress that political fights about aid were counterproductive to national security. This would build consensus for an expanded aid program around the almost universal idea that the United States had to win the Cold War. But this is not what happened.

In December 1961, Kennedy asked retired general Lucius Clay to lead the new commission. Clay had been Eisenhower's deputy during World War II and the postwar commander of the US forces in Europe. He ran the US occupation of Germany, and in that role organized the Berlin airlift. In September 1961, Kennedy had sent Clay back to Berlin to be his official representative during the Berlin Crisis.[63] Successful in that effort, Kennedy anticipated that his stature in Washington might give the aid committee the necessary gravitas to convince legislators to follow its advice.

To get the process started, in January and February 1963, Clay received briefings from administration officials, along with his committee (which included former Secretary of Defense Robert Lovett, former Treasury Secretary Robert B. Anderson, the president of the AFL-CIO George Meany, and the outgoing president of the World Bank Eugene Black).[64] Unfortunately for Kennedy, following these briefings, Clay and the rest of the committee took their job a bit too seriously and did their own investigations. Rather than trumpeting Kennedy's view about the relationship between aid and the security of the free world, they constructed a report that contained serious criticisms of US aid. Their conclusions even suggested Kennedy's 1963 foreign aid budget request (for 1964) should be cut by $500 million. That is, instead of writing a report that embraced the expansive claims inherent in modernization theory, they adopted a position that leaned toward Passman's. They wrote, foreign aid's "burden on the already pressed taxpayer, and the prospect of its prolonged continuation … [raises] questions concerning the nature and conduct of these programs. There has been a feeling that we are trying to do too much for too many too soon, that we are overextended in resources and under-compensated in results, and that no end of foreign aid is either in sight or in mind." Clay's report continued,

> Many of the countries which have received our aid have not fully performed their part of the assistance bargain with their own resources. Moreover, we have not adequately conditioned our aid in many cases on the achievement of such performance. Indeed, we may find ourselves, in effect, granting a number of continuing subsidies because it is argued that their denial would create instability and a loss of good will.[65]

Given the publicity and high expectations for the Clay Report, and its rather harsh criticisms, it was not entirely surprising that many congressional leaders felt more comfortable joining the anti-aid chorus. For example, Senator George D. Aiken (R-VT), who had voted for most aid in the past, began to call for a scaled-down program. He asked in April 1963, "why shouldn't we concentrate our efforts on the Western Hemisphere and certain other areas where we have mutual interests." He continued, "why should we have any responsibility in Africa? … [W]hy should we pay for economic aid to the Congo where we have practically no investment."[66]

As it became clear there was little political upside to backing aid spending programs in Congress, and as the Clay Committee suggested reduced aid spending, Kennedy had to pare down his request for the 1964 budget year.[67] In January 1963 he had called for a $4.95 billion program; following the Clay Report in April he dropped that to $4.525 billion. By June, as House and Senate committees held their hearings, and it became obvious there would be more cuts, Kennedy signaled he would be willing to "live with" a reduced aid program of $4.1 billion.[68]

FIGURE 4.2 *In Surgery*. This *Baltimore Sun* cartoon highlighted that while Kennedy was willing to make small cuts in 1963 to his aid program, Clay proposed bigger cuts, but Passman's cuts were the most substantial and most aggressive.

Source: *Baltimore Sun*, April 19, 1963.

The situation frustrated Kennedy, who maintained in a press conference on August 20, 1963, that "Our foreign aid program is essential to the continued strength of the free world. It gives us increased military security at a cost far lower than if we had to carry the entire burden alone." It was vital to the Cold War in giving "protection against Communist internal takeover of free people who are … not able to build solidly without outside help." Speaking directly to opponents in Congress, he asked, "One wonders which concrete actions critics would like to stop. Should we scrap the Alliance for Progress, which is our best answer to Communism in this hemisphere? Should we deny help to India, the largest free power in Asia as she seeks to strengthen herself against Communist China?" He seemed to appreciate that legislators were tired of dealing with foreign aid and debating its funding year after year, but he insisted, "however tired we may get of this program our adversaries are not tired … . The cause of freedom should certainly not be fatigued." It was "necessary and essential," he insisted, to pass a bill with at least a $4.1 billion authorization request (though he had said as much about his earlier $4.95 billion and $4.525 billion requests).[69]

Kennedy's plea did not sway the House, which voted 222 to 188 on August 23 to cut $585 million from the aid bill to take it down to $3.502 billion. Immediately after the vote, Kennedy called reporters to a special news conference where he was visibly angry. He said the House action was "unprecedented, unwarranted, and unwise," and added it was a "short-sighted, irresponsible, and dangerously partisan action." The partisan charge was relatively new, though accurate, as Republicans voted 156 to 16 for the cut while Democrats voted 172 to 66 against.[70] Republicans countered that Kennedy bore some responsibility for making aid budgets a party matter, citing the case of Walter Judd of Minnesota (R). In 1962, at the same moment that Judd was pushing his colleagues on the House Foreign Affairs Committee to back Kennedy's full budget request, Kennedy was in Judd's district campaigning for his Democratic challenger. Judd lost the election, Kennedy lost an enthusiastic foreign aid supporter, and Republicans learned to be more cautious about bipartisanship.[71]

In the Senate, Kennedy started better. The Senate Foreign Relations Committee reported out an authorization bill in late October 1962 for $4.2 billion.[72] Yet again there was opposition, and leaders of both parties agreed to a $385 million cut, which took the bill down to $3.815 billion. Their goal had been stopping proposed amendments, including one that called for a larger $1.8 billion cut. Felix Belair, the *New York Times* reporter who most closely followed this story, wrote that the cut was "simply a matter of steadily mounting pressure for a cutback that had to be satisfied to prevent the boiler from blowing apart." Senators, even ones who had backed foreign aid, were frustrated with the program, the lack of gratitude from recipient countries, and angry that year after year they needed to commit so much time to the same issue.[73]

There was a deep disconnect between Congress and Kennedy's approach. Just before his death, on November 9, 1963, Kennedy told an audience at the

Protestant Council in New York City that "foreign aid would be a way to save the world." There were global problems that transcended the Cold War and had little to do with the conflict between the United States and the Soviet Union. The "family of man," he said "can survive differences of race and religion … it can accept differences of ideology, politics, and economics. But it cannot survive, in the form we know it, a nuclear war, and neither can it long endure the growing gulf between rich and poor." His pitch was that "The rich must help the poor, the industrialized nations must help the developing nations. And the United States, along with its major allies must do better – not worse – by its foreign aid program." Peace relied on aid, as poverty was "an invitation to agitators, aggressors, and subversives. It encourages the ambitions of those who desire to dominate the world." But the members of Congress understood aid spending as a fiscal matter and had difficulty embracing Kennedy's views.[74]

On November 21, 1963, a day before Kennedy's assassination, House and Senate negotiators met for their first session to work out a compromise authorization bill. The tumult following the president's death understandably slowed work, and it was not until December 13 that both bodies passed a compromise $3.599 billion authorization bill. After the vote, Belair, the *New York Times* reporter, connected the wide support for such a substantial cut to Kennedy's death. He suggested, "the 'decade of development' which President Kennedy proudly proclaimed at the beginning of his administration began to look like an empty dream." But the cutting was not done, of course. On the same day that the $3.599 billion compromise passed both houses, Passman announced his committee was recommending a $2.8 billion appropriation bill, $900 million less than the authorization bill.[75]

As one of his first acts, President Lyndon B. Johnson tried to induce Passman to introduce a larger figure. In early December, the new president held conversations with the Speaker of the House, John McCormack (D-MA), to develop a compromise that everyone, including Passman, could accept. McCormack suggested a $3.4 billion bill, which Johnson approved. Johnson then called Passman to ask for his support, but Passman held firm. Trying a more direct approach, on December 11, Johnson asked Passman to come to the White House to get Passman to accept the $3.4 billion figure. In the meeting Passman again said no, even though Johnson promised a fight over anything less than McCormack's compromise. The following day Passman defiantly told his colleagues, "I'll go to the White House when I'm invited and I'll be polite and listen. But if the day comes when I have to yield my own convictions, fully supported by the facts, then I'll go home." He insisted he had not been softened, and any reports that he would call for a larger bill were false. Johnson, realizing he would lose, opted not to fight. An anonymous source with access to congressional leaders told the press that Johnson would likely play it "soft" because an all-out fight would lead to even more cuts. This gave Passman the opportunity to dominate the House debate and get a $3 billion authorization passed, $1.95 billion less than Kennedy had originally proposed, almost a 40 percent cut.[76]

While critics bemoaned his successes, Passman was becoming something of a folk hero in Congress, and there was a growing chorus of observers who admitted they marveled at his knowledge, energy, and power over foreign aid. Bill Henry, a columnist for the *Los Angeles Times*, wrote that while Congress was "mighty dull most of the time," when Passman had the floor it was the "best show in town." Henry added that when Passman spoke "it's rather hard to take your eyes off him. Otto is forceful, factual, and fidgety." Speaking of the session dedicated to the aid bill, Henry continued that Passman dominated the proceedings, starting with a "devastating, factual report which is such a combination of facts and figures with colorful illustrations and caustic criticism that the opposition is pretty well licked before it starts."[77] Journalist Murray Kempton, writing in *The Spectator*, agreed. A far larger group of representatives showed up on the House floor than usual when Passman was speaking. "They come early," he explained, "even though they would not have to vote for two hours because Otto Passman amuses them." But they also listened to the substance of what he said and voted with him. Chalmers Roberts, writing for the *Washington Post*, echoed this sentiment. He explained that Passman "talks like an auctioneer, tossing off figures in rapid-fire fashion. He is both ingratiating and obfuscating." No one, it seemed, had the fortitude to stand up to him, and as a consequence, he mostly got his way.[78]

The votes in December 1963 marked a final dramatic triumph for Passman. A few months later, his patron, Clarence Cannon, died in May 1964, and Johnson's fellow Texan, George Mahon (D), replaced him as chair of the House Appropriations Committee. Johnson and Mahon then pressured members of Passman's subcommittee to reject cuts in 1964 as they worked on the 1965 budget. In his first year, Johnson asked for $3.5 billion, and Passman wanted a reduction to $2.6 billion, but the committee rejected that, and in a 7 to 5 decision agreed to recommend a $3.317 appropriation. Following the vote Passman stormed off, telling a reporter "Johnson is as confused about foreign aid as the country boy who dropped his chewing gum in the chicken house."[79] But this was not the end for Passman. He retained the chair position on his subcommittee and continued to push for cuts. He also maintained his place as the de facto leader of the anti-waste, anti-foreign aid movement. He continued to work with the Citizen's Foreign Aid Committee and appeared on television and wrote extensively about aid's problems. He remained vocal, but had far less power over the process.

There is a danger in focusing too much on Passman as the architect of aid cutting in the early 1960s. He was the dominant and most energetic of the aid antagonists, but his power came from a much wider acceptance that aid budgets were too big. He was not alone in rejecting Kennedy's belief that the United States could transform the world and that its peace and security were dependent on that transformation. Passman and his colleagues just said no, aid did not work, it was riddled with inefficiency and waste, and it was not a national responsibility to "fix" other people and their societies. Their refrain was that taxpayers should keep their money and government should stop trying to transform the world.

Notes

1 Latahm, *Modernization as Ideology*; Taffet, *Foreign Aid as Foreign Policy*; Stephen G. Rabe, *The Most Dangerous Area in the World: John F. Kennedy Confronts Communist Revolution in Latin America* (Chapel Hill, 1999).
2 John F. Kennedy, "Inaugural Address, January 20, 1961," Peters and Wooley, eds, APP, www.presidency.ucsb.edu/node/234470 (accessed October 19, 2020).
3 John F. Kennedy, "Address at a White House Reception for Members of Congress and for the Diplomatic Corps of the Latin American Republics, March 13, 1961," Peters and Wooley, eds, APP, www.presidency.ucsb.edu/node/236146 (accessed October 19, 2020); John F. Kennedy, "Special Message to the Congress Requesting Appropriations for the Inter-American Fund for Social Progress and for Reconstruction in Chile, March 14, 1961," Peters and Wooley, eds, APP, www.presidency.ucsb.edu/node/236158 (accessed October 19. 2020); John F. Kennedy, "Special Message to the Congress on the Peace Corps, March 1, 1961," Peters and Wooley, eds, APP, www.presidency.ucsb.edu/node/236086 (accessed October 20, 2020).
4 Nils Gilman, *Mandarins of the Future: Modernization Theory in Cold War America* (Baltimore, 2007).
5 Walt W. Rostow, *The Stages of Economic Growth: A Non-Communist Manifesto* (Cambridge, UK, 1960).
6 Rostow to Kennedy, February 28, 1961, Foreign Aid 2/24/61–2/28/61, Staff Memoranda, Walt W. Rostow, Box 324, Meetings and Memoranda File, National Security File, John F. Kennedy Library, Boston, MA (hereafter JFKL); Memorandum on a New Organization for the US Foreign Aid Program, Foreign Aid 1–10/61, Staff Memoranda, Walt W. Rostow, Box 324, Meetings and Memoranda File, National Security File, JFKL; Jeffrey F. Taffet, *Foreign Aid as Foreign Policy: The Alliance for Progress in Latin America* (Routledge, 2007).
7 John F. Kennedy, "Special Message to the Congress on Foreign Aid, March 2, 1961," Peters and Wooley, eds, APP, www.presidency.ucsb.edu/node/236184 (accessed October 20, 2020).
8 John F. Kennedy, "Special Message to the Congress on Urgent National Needs, May 25, 1961" Peters and Wooley, eds, APP, www.presidency.ucsb.edu/node/234560 (accessed October 20, 2020).
9 Dean Rusk testimony to Senate Foreign Relations Committee, May 31, 1961, US Senate, *Hearings before the Committee on Foreign Relations on the A Bill to Promote the Foreign Policy, Security, and General Welfare of the United States by Assisting Peoples of the World in their Efforts Towards Economic and Social Development and External Security, and for Other Purposes, United States Senate, Eighty-Seventh Congress* (Washington, 1961), 30–31.
10 *CR*, August 4, 1961, 14719, 15552, 15553; Goldwater would later say about foreign aid, "I don't want to give it – period … . I can take polls that will show you 90 percent of the people are against foreign aid, because I know how to make a poll. If foreign aid could be voted on by the American people, they would reject it. Just like the Civil Rights bill. If they could have locked the doors to the Senate and turned the lights off, you wouldn't have gotten 25 votes." From "Transcript of Unpublished Part of *Der Spiegel*'s Interview With Goldwater," *NYT*, July 11, 1964.
11 *CR*, August 11, 1961, 155466; Taffet, *Foreign Aid as Foreign Policy*.
12 James C. Dewey, "Obituary, Patrick V. McNamara," *Detroit Free Press*, May 1, 1966; *CR*, August 11, 1961, 15508.
13 *CR*, August 11, 1961, 15552, and 15553.
14 *CR*, August 11, 1961, 15032.
15 *CR*, August 11, 1961, 15546; *CR*, August 16, 1961, 15594; *CR*, August 18, 1961, 16411; Felix Belair, "Aid Measure Sent to Senate Floor," *NYT*, July 25, 1961; E. W. Kenworthy, "Fulbright Terms Aid Bill Best Yet," *NYT*, August 5, 1961; E. W. Kenworthy, "Congress Votes Conflicting Bills on Long Term Aid," *NYT*, August 19, 1961.

16 *CR*, August 14, 1961, 15748; *CR*, August 15, 1961, 15823, 15850–15851.
17 *CR*, August 16, 1961, 16060, 10672–16073; Tom Patterson, "Triumph and Tragedy of Dalip Saund," *California Historian*, 1992.
18 John F. Kennedy, "Statement by the President Urging Bipartisan Support for Long-Term Foreign Aid, August 17, 1961," Peters and Wooley, eds, APP, www.presidency.ucsb.edu/node/235384 (accessed October 20, 2020); E. W. Kenworthy, "Congress Passes Aid Bill," *NYT*, September 1, 1961.
19 Martha Williams to Passman, January 3, 1957, F28-Aid Subcommittee, Box 1958–02, General Files, Otto Passman Collection, University of Louisiana at Monroe, Monroe, LA (hereafter OPC).
20 Samuel P. Huntington, "Congressional Responses in the Twentieth Century." In David B. Truman, ed., *The Congress and America's Future* (Englewood Cliffs, NJ, 1965), 5–31.
21 Rowland Evans, Jr., "Louisiana's Passman: The Scourge of Foreign Aid," *Harper's Magazine*, January 1, 1962.
22 Randolf Jones, "Otto Passman and Foreign Aid: The Early Years," *Louisiana History* 26, 1 (Winter 1985), 53–62; Passman, "Address at the University of the Americas Graduation Exercises," June 9, 1973, F07, Box 1966–09, General Files, OPC.
23 Passman, "Speech on KNOE," October 25, 1951, F07-Speeches, Box 1951, General Files, OPC.
24 Passman, "Radio Speech," March 1, 1948, F09-Speeches, Box 1951, General Files, OPC; Jones, "Otto Passman and Foreign Aid," 58–59.
25 Jones, "Otto Passman and Foreign Aid," 60–61.
26 Evans, "Louisiana's Passman," 78–83; "Interview with Maurice Williams, 1996," United States Foreign Assistance Oral History Program, Association for Diplomatic Studies and Training, collection housed in the Lauinger Library, Georgetown University, Washington, DC.
27 Passman, "Radio Broadcast," April 1, 1951, F07-Speeches, Box 1951, General Files, OPC.
28 Passman, "New Glory for Old Glory, KRUS radio speech," November 10, 1948, F09-Speeches, Box 1951, General Files, OPC.
29 Passman to Richards, August 30, 1968, F01-Campaign Support, Box 1968–10, OPC; Passman, "Where is the Reign of Terror," 1957, F05-Speeches, Box 1956–1958, General Files, OPC.
30 Passman, "Where is the Reign of Terror."
31 Passman, "Monroe Speech," November 11, 1960, F23-Speeches, Box 1960–03, General Files, OPC.
32 Amanda Schlumpberger, "Respecting the Separateness of Others: Segregationist Opposition to American Foreign Aid and the Formation of a Southern Internationalism, 1946–1973" (PhD dissertation, University of Kansas, 2015), 4, 112–113; Thomas Noer, "Segregationists and the World: The Foreign Policy of the White Resistance," in Brenda Gayle Plummer, ed., *Window on Freedom: Race, Civil Rights, and Foreign Affairs, 1945–1988* (Chapel Hill, 2003); *CR*, August 18, 1961, 16412.
33 Amanda Schlumpberger, "Respecting the Separateness of Others," 112–113; Thomas Noer, "Segregationists and the World: The Foreign Policy of the White Resistance," in Brenda Gayle Plummer, ed., *Window on Freedom: Race, Civil Rights, and Foreign Affairs, 1945–1988* (Chapel Hill, 2003); *CR*, August 18, 1961, 16412.
34 Passman, "New Glory for Old Glory, KRUS radio speech," November 10, 1948, F09-Speeches, Box 1951, General Files, OPC.
35 Billy James Hargis, "Hargis Condemns Foreign Aid," *Christian Crusade*, September 1957; Billy James Hargis, "The United States… Alias the Prodigal Son," *Christian Crusade*, January 1957; Billy James Hargis, This I Believe (Tulsa, no date); Lee Roy Chapman, "The Strange Love of Dr. Billy James Hargis," *This Land*, October 2, 2012, thislandpress.com/2012/11/02/the-strange-love-of-dr-billy-james-hargis (accessed

October 15, 2020); Thomas Wayne Dehanas, "America's Modern Day Messiah: Billy James Hargis and his Christian Crusade-A Case Study in Extremism," MA thesis, Oklahoma State University, July 1966.

36 "Otto the Terrible," *Newsweek*, September 10, 1962.

37 "Interview with Maurice Williams, 1996," United States Foreign Assistance Oral History Program, Association for Diplomatic Studies and Training, collection housed in the Lauinger Library, Georgetown University, Washington, DC. Williams claimed that Passman engaged in questionable ethical lobbying efforts, using his power to gain favors or force adjustments in aid bills to accommodate friends. Williams claimed Passman steered a boat contact for Pakistan to a small manufacturer in his district, and when the boats did not meet the specifications of the AID contract, he pushed AID to resolve the issue favorably for the manufacturer.

38 "Otto the Terrible," *Newsweek*.

39 "Manion Weekly Broadcast Transcript," July 20, 1958, F28-Foreign Aid Subcommittee, Box 1958–02, General Files, OPC; Bonner Fellers to Passman, June 25, 1959, F19-Foreign Aid Subcommittee, Box 1959–03, OPC; Passman "Dear Colleague Letter, December 1, 1958," Congressional Reports, Box 1, Flies of Joseph M. Dodge, DDEL; "Meet the Press Transcript," August 6, 1961, F30-Foreign Aid Meet the Press, Box 1963–07, OPC.

40 Henry Nettles to Passman, June 25, 1960, F04-Correspondence, Box 1959–03, OPC; John Daly to Passman, July 8, 1956, F14-Foreign Aid, Box 1956–01, OPC.

41 Mrs. Robert Colin to Passman, July 29, 1959, F20-Foreign Aid Non-Constituent Support, Box 1958–01, OPC.

42 Anonymous Letter "Indifference and Apathy Can Mean National Suicide" to Passman, No Date, F20-Foreign Aid Non-Constituent Support, Box 1958–01, OPC.

43 George Johnson to Passman, July 15, 1959, F20-Foreign Aid-Non Constituent Support, Box 1958–02, General Files, OPC; Dean V. Thompson to Passman, July 19, 1959, F20-Foreign Aid-Non Constituent Support, Box 1958–02, General Files, OPC; Anna Marie Schiff to Passman, February 13, 1959, F-22 Foreign Aid – References used for March 25, 1958 speech, Box 1958–02, General Files, OPC.

44 Robert Walcott to Passman, July 23, 1959, F20-Foreign Aid-Non Constituent Support, Box 1958–02, General Files, OPC; Arnold Krochmal to Passman, July 24, 1959, F20-Foreign Aid-Non Constituent Support, Box 1958–02, General Files, OPC; Frank Mickadeit to Passman, July 24, 1959, F20-Foreign Aid-Non Constituent Support, Box 1958–02, General Files, OPC; John E. Owen to Passman, August 11, 1961, F19-Foreign Aid Backdoor Spending, Box 1963–07, OPC.

45 Passman response to Rusk, US House of Representatives, *Part I, Hearings in the Subcommittee on Foreign Operations Appropriations of Committee on Appropriations, 87th Congress, June 29, 1961* (Washington, 1961), 7, 14–16, 23; Willard Edwards, "Aid Figure Cut to 3.5 Billion by House Unit" *Chicago Tribune*, September 2, 1961; Felix Belair, "Foreign Aid Hits New House Snag," *NYT*, July 12, 1961; "Mr. Passman Proves a Point," *New York Herald Tribune*, September 4, 1961.

46 E. W. Kenworthy, "House Unit Backs Foreign Aid Cut of 896 Millions," *NYT*, September 2 1961; John F. Kennedy, "Statement by the President Urging the Congress To Appropriate Requested Foreign Aid Funds, September 02, 1961," Peters and Wooley, eds, APP, www.presidency.ucsb.edu/node/235559 (accessed October 20, 2020); Drew Pearson, "Foreign Aid Cuts Please Moscow," *Washington Post*, September 9, 1961.

47 *CR*, September 5, 1961, 18134.

48 Evans, "Louisiana's Passman." Passman exaggerated the issue of unspent money. It was a problem that appropriations were not spent in the year in which they had been appropriated – the amount of time necessary to plan, and make agreements with foreign governments and other organizations, made delays inevitable. Money "in the aid pipeline" but not spent in a fiscal year was automatically re-appropriated, usually in the following year. Thus, there was no pot of $5.3 billion dollars sitting in an account ready to be spent because that

money it had already been assigned to previously appropriated purposes. Still, Passman had a point in saying that if the government could not spend the money authorized for a fiscal year in that fiscal year, it might make sense to only appropriate money in the year it could be spent. He was also correct that spending for 1961 would not be limited to the appropriation, as all the unspent money would still be dedicated to advancing Kennedy's foreign policy aims.

49 *CR*, September 5, 1961, 18134–18137.

50 Lawrence F. O'Brien Oral History Interview, September 18, 1985, Lyndon Baines Johnson Library Oral History Collection, Lyndon Baines Johnson Library, Austin, TX.

51 *CR*, September 5, 1961, 18182, 18183, 18151.

52 Felix Belair, "Senate Restores Most of Aid Cuts: Passes Bill, 62–17," *NYT*, September 16, 1969.

53 *CR*, September 15, 1961, 19648.

54 Felix Belair, "Conferees Break Off Talks On Funds for Foreign Aid," *NYT*, September 22, 1961; Felix Belair, "Passman Blocks Accord on Funds for Foreign Aid," *NYT*, September 23, 1961; Felix Belair, "Aid Compromise Blocked by Foe," *NYT*, September 24, 1961; Felix Belair, "Conferees Fail to Agree on Sum for Foreign Aid," *NYT*, September 26, 1961.

55 Felix Belair, "Congress Votes Aid Compromise of $3,900,000,000," *NYT*, September 27, 1961; Evans, "Louisiana's Passman."

56 Hans Morgenthau, "A Political Theory of Foreign Aid," *American Political Science Review* 56, 2 (June 1962), 301–309.

57 John F. Kennedy, "Special Message to the Congress on Foreign Aid, March 13, 1962," Peters and Wooley, eds, APP, www.presidency.ucsb.edu/node/236977; Felix Belair, "Foreign Aid Plan is Near 5 Billion," *NYT*, January 19, 1962; Felix Belair, "Kennedy Chides Critics who seek Foreign Aid Cuts," *NYT*, March 15, 1962.

58 Felix Belair, "4.6 Billion Voted by Senate Panel for Foreign Aid," *NYT*, May 23, 1962; Felix Belair, "4.6 billion Aid Bill Voted by House Unit," *NYT*, May 25, 1962; Felix Belair, "Latin Aid Cut 20% by Panel in House," *NYT*, May 24, 1962; Felix Belair, "Aid Bill Voted by Senate; Red-Bloc Ban is Modified," *NYT*, June 8, 1962; Felix Belair, "House Supports Kennedy's Power to Aid Red Lands," *NYT*, July 13, 1962; Felix Belair, "Conferees Grant Kennedy Leeway to Aid Red Lands," *NYT*, July 19, 1962; Felix Belair, "Senate Thwarts Foes of Aid Bill," *NYT*, July 20, 1962; Felix Belair, "4-Billion Aid Bill Sent to Kennedy by House, 221–162," *NYT*, July 25, 1962; "Kennedy Signs Bill Authorizing 4.6 Billion in Aid," *NYT* August 2, 1962.

59 "Passman Asks Cut in Foreign Aid Fund," *NYT*, July 26, 1962; Felix Belair, "1.5-Billion Aid Reduction Planned by House Group," *NYT*, August 24, 1962; Felix Belair, "House Unit Votes $1,500,000,000 Cut for Aid Program," *NYT*, August 18, 1962; Felix Belair, "1.1 Billion Aid Cut is Sent to House," *NYT*, September, 19, 1962; Felix Belair, "House Approves Foreign Aid Bill; Retains All Cuts," *NYT*, September 21, 1962; "Roll-Call on Sending Aid Bill Back to Committee," *NYT*, September 21, 1962.

60 Felix Belair, "792 Million Cut in Aid Restored by Senate Group," *NYT*, September 28, 1962; Felix Belair, "Senate Rejects Aid Cuts and Ban on Help for Reds," *NYT*, October 2, 1962; Felix Belair, "Foreign Aid Bill Cut by Conferees to $3,928,900,000," *NYT*, October 5, 1962; John D. Morris, "House Approves Aid Compromise; Vote is 171 to 108," *NYT*, October 7, 1962; John D. Morris, "Foreign Aid Bill Goes to Kennedy," *NYT*, October 9, 1962.

61 David Bell, "Foreign Aid and US National Security," *International Development Review* 5, 2 (June 1963), reprinted by the Agency for International Development; "Speech to Foreign Policy Association, May 23, 1963" David Bell-Speeches 1963, Box 1, Speeches and Press Releases 1963–1976, RG 0286, NARA

62 "A New Program of Free-World Aid for the Decade of Development to Help the Underdeveloped Free Nations of the World become Self-Sustaining," Citizens

Committee for International Development, No Date. Container 24, USAIA/Congressional Liaison Staff, Congressional Correspondence, 1954–1962, RG 0286, NARA; There was also a separate independent group formed in 1956, the Citizens' Committee for Expanded Foreign Aid; "Foreign Aid Plan Held Too Limited," *NYT*, March 27, 1956.

63 J. Emlyn Williams, "West Berliners Cheer Clay," *Christian Science Monitor*, September 20, 1961; "Gen. Clay, Top Eisenhower Aide in WWII Dies at 80," *Los Angeles Times*, April 17, 1978.

64 Papers of John F. Kennedy. Presidential Papers. National Security Files. Subjects. Foreign Aid: Clay Committee: Summaries of proceedings, January 1963, Digital Identifier JFKNSF-297–013; "Kennedy Names Panel to Study Economic, Military Aid Abroad," December 11, 1963.

65 US Committee to Strengthen the Security of the Free World, "The Scope and Distribution of United States Military and Economic Assistance Programs" (Washington, 1963), 1–2; "Text of President Kennedy's Message to Congress on his Foreign Aid Program," *NYT*, April 3, 1963.

66 E. W. Kenworthy, "Foreign Aid Cuts Now Seen Likely," *NYT*, April 4, 1963; "Aid Cuts Sent to Congress," *NYT* April 12, 1963.

67 Felix Belair, "Congress Reflects a Growing Opposition to Foreign Aid," *NYT*, April 21, 1963.

68 Felix Belair, "Kennedy to Ask for 4.9 Billion Fund for Foreign Aid," *NYT*, January 16, 1963; Felix Belair, "President Cuts Foreign Aid Plea," *NYT*, April 3, 1963; Felix Belair, "Kennedy Agrees to Aid-Fund Cuts," *NYT*, June 26, 1963.

69 "Transcript of the President's News Conference," *NYT*, August 21, 1963.

70 "House Roll-Call on Aid Cut, *NYT*, August 24, 1963; "Kennedy's Aid Statement," *NYT*, August 24, 1963; "Setback on Aid," *NYT*, August 25, 1963; The Kennedy administration's press against the cut continued with an editorial by David Bell, "A Reply to Opponents of Foreign Aid," *NYT*, September 1, 1963.

71 Felix Belair, "Foreign Aid: Major Opposition Rises in Congress," *NYT*, August 25, 1963.

72 Felix Belair, "Halleck Warns Senators on Aid," *NYT*, October 25, 1963.

73 Felix Belair, "Aid Opposition Grows," *NYT*, November 3, 1963; "Comparison of Two Aid Bills," *NYT*, November 16, 1963.

74 "President's Address on Foreign Aid," *NYT*, November 9, 1963.

75 "Senate Roll-Call Vote on Foreign Aid Limit," *NYT*, December 13, 1963; Felix Belair, "US Foreign Aid Concept is Dealt a Serious Blow," *NYT*, December 22, 1963; "Funds for Foreign Aid," *NYT*, December 14, 1963.

76 Robert Allen and Paul Scott, "Foreign Aid Truce Urged," December 4, 1963. The $3.4 number is alternatively presented as $3.3 in other sources. Felix Belair, Jr., "President Offers Deal to Passman," *NYT*, December 13, 1963; Felix Belair, Jr., "Johnson Calls in Passman on Aid," *NYT*, December 12, 1963; Willard Edwards, "Still Foe of Big Aid: Passman," *Chicago Tribune*, December 13, 1963; Passman Adamant on Aid Stand," *Philadelphia Inquirer*, December 13, 1963; Felix Belair, Jr., "Johnson Brands Foreign Aid Cuts 'Setback' for US," *NYT*, December 15, 1963.

77 Bill Henry, "Congress, Best Show in Town," *Los Angeles Times*, December 12, 1963.

78 Chalmers Roberts, "When Passman Talks on Aid, the House Listens and Obeys," *Washington Post*, December 12, 1963; Murray Kempton, "No Miracles for Mr. Johnson," *The Spectator*, December 27, 1963.

79 Felix Belair, "Johnson to Resist Foreign Aid Cuts," *NYT*, June 18, 1964; Felix Belair, "House Unit Votes $3.3 Billion in Aid, Defying Passman," *NYT*, June 24, 1964.

5

WAYNE MORSE AND AID AS IMPERIALISM

In 1963, Kennedy's final year as president, and throughout the rest of the 1960s, the dynamic opposition to foreign aid shifted from the House of Representatives to the Senate. Passman had been effective in the 1963 fight, but his arguments had changed little over time, and they would remain consistent during the rest of his tenure. In the Senate, the Oregonian, Wayne Morse, was leading a different, new kind of battle against aid. He pushed his colleagues to think about more than problems of waste, inefficient bureaucracies, and corruption. Throughout the 1960s, in the annual Senate debates about aid, he argued that aid spending needed to reflect moral values.

Morse believed that the United States needed to be globally engaged and that aid could help advance US Cold War objectives, but he also argued that by backing dictatorships and totalitarian governments, just because they were anti-communist, the United States was violating its claim to support democracy and freedom as objectively good. He said the United States needed to abandon anti-communism as its essential Cold War strategy and instead pursue moral global engagement. This was similar to Henry Wallace's argument in the late 1940s that knee-jerk anti-communism was intensifying global tension. Unlike Wallace, though, who said the United States should engage with everyone, including communists, Morse said aid programs should only back governments that shared its values, and in granting foreign aid, consider ethical factors as paramount. Aid to dictatorships had to be stopped; that meant both communist and non-communist ones. By 1968, when Morse lost his reelection bid, other senators, most notably Frank Church (D-ID) and J. William Fulbright (D-AR) had become leaders in this fight, and in the early 1970s they tried to finish what he had started.

Their critique was not only about foreign aid; it was also an attack on Cold War policymaking, and it raised questions about the nature of the state in the global arena. Morse, and the senators who followed in his footsteps, were not just saying that the United States needed power to protect itself, but that its power had to serve a higher purpose.

Morse's Fight

That Morse joined Passman as a central figure in fighting spending suggests how opposition to foreign aid made unlikely bedfellows. Passman employed a folksy anti-intellectual rhetoric. He often referenced his hardscrabble education, legitimately suggesting he had humble origins and that he wanted to help his fellow citizens keep their taxes low and the bureaucrats accountable. His place in the Democratic Party's white Southern wing also defined his place in Washington. He was antagonistic to civil rights legislation and the exercise of federal government power, believing it was inherently dangerous and often destructive. Morse, by contrast, was an intellectual and urbane law professor with a deep self-righteous contrarian streak and a powerful instinct against compromising in quests for justice. He was an early and aggressive supporter of the civil rights movement and believed that government could be a transformative force for good. He proudly self-identified as a liberal.

There were other differences. Whereas Passman was essentially a one-dimensional legislator (in that he only had stature on questions of foreign aid), Morse was heavily involved in crafting labor, agriculture, and educational policy. This reflected Morse's broad concerns, and it was also a function of the greater responsibilities and power of individual senators. He was also obviously engaged in foreign affairs, serving on the Senate Foreign Relations Committee from 1955 to 1969. In addition to using his role on that committee to fight foreign aid, he was an early critic of the US war in Vietnam, and is most well known as one of the two senators, along with his consistent ally, Alaska's Ernest Gruening (D), to vote against the Gulf of Tonkin resolution in 1964. They stood alone in proclaiming it was a mistake to authorize increasing US involvement in Vietnam. Morse could see a national disaster looming.

Passman and Morse shared a commitment to challenging institutional power and both seemed to find joy in their contrarianism, though they operated quite differently. Passman worked within the committee system, using his relationships with powerful leaders like Clarence Cannon to advance his agenda. Morse operated independently, finding or picking up allies as he could, often seeming to care less about the victory than his integrity. He was routinely alone (or nearly alone), and seemed to believe that if his colleagues all agreed about something, they were probably wrong. One Senate colleague joked that if Morse "found himself on the same side as the Father, the Son, and the Holy Ghost, he would fear he was just going along with the crowd."[1]

Raised on a farm in Wisconsin, Morse excelled in school, especially in debate competitions. He attended the University of Wisconsin, then earned a law degree at the University of Minnesota, and finally got a doctorate in law from Columbia

University in New York City. He later explained that as a young man he had been inspired by Robert LaFollette, the powerful Wisconsin progressive politician, and by independent leaders like Nebraska's George Norris and Oregon's Charles McNary. Their dogged pursuit of justice, emphasis on principle, and independence from party leaders provided Morse a model for his public career. He would make his own determinations about right and wrong, always looking for the moral path, and then begin fighting. This was the core of his political vision.[2]

Following his graduation from Columbia in 1929 he took a position at the University of Oregon, and two years later became dean of its law school. His ascent toward the Senate began when Roosevelt's Secretary of Labor, Francis Perkins, appointed him Pacific Coast arbitrator for maritime disputes. He was successful in this role, consistently finding common ground between unions and businesses in their negotiations. As a result, Roosevelt asked him to settle a national dispute between railway companies and unions in 1941. This led to his appointment to the National War Labor Board, a panel constructed following US entry into World War II dedicated to arbitrating labor issues and averting strikes and lockouts that might hinder the war effort.[3]

As a member of this 12-person board, Morse's stubborn pursuit of principle gained national attention. In 1943, he alone refused to vote for an agreement with coal unions that promised them a better contract than other unionized workers. His colleagues, and Roosevelt administration officials, had hoped to pacify the combative coal union leadership and keep them from striking, but Morse thought this was capitulation in the face of a threat. His dissent, extensively covered in the press, focused on the injustice of the decision and his personal need to preserve his integrity. One Oregon newspaper cheered his vote with a headline, "Wayne Morse takes firm stand for government by law, not by political intimidation." Another Oregon paper wrote glowingly that the country needed more men like him, "with vision and courage" to "exercise independent judgment."[4]

This publicity gave him the opportunity to run for, and win, a US Senate seat from Oregon as a Republican, albeit one who had been close to Roosevelt and who spoke about inclusive and progressive politics. At the time, Oregon was solidly Republican, Morse less so. In January 1953, two years into his second term, he bolted the party and became an independent. He was horrified that Eisenhower had selected Richard Nixon as his vice-presidential running mate; Morse thought Nixon was a vapid anti-communist grandstander. Later, in 1956, he formally joined the Democratic Party, though he was always more independent than anything else. One reporter described him as "brilliant but cantankerously independent," and noted he "made it a virtue of going it alone rather than going along." He added, Morse "probably has less respect for the axioms of party unity, of compromise, and of log-rolling" and "a more thorough disregard of what his fellow may think" than anyone else in Washington.[5]

Morse on Foreign Aid

As a first-term senator, Morse backed the Marshall Plan and the Truman Doctrine. He later explained he thought both had been necessary and effective, but in the early 1950s he started making conventional anti-aid arguments that focused on costs and outcomes. For example, in 1953 he attacked, as Passman later would, the problem of authorizing and appropriating new funds before all previously approved money had been spent. He noted that the Eisenhower administration had close to $2 billion available in unspent but appropriated funds that year, and it did not make sense to authorize more spending when there was still money in the aid pipeline. He also highlighted data suggesting Europeans no longer needed aid. Using US government data, he joined Allen Ellender (D-LA), a close Passman ally, in arguing that European agricultural production and industrial production had substantially exceeded prewar levels. It did not make sense, Ellender told the Senate, to "continue to send our treasure abroad and eventually bankrupt ourselves."[6] Morse agreed, claiming he was sympathetic about a need to rebuild infrastructure, but the United States need not pay. Europeans could raise revenue through taxation. He said, "there is something morally wrong in taxing our American taxpayers on the basis of their ability to pay, when our allies who are receiving aid are not requiring their citizens to pay the taxes they should pay."[7]

In the late 1950s Morse opened up a new line of attack, more closely aligned with his ideas about justice and law, suggesting that aid might be immoral and could damage US power. Focusing on aid to totalitarian dictatorships, he said assisting these regimes undermined US claims that the Cold War was a struggle about democracy and freedom.[8] He argued that even if aid was economically transformative, advanced development objectives, and strengthened US allies, it could still be a mistake. This led him to introduce an amendment to the 1959 foreign aid bill to eliminate aid for authoritarian governments in Yugoslavia, the Dominican Republic, and Saudi Arabia. He also told the Senate that the United States should not back Generalissimo Francisco Franco's dictatorship in Spain, arguing "that when the chips are down we cannot count on any dictatorship in the great contest between freedom and totalitarianism."[9] This was a novel kind of anti-aid argument. While there had been objections to funds for Poland and Yugoslavia because they had communist governments, before Morse's amendment there was little discussion about the problems of sending foreign aid to repressive anti-communist regimes since the early Marshall Plan debates. In the context of the Cold War, as long as dictators were anti-communist they were friends who needed backing. This was not an argument against all aid, and Morse's position was still evolving, but it was the start of a new movement.

Nothing immediate came of Morse's amendment, which most of his colleagues on the Senate Foreign Relations Committee rejected, and Morse still seemed comfortable with most US economic aid. He was much more critical of military aid, which he saw as wasteful and ripe with opportunities for corruption. When Kennedy began calling for more aid, new programs, and reform, Morse was supportive. He was proud of his role in the development of the Alliance for Progress as chair of the Senate Foreign Relations Committee's Subcommittee on Latin America. Kennedy had been a member of this subcommittee, and Morse felt, with some justification, that it had been instrumental in establishing a framework for how a regional development plan could alleviate poverty and destroy the conditions that had allowed communism to breed. Morse worried about aid to dictatorships, but he also believed in the tenets of modernization theory.[10]

The 1963 Fight

In the early 1960s, Morse waged a mostly lonely fight to convince his colleagues to cut aid to dictatorships, but he had few successes. His colleagues in the Senate were not particularly interested in this concern, and despite his speeches and proposed amendments, he was unable to shift the debate and modify aid bills. This began to change in 1963. As the previous chapter explained, the legislative fight in 1963 represented the greatest success of anti-aid forces in pushing aid spending lower. Kennedy had initially requested $4.95 billion, and Congress only appropriated $3 billion. It was also the final year that Passman dominated the aid conversation. In the Senate, at the same time, Morse's position finally began to gain supporters as his colleagues started to agree with the wisdom of his concerns.[11]

A debate about aid for Egypt was key to this change. Through the early 1960s, Kennedy desperately hoped that Egypt's president, Gamal Abdel Nasser, might lean toward the United States and away from the Soviet Union. This could have a powerful impact across the Middle East as Egypt was the region's largest country, and Nasser its most influential leader. It could also help shift global opinion. Nasser had been a hero throughout Asia, Africa, and the Middle East for standing up to the British and the French during the 1956 Suez Crisis; gaining his friendship could demonstrate that the United States supported Arab nationalism and show that the United States backed decolonization movements. Foreign aid, Kennedy hoped, might be important in swaying Nasser's loyalties.[12] But many senators, beyond Morse, were critical of Kennedy's approach because of Nasser's hostility toward Israel. The New York Republican, Jacob Javits, was most aggressive in arguing that the United States needed to use its aid, and the threat of eliminating aid, as a way of forcing Nasser to accept the "futility of his dream of destroying Israel and the expensive vanity of his huge arms preparations."[13] Javits' case seemed easy to make, and his argument bolstered the larger idea Morse had been pushing, that certain allies, or potential allies, could not be treated as such. Other senators agreed, and noted that a recent book, *Behind the Egyptian Sphinx: Nasser's Strange Bedfellows*, made the convincing case that Nasser had allowed Nazis to emigrate to Egypt and escape justice, and that many were serving in his government in powerful positions.[14]

Morse insisted he would never support aid for Nasser. The United States needed to tell the other Arab states, who were also threatening Israel, "We will give you support. We will help you build up a system of political and economic freedom in your country just as rapidly as you want us to help you build it – subject to the condition that we have a commitment from you, namely your pledge, that you do not intend to make war in the Middle East."[15] This reflected a new idea, which would also become important to Morse and his supporters, that no country that threatened the status quo should receive economic aid.

For Morse, the problems with the Egyptian leader were indicative of larger issues. He also focused on Indonesia's Sukarno as "one of the most corrupt men on the face of the earth." Sukarno had led his country to independence in the 1940s, but in the late 1950s and early 1960s he assumed dictatorial power and began accepting Chinese and Soviet assistance. Eisenhower and Kennedy had both hoped that aid might counter his drift away from the US orbit. Morse saw this differently. Sukarno, a dictator who did not respect democratic values, was manipulating the United States. He said, if Sukarno "did not believe he could get aid from the United States by way of a payoff … he would be 'in bed with' the Communists now." The United States sent aid to other dictatorships, and those were also a problem, but Morse thought helping Sukarno and Nasser seemed especially egregious and impossible to defend.[16]

Morse's attacks on funding to Indonesia and Egypt helped sway other senators, especially the ones most committed to civil rights and humanitarian values and who self-identified as liberals. In June 1963, Idaho's Frank Church (D) told the Senate Foreign Relations Committee that he had always backed aid spending, even though the people of his state seemed deeply opposed, because he understood its importance in fighting the Cold War. Yet he was beginning to falter after listening to Morse, and starting to think there was a basic flaw in US strategy. He said there was an "inability of administrators or administrations, be they Democratic or Republican, to make significant changes in course," and rhetorically asked, "now that we have put vast sums of money over an extended period of years in many countries, where has the theory been proven?" Aid had not made the world a better place. Rhetorically again, he asked, "Where has the program worked? Where are we going to stop?" If the answer to the first question was "nowhere," the program needed to end.[17]

This empowered Morse, who delivered blistering daily speeches on the Senate floor in July and August 1963 that, like Church's comments, went beyond attacking just elements of aid programming, but called for a wholesale revision in the US approach. He said there was "no political issue more vital to the welfare of the American people than the issue of foreign aid" because it "violates the oft-repeated professings of the Government of the United States that we support freedom around the world, and oppose tyranny and denial of self-government."[18] The problem of aid spending was not about where the United States put its money; it was about national ideals. The United States had lost its way in fighting the Cold War, and in its quest to halt communism it failed to appreciate the greater goal of advancing liberty and democracy.

Morse also made other, Passman-like critiques about corruption, inefficiency, waste, and limited results. He argued the United States needed to "clean the slate" and "stop running around the world ... trying to cram aid down throats of various governments." Instead, the United States should say, "Come on in, if you have a set of proposals or list of projects which you think are meritorious, which are economically sound, which will help raise the standard of living of the masses of your people, which will benefit the productive power of your economy, which will strengthen democratic government. We will listen favorably and will make you loans, and in some instances grants, on the basis of conditions which will protect the American taxpayer and best serve the long-term interests of your country." He argued a few days later that it was "a sad and disheartening fact of American foreign policy that more and more we are relying upon the 'purchase' of friends and allies ... . In return we have received so little that our Government propagandists have tried to mislead the American people in what amounts to a program of deception."[19]

Morse's solution was greater oversight, which could lead to reform. Congress had delegated its responsibility to the executive branch to determine how government should use its money, and when faced with annual requests for more spending, despite no proof of success, it kept voting to give the executive more. He noted the Senate Foreign Relations Committee had been debating a request to authorize $1 billion for India to help build a steel mill, despite evidence that Indian steel mills were operating below capacity, that the country lacked the raw materials to supply such a mill, and that they did not have the trained personnel to operate it. Nevertheless, the Kennedy administration wanted to fund it, and Morse feared Congress might not have the courage to reject the request. "Enactment of the bill," he said, "would perpetuate the shocking waste and gross inefficiency which for years have characterized the administration of American foreign aid."[20]

As he had in the past without success, Morse again offered amendments as the Senate considered the authorization bill in late October 1963. Perhaps the most important amendment, and indicative of his major long-term contribution to debates about aid, was his proposal to insert a clause into the bill that would halt aid to any country whose government came to power by overthrowing a freely elected constitutional regime. This would automatically ban aid to Burma, Pakistan, Egypt, Spain, and multiple Latin American countries (including Ecuador where there had been a *coup d'état* in June 1963, and the Dominican Republic which had one at the start of October). Given the debate about Egypt, this clause resonated with his colleagues and it passed 65 to 13. It led to more amendments that restricted aid to Yugoslavia and Indonesia, and another one that barred aid to countries that extended their territorial limits beyond those recognized by the United States.[21]

The "Liberals' Revolt"

Morse's short-term victory, his ambition to cut spending dramatically, and his hope to recast the entire aid program along more ethical lines led him to suggest that the bill be sent back to the Senate Foreign Relations Committee in a process called "recommittal." The Committee could then completely rewrite the bill based on his objections. This was a radical step, and would have added months to an already long-delayed process. Morse said there was no urgency in getting a bill passed, and a flawed bill was worse than no bill at all. This tactic did not work. Montana's Mike Mansfield, the Senate Democratic majority leader, and Everett Dirksen, the Republican minority leader, both agreed to prune an additional $385 million from the authorization bill as an enticement for senators to reject Morse's gambit, and the recommittal vote failed. Morse then tried other procedural delaying tactics. He refused to agree to unanimous consent requests that sped up Senate business, and insisted on full debates and floor votes on a long list of amendments (both that he offered and that others offered). As a result, the foreign aid debate took over the Senate calendar in late October and early November 1963.[22]

The strategy was controversial because of accusations that it would hurt progress in passing a civil rights bill. One reporter, Joseph Kraft of the *Washington Post*, suggested that Southern Democrats hoped that by backing Morse, and "by slowing down all business, by prolonging all debate, they will put off the civil rights issue to the point where the North and the Negroes, tired and frustrated, lose heart." Kraft did not accuse Morse of disingenuousness, explaining that he was "no nitpicking Passman," whose attacks were "swollen with trivial details of obscure transactions arising from unheard-of projects in un-heard of countries." Quite the opposite, Morse was "noted for doughy fights on behalf of lonely causes, and serious with a vengeance." But he was being used by the Southerners and was their "dupe."[23] The accusation angered Morse. He argued that the aid debate was fundamentally important and a question of national morality and justice, just as the civil rights issue was, and that the Senate could handle both.

Senate Democratic leaders had no effective way to stop Morse from controlling the agenda, and to a large extent they admitted they agreed with his concerns. Fulbright, the chair of the Senate Foreign Relations Committee, explained that even though he was supposed to be defending the bill, he had misgivings. He said that the aid program was becoming "obsolescent," but added the caveat that an immediate change would "pose unacceptable risks to our entire foreign policy mission." He said he would vote for the bill then under consideration, but wholesale changes were necessary for the future.[24] Fulbright was not ready to join the opposition yet, and argued that aid's critics had oversold the problems. Opponents like Morse were claiming "we had been spending our time over the last decade throwing away billions of dollars in a fruitless effort" that failed and undermined US global power. He insisted that aid had been a big part of US successes in fighting the Soviets and their allies to "better than a standstill," and it remained a valuable foreign policy tool, albeit one that needed substantial reform.[25]

Morse's push for a fight, coupled with growing acceptance of problems in the aid bill, spurred other senators to try to rewrite the bill on the Senate floor. The press and some senators called this the "Liberal Revolt." Led by Morse, key liberals, including Church, Gruening, and Albert Gore (D-TN), introduced roughly fifty amendments, mostly dedicated to cutting aid to non-democratic regimes. The effort gained steam as more senators, beyond the initial core, joined the effort. Church insisted that the "revolt" was not directed at Kennedy. He admired the Peace Corps and backed Kennedy's ideas about modernization; the issue was, as he put it, "a gathering impatience and frustration," coming from years of lack of real reform and growing excesses in aid spending.[26]

The nature of the amendments and the wide number of sponsors demonstrates that Morse's ideas were beginning to catch on, at least among the most liberal senators. One amendment sponsored by Morse, Gruening, and Javits, as well as Clifford Case (R-NJ), Abraham Ribicoff (D-CT), Stephen Young (D-OH), Kenneth Keating (R-NY), Paul Douglas (D-IL), Edmund Muskie (D-ME), and Thomas Dodd (D-CT), would have eliminated funding for countries engaged in or planning aggression against their neighbors. Another tried to cut military aid to Latin America. The sponsors, Morse and Gruening, along with William Proxmire (D-WI), Sam Ervin (D-NC), George Smathers (D-FL), Howard Cannon (D-NV), and George McGovern (D-SD), argued that Latin American militaries did not need US weapons for hemispheric defense. They had been using them mostly to launch *coups d'état* against democratically elected governments, and that was contrary to US interests.[27]

Despite the revolt, most of the Morse-supported amendments failed narrowly, and in some cases badly. In the end, the bill changed little. One example was an amendment that, following a military *coup d'état* in a country receiving aid, the US president would need to formally declare that sending aid to a new regime was vital for national security. Congress would also have to pass a similar resolution within 30 days. Otherwise, all aid would automatically stop. Fulbright challenged the amendment and said this would limit presidential power too much, and it lost 78 to 11. A similar catch-all amendment to prohibit aid to regimes that came to power by ousting elected constitutional governments did pass in the Senate, but failed to make it into the final bill. Instead, as a compromise measure, the bill carried a weak provision that if the president determined that a government was attacking, or planning to attack, another country, it should not get new aid. In the end, despite initial fanfare and seemingly interminable debate, the "Liberals' Revolt" had little impact on the bill.[28]

The Aftermath of the "Liberals' Revolt"

Though a failure, the "Liberals' Revolt" set the tone for two developments. In the short term, it led to more disciplined presidential efforts to pass bills. In the long term, it emboldened criticism of US policies that failed to distinguish between democratic and authoritarian allies. This criticism was central to the debates about US commitments to Vietnam that were just beginning.[29]

At first, it appeared that 1964 might be a repeat of the 1963 situation. Morse indicated that he would push to include language about dictatorships just as hard as he had the year before, but Johnson's engagement in the process, and a much smaller request, limited senators' enthusiasm to have the same exact conversations again.[30] Morse only notched two victories in 1964, and neither was significant. He convinced his Senate colleagues to back an amendment that banned aid to Indonesia, though it did not make it into the final House-Senate compromise authorization bill. His other victory was pushing an amendment that increased interest rates in aid loans for recipient nations. This was a complex issue driven by the US government using high-interest bonds to fund its operations, and then lending money to other countries (as part of foreign aid) at rates lower than it was paying in interest.[31] Morse's success here came because this amendment appealed to fiscally minded conservatives, as well as to liberals worried about waste. The *Los Angeles Times* reported colorfully on this victory, amid Morse's larger failure to change the authorization bill, that the senator must have felt lonely when shouting he was "against the shakedown of the American taxpayer," and slightly invigorated when "the boys voted with him" to do "something about the scheme under which this country lends abroad at less interest than it pays to get the money in the first place." But this was not much of a success, and did little to address Morse's larger concerns about aid and national values.[32]

Debate in the Senate on the aid authorization bill coincided with the discussion of the Gulf of Tonkin resolution. On August 4, 1964, Johnson announced to a national television audience that North Vietnamese ships had attacked two US naval vessels, *Maddox* and *Turner Joy*. Johnson explained that this was a hostile act by an antagonistic enemy, and that the United States needed to respond to protect itself and its allies. He then asked Congress to pass a resolution (the Gulf of Tonkin Resolution) that allowed him to "take all necessary measures to repel any armed attack against the forces of the United States," and to "take all necessary steps, including the use of force," to help any country "requesting assistance in defense of its freedom."[33]

In criticizing the resolution, Gruening, Morse's strongest ally, emphasized the point they had made in objecting to foreign aid for non-democratic regimes. He said, "the allegation we are supporting freedom in South Vietnam has a hollow sound. We have been supporting corrupt and unpopular puppet dictatorships" via foreign aid that had "scant support from their own people, [and] who have shown little disposition to fight" for freedom. He added, "I do not consider this our war and I feel that Vietnam is not worth the life of a single American boy."[34] Morse explained that Johnson was insisting the issue in Vietnam was backing freedom, but there was "not one iota of freedom in South Vietnam, for the South Vietnamese people do not know what the word means." He continued colloquially, "the average man of North or South Vietnam would not know what democracy looked like if he met it on the main street of Saigon." If South

Vietnam was not a democracy, and not free, the United States had no business getting involved.

Morse said that the United States had been using its foreign aid to prop up the South Vietnamese military, as it was doing throughout the world, instead of "preparing the seedbeds of economic freedom," which would be the basis for political freedom.[35] Thus, the Vietnam problem was a symptom of the exact thing he had been saying about aid since the late 1950s. The United States was not supporting its national values, it was pushing anti-communism, and those were not the same things. Morse and Gruening also spoke at length about how the war was likely to be a costly quagmire, the questionable legality of US involvement in Vietnam, and their hope that the United Nations could get involved, but their previous anti-foreign aid efforts provided the structure for their opposition to the Gulf of Tonkin Resolution.

In this case, Morse's fealty to his convictions, belief in his own judgment, and willingness to fight for principle took extraordinary courage; Gruening did back him, but as in debates about foreign aid, Morse was the leader. In the House, the Gulf of Tonkin Resolution passed 416 to 0, and in the Senate the vote was 88 to 2, and the ten absent members all requested that the record reflect their intent to have voted for the resolution. Resigned to failure, Morse told the Senate at the end of the debate that they were giving "war-making powers in the absence of a declaration of war" to the president in Vietnam, which was "a historic mistake." He predicted "that within the next century, future generations will look with dismay and great disappointment" at the Congress which had failed so badly to see the obvious dangers in backing the resolution.[36] His only error on this point was that instead of that process happening over generations, it happened over the space of just a few short years; many of his colleagues would soon admit he had been right. They would also recognize that he was correct about the larger point, which was connected to aid, that US backing for dictatorship had led to the Vietnam problem in the first place.

After the Tonkin Vote

As in 1964, it seemed that 1965 might be a transformative year for foreign aid. When the Senate Foreign Relations Committee began considering the bill, Fulbright announced that he would not serve as its floor manager, effectively opposing Johnson's funding request from the start and making it unlikely that the process would go smoothly. Fulbright was shifting, albeit slowly, into an aid critic.[37] That Fulbright's concerns and rhetoric moved closer to Morse's was meaningful because the Arkansas Democrat was the most influential voice on foreign policy in the Senate. Fulbright explained that he was increasingly worried that aid was going to countries that did not respect the rule of law, and hoped the Johnson administration would be more aggressive in pushing recipient countries to embrace US moral leadership. He said he appreciated that aid could be counterproductive to US aims in that it might lead to growing anti-Americanism, and suggested colorfully that it was "well acknowledged – certainly since the days of Shakespeare – that a borrowing relationship between friends ... very often results in some resentment." He added that lenders expect to be repaid, as "personal feeling goes with a loan, and the borrower feels that he is obligated in a way beyond mere repayment of a loan." At the same time, "the lender feels that he has done a personal favor, which is aside from business, to the borrower."[38] Aid was not improving relationships, instead it was antagonizing the very people the United States needed as allies in the Cold War. But Fulbright's political instincts and loyalty came into play as Johnson successfully pushed him in early June to relent and manage the bill. Fulbright had a long and close relationship with the president, and his responsibility as a party leader, at least temporarily, led him to agree to back the bill. He ended up fighting both Morse's plans for substantial cuts to the bill and bans on aid to Egypt and Indonesia[39]

Fulbright's back-and-forth on aid was connected to his well-documented gradual shift from a pro-war to an anti-war position between late 1964 and 1966. As historian Randall Woods wrote, Fulbright slowly determined "that the war in Vietnam was essentially a civil war and that the United States was merely supporting one side against the other." Fulbright had backed the Tonkin Resolution and publically supported the administration's positions in 1964 and into 1965, yet he privately started to say that the war was reckless and unnecessary.[40]

These concerns about foreign policy's direction grew after Johnson sent US forces into the Dominican Republic in April 1965. Fulbright feared (presciently) that the president was misleading the public about the threat to US lives in order to justify the invasion. This led Fulbright to tell the Senate in September that the intervention was a "grievous mistake" and the "policy that purported to defeat Communism in the short run" was "more likely to have the effect of promoting it in the long run." Johnson badly misread the situation, Fulbright explained, and then made the problem worse through his clumsy actions. Johnson was livid about the criticism. Woods writes that Fulbright's speech destroyed their relationship. Johnson banned Fulbright from the White House and attacked him mercilessly. This freed Fulbright to adopt a more critical perspective on Vietnam, and also on foreign aid. He subsequently hewed even more closely to Morse's position that the United States needed to be a responsible moral force.[41]

Because Fulbright's break with Johnson did not come until September, though, it left Morse in a much weaker position during the aid bill hearings earlier that summer. If Fulbright had joined the opposition, Morse might have been able to force meaningful changes in the bill. Without much chance of success, though, and used to fighting alone, Morse soldiered on. In a blistering speech on June 11, 1965, he attacked waste and mismanagement by discussing internal classified government reports that cataloged US military aid failures. He explained that while the reports could not be distributed, he had asked for permission to read their titles on the Senate floor. Using Passman-like specificity he recited their names: "Inadequate

Planning, Programing, and Contracting for a Fixed Communications System for the Government of Indonesia Under the Military Assistance Program ..., Waste of Military Funds in Construction of Shahabad Depot in Iran Under Military Assistance Program ..., [and] Inadequate Consideration Given to Utilizing Reserve Fleet Ships in Lieu of Providing New Ships to Iran Under the Military Assistance Program." There were so many, he claimed, that he did not have time to even read all their titles for the record. He explained, "I am at a loss to understand how these devastating reports showing shocking waste in the administration of the foreign aid program could continue to exist and the White House not insist on cleaning it up." Then, focusing on a report about extensive US aid to Thailand, he chided that he could not help but find it funny to listen to "the bleeding hearts for freedom talking about freedom in Southeast Asia, for in Southeast Asia we do not support freedom. We support totalitarianism ... we are not supporting a free society; we are supporting a society that lives under a form of totalitarian government."[42]

But with Fulbright's backing, the authorization bill moved forward quickly, with limited revision or amendments. Morse was predictably furious. He argued, as he had in earlier years, that there was "a rapid trend ... toward the development of a country by executive supremacy, thereby weakening and undermining and undercutting our system of three coordinate and coequal branches." The aid program was an executive "deception" and fundamentally anti-democratic, but few in Congress cared to point out that deception or fight against it. That needed to stop, and he called for "a congressional review of aid in all its manifestations," and insisted that unless "this Congress assumes full responsibility for a review of aid" there would be no change. The State Department staff, and the USAID staff, could never, and would never, conduct a critical review of aid spending. It was their job to run aid programs, and more money would allow them to run more of them. It did not matter if aid was in the US government's long-term interest, or if it worked or not. The bureaucrats were only supposed to do, not assess, and without assessment and revision, the program had lost its way. This was not an abstract problem; it was at the core of US foreign policy failures. As the United States misused its aid, which included supporting dictators, it became "causative ... of revolutions that play into the hands of Communism." He repeated his core objection, "we talk a good 'game' about freedom, but we frequently fail to practice it abroad – as we have failed for years, in South Vietnam, to practice our ideals of freedom. When history is through with us, it will not be pleasant reading for future generations."[43]

The 1965 aid process was Johnson's most successful, in part because of Fulbright's help, but also because he had earlier weakened Passman. He had initially requested $3.38 billion, and following the long process, in October, Congress passed a $3.218 billion appropriation bill, an unusually small cut.[44] But the nature of aid battles were that they never really ended, and as the 1965 fight was ending, the 1966 one was just about to start, and Morse's position was getting stronger.

The Senate Foreign Relations Committee Hearings

The 1966 aid debate kicked off, not with Johnson's request for funds, which would occur on January 24, 1966, but with a request on January 19 for a supplemental emergency appropriation.[45] Johnson wanted $13.1 billion in additional funds for fiscal year 1966 (ending on June 30, 1966), to cover military spending in Vietnam; included in this sum was a relatively small request for an additional $400 million in foreign aid, also mostly for Vietnam, but not exclusively. On the Senate side, the military request went to the Senate Armed Forces Committee and the Defense Department Subcommittee of the Senate Appropriations Committee, both chaired by Georgia's senator Richard Russell (D).[46] The smaller foreign aid request went to Fulbright's Senate Foreign Relations Committee.

Johnson's request played into Fulbright's growing sense that there needed to be a national conversation about the war, and following the Dominican Republic speech the previous September he felt freer to challenge Johnson. Fulbright was also clearly thinking more about Morse's concerns about aid and their role in leading to the US commitment in Vietnam. Fulbright's staffer, Pat Holt, explained that the point of the hearing was investigating the war, not attacking it. He said, "carefully prepared public hearings could have a valuable educational effect for both the Congress and the public" for understanding what was happening in Vietnam. He added, hinting at the criticisms to come, that "public hearings on Vietnam are not only appropriate for the Foreign Relations Committee but can even be regarded as a Committee responsibility."[47]

In the first session, Secretary of State Dean Rusk met the committee on January 28 to argue that the supplemental appropriation was fundamental for US success and necessary for two reasons. First, the money would allow the Vietnamese government to import basic goods that included rice, oil, medicines, fertilizer, and construction materials. This would address local shortages and support "morale essential to the entire effort." Second, the money would fund medical services, refugee support, and infrastructure projects. He argued, "Without our aid programs we could win the major military battles in Vietnam and still lose the war and the peace." The economic programs were just as necessary as the military ones, he said, because they allowed the United States to "reinforce the economic and social progress that South Vietnam has been making during a brutal war and in spite of unremitting destructive efforts by the enemy."[48]

But the senators had big questions. Church told Rusk that "you can look at the war in Vietnam as a covert invasion of the South by the North, or you can look at it as some scholars do, as basically an indigenous war to which the North has given a growing measure of aid and abetment, but either way it is a war between Vietnamese to determine what the ultimate kind of government is going to be for Vietnam." He wanted to know why the United States should care. Rusk replied that the United States had a responsibility to Vietnam based on its "specific commitments" to Vietnam, and Southeast Asia, as part of its obligation to fight global communism. Fulbright, picking up Church's case, challenged Rusk. He said there was no clear "specific commitment" that obligated the United States engagement. Fulbright mentioned that 15 senators had just sent Johnson a letter asking this same thing, what was the justification for war. Fulbright said that like them, he was "not quite clear" about US purposes in Vietnam. He said he was not necessarily opposed to the fighting, he just wanted "an opportunity to examine the objective further" before voting "on commitments which are irrevocable."[49] Quickly, the hearing about aid was becoming a hearing about the biggest question of US global engagement of the era.

Fulbright asked Rusk, "would the approval of this very large increase in [the aid] authorization be interpreted as an approval of our policy … would it be interpreted as an approval of an all-out war. Would you think it should be interpreted that way?" Fulbright wanted to know if more aid would strengthen the idea that the United States had a preexisting commitment to Vietnam. Rusk answered blandly that given the nature of the decision, "the Executive and Congress must at all times move together on these matters as they have in the past." Fulbright, frustrated and hoping for something more, replied, "I do not think that is responsive. You do not have to answer if you do not like." But added again for emphasis that the Secretary of State's answer was "not responsive" and said that the Senate could not move forward on the aid authorization without a good answer to the question.[50] Fulbright's disappointment carried over to a closed meeting of the Committee in which members agreed to subsequently hold televised meetings about the authorization. In a line of thought similar to what Morse had been saying about congressional power over foreign affairs, they were angry that Johnson just wanted them to "consent" to his policy, and did not want their "advice." A more public forum would force the Johnson administration to give better answers.[51]

Bell on Television

Thus, at the Committee's invitation, both the CBS and NBC television networks broadcast the next session on February 4 to a national audience, at which David Bell, the administrator for the Agency for International Development, testified. The senators mostly wanted to talk about US strategy in Vietnam, but Bell was not really capable of discussing anything other than foreign aid and the specific supplemental aid request, so the hearing turned into a long televised conversation about US aid.

Fulbright opened the session by asking questions about the overall costs of the war, but Bell replied he could only authoritatively speak about the aid authorization. Asked about the fighting itself, he made some general observations of the difficulties connected to aid programing, but insisted he did not have the competency to go into depth. This frustrated the senators and made the hearing conflictual, which made for compelling television.[52]

Church said that despite his "very real difficulty with the policy in Southeast Asia," he would vote for the supplemental aid request because of "the American men committed there," and because there was a "war in progress." Elsewhere though, he said he was "very skeptical" about aid budgets that seemed to be leading to cuts in domestic programs "in order to finance the spiraling costs of the war in Southeast Asia." He added, "If these domestic programs are going to be cut, then I think that the foreign aid program ought to be brought under the same kind of scrutiny, and that the Congress should consider cutbacks in that program as we will consider cutbacks in domestic programs."[53] To make his point, Church emphasized the costs as he understood them and repeated his concern:

> Last year the President requested $103 million for the school milk program. This year he requests $21 million. That is in the neighborhood of an 80 percent cut. In the agricultural conservation program … last year the Congress voted $220 million for that program. This year the President requests $120 million, or a $100 million cut… Last year the President requested, for land-grant colleges, $12 million. He requests nothing this year … . The requests for Veterans' Administration hospitals is down from $90 to $52 million … the time has come to begin to consider where we can cut back on these programs in other foreign lands, even as we are cutting back on the school lunch program and the milk program and the educational programs here in the United States.[54]

Church was not particularly specific about what he wanted, but Fulbright and Morse explored areas to cut in more detail. In a conversation about Zambia, Fulbright asked critically, "What are we doing there?" Bell replied that the United States was helping out the British, who had asked for assistance in financing petroleum imports into the country. Fulbright said this was overreach, and part of the Johnson administration's efforts to "carry out a Pax Americana" and "keep peace all over the world and in every place where some controversy might arise." Bell pushed back, saying that "in the African countries generally we do have a US interest which is sufficient to warrant the expenditure of some funds, in most cases very limited funds." Zambia, he added, was one of those cases.[55]

Morse, in his time, focused on Thailand and the $7.5 million in the supplemental budget for local police, air traffic system improvements, and the construction of water system improvements. Bell defended this request as central to US efforts to support counterinsurgency in that country as they provided a means "for the strengthening and improvement of the local government and of the economic circumstances of the people of these villages." Bell painted a picture of US aid as a success, saying he had visited recently and he "saw villages in northeast Thailand which had been connected for the first time by all-weather roads with the nearest towns … . It was much like the effect of our own county roads out in the Middle West and the Far West." He said, "This meant that the farmers who lived in these villages could obtain better markets for their crops, larger income for their families. It meant that for the first time they could send their youngsters not just to the primary school, which was in the village, but to the secondary school, which was in the nearest town. It meant that they could reach the stores and other markets from which they could buy fertilizer, better seed, and other kinds of goods." Morse countered, consistent with his previous critiques, that "we have been pouring these millions and millions of the taxpayers' money into a police state." He continued, "We put ourselves in a very difficult posture in our image around the world when we continue to do that … . As far as I am concerned, I am no more anxious to support a police state of the totalitarian, Fascist type than the Communist type, because human freedom is nonexistent in all these states."[56]

Even when the conversation addressed Vietnam, it was focused on aid. Morse asked, for example, about Vietnamese import duties. Bell claimed that no US money went to pay import duties, that Vietnamese consumers paid them. He claimed that the United States had "a substantial number of auditors and inspectors on the scene in Saigon and the other ports, and we are reasonably confident that the goods we are paying for in fact get to the importers to whom they are supposed to get, and into the markets of Vietnam." He admitted, however, that "once the goods are in the markets in Saigon and other cities, one cannot be sure they cannot be purchased or hijacked and taken by the Vietcong."[57] This was effectively explaining, to a live national television audience, that there was corruption in the aid process.

The hearing was awful for the administration as Bell struggled to defend the aid program against consistent attacks, especially from Morse and Fulbright. Having watched the testimony, an angry and upset Johnson telephoned Larry F. O'Brien, a key Democratic Party strategist, to complain about how this "very, very disastrous break" hurt his ability to move legislation through Congress. The senators were "having a field day" and "running wild."[58] He told Vice President Hubert Humphrey that "we're going to have some real rough days" because the press wanted to "murder" him, as did the senators. "Everybody," he said, "wants to be the authority in foreign relations."[59]

The Case Against Aid as the Case Against Vietnam

Following the Bell testimony, the Senate Foreign Relations Committee shifted more aggressively toward a discussion of US policy in Vietnam through televised hearings with former chief of Army Research and Development James Gavin, the well-known retired diplomat George F. Kennan, and the former chair of the Joint Chiefs of Staff Maxwell Taylor. In asking about the request for the supplemental appropriation, they continued to focus on US interests in Vietnam, and how those interests could be reflected in policy action. Gavin argued that vital US interests were not at stake, but that the United States had a moral commitment to act. This was not a full-throated endorsement. He suggested caution, noting that "it is time that we stop and take a look at where we are, in terms of our total global commitments, and realize that if we are going to really do well in this confrontation in the long run, we had better be restrained and wise in what we do."[60] Kennan was clearer in suggesting that the United States was making a mistake. Like Gavin, he agreed that US commitment obligated some kind of continued effort. He argued, "I think our military involvement in Vietnam has to be recognized as unfortunate, as something we would not choose deliberately." He wanted US involvement to end soon. He said, "I think it should be our Government's aim to liquidate this involvement just as soon as this can be done without inordinate damage to our own prestige or to the stability of conditions in that area." Making the connection to foreign aid, he claimed, "our country should not be asked and should not ask of itself, to shoulder the main burden of determining the political realities in any other country, and particularly not in one remote from our shores, from our culture, and from the experience of our people. This is not only not our business, but I don't think we can do it successfully." He closed by referencing John Quincy Adams's July 4, 1821, address. Adams said the United States does not go "in search of monsters to destroy. She is the well-wisher to the freedom and independence of all. She is the champion and vindicator only of her own."[61]

Finally, on February 18, Rusk returned to the committee to testify again, and for the first time on television. He was more responsive. In his opening statement he seemed to reply to Kennan's question, "Why are we in Vietnam?" and the purpose of the US commitment by saying,

> Certainly we are not there merely because we have power and like to use it. We do not regard ourselves as the policeman of the universe. We do not go around the world looking for quarrels in which we can intervene. Quite the contrary. We have recognized that, just as we are not gendarmes of the universe, neither are we the magistrate of the universe. If other governments, other institutions, or other regional organizations can find solutions to the quarrels which disturb this present scene, we are anxious to have this occur. But we are in Vietnam because the issues posed there are deeply intertwined with our own security and because the outcome of the struggle can profoundly affect the nature of the world in which we and our children will live. The situation we face in Southeast Asia is obviously complex but, in my view, the underlying issues are relatively simple and are utterly fundamental. I am confident that Americans, who have a deep and mature understanding of world responsibility, are fully capable of cutting through the underbrush of complexity and finding the simple issues which involve our largest interests and deepest purposes.[62]

Fulbright and other senators were coming to an alternative answer, that while the United States had a kind of "responsibility" for the situation in Vietnam, that responsibility emerged not from conditions in Vietnam, but from a history of granting aid packages that had ensnared the United States. That is, Vietnam only mattered because the United States had previously made financial commitments there. Its initial investment necessitated secondary investments to demonstrate that the initial investments had been wise. Still, at this point it was hard to not give Johnson the money he wanted as US troops were already in Vietnam and needed the chance to succeed. The Committee voted 18 to 1 to pass the supplemental authorization, with only Morse objecting.[63] The full Senate held a cursory debate lasting less than a day, and in the end, only Morse and Gruening voted against it.[64]

The hearings were a vital part of the developing national conversation on Vietnam. The major networks consistently preempted coverage of their regularly scheduled programming to broadcast them, and by the time the Committee had finished, the NBC network had put on the air more than 69 hours of hearings, while CBS broadcast more than 27 hours and ABC more than 22 hours. The networks also played extensive clips on their evening news shows, reaching an even larger audience. The senators' critical questioning opened up more and more people toward rethinking Vietnam, because, as Randall Woods writes, "Fulbright… and the other witnesses were not irresponsible students or wild-eyed radicals but conservative, establishment figures." But the context for their questions, which sometimes got lost in the conversation, was the long debate about foreign aid and its place in US policy.[65]

It does seem likely, beyond the Vietnam issue, that the hearings had an impact on popular views about foreign aid, as tables 5.1 and 5.2 demonstrate. These polls, taken by Gallup and Louis Harris & Associates, suggest shifting opinion.

TABLE 5.1 General Opinions about Foreign Aid (in percent)[66]

In general, how do you feel about foreign aid – are you for it or against it?

	January 1963	*February 1965*	*February 1966*
For it	59	57	53
Against it	30	33	35
No opinion	11	10	11

TABLE 5.2 Opinions about President Johnson's Handling of Foreign Aid (in percent)[67]

How do you rate the job President Johnson is doing – excellent, pretty good, only fair, or poor on handling foreign aid?

	August 1964	*November 1964*	*October 1965*	*July 1966*
Excellent/Pretty good	58	50	48	38
Only fair/Poor	42	50	52	62

The wording of the poll in Table 5.2 is problematic because it is possible that those responding "Only fair/poor" might have given a negative response because they thought Johnson was not doing enough to promote aid. However, the larger trend is clear and significant, though it was likely about more than aid and a function of Johnson's overall falling approval rates. According to the Gallup Organization, his job approval rate in 1964 was mostly above 70 percent, gradually dropping in 1965, and then falling rapidly in early 1966, from about 61 percent in late January to 46 percent in early May. The Fulbright Committee hearings were part of that shift, and notably, Johnson's overall approval rate was between 12 and 20 percentage points better than his approval rate specific to foreign aid.[68]

Toward a New Aid Bill

Despite the success of the supplemental request, the hearings had an impact on the larger aid debate in 1966, which was even more contentious than the 1963 fight. For 1967 Johnson made a smaller request ($3.386 billion) and called for separate military and economic bills that might be easier to pass than a single bill. He also renewed a request for multiyear appropriations. He said this strategy was necessary to clarify "the goals and functions of these programs in the mind of the public and the Congress," and to signify the "depth of our commitment" to global progress. Yet the tone had changed, and one reporter explained that senators no longer felt "disenchanted" with aid policy, they were ready for "rebellion," and it "required no psychoanalyst to identify the source of the trouble." Waste had always been a problem; this year it was something else, "a distrust of the foreign policy course on which President Johnson has been embarked since his commitment to the Vietnam war."[69]

One major sign of the change was that Fulbright finally came out publicly against the bill and remained in the opposition. "Each year," he said, "it becomes more difficult for those of us who believe in the desirability of a foreign assistance program to support a continuation of the program as now conceived and administered." He admitted that Johnson's unilateral actions in Vietnam had forced him to reassess, but that helped him see that there were much larger issues.[70] He explained, in words that echoed Morse,

> I have always supported foreign aid, beginning with the Marshall Plan. But as time passed, it became more evident, in my view, that something basic is wrong with the aid program. The program has not achieved its purpose in the underdeveloped world, as it did in Europe. I believe that the experience with the Marshall Plan misled some of us to believe that we can do with money what we did in Europe. The difference, of course, has been commented upon often: The situation in Europe involved a highly developed economy and society which was severely damaged by the war. That society contained the manpower, the

> know-how, the men and the traditions – everything except the capital. All it needed was the infusion of capital. We supplied that and the aid program worked well. The situation in the rest of the world is not comparable to that in Europe after the war. I do not believe that a bilateral approach by a great nation assuming a kind of patronizing attitude – a new kind of colonial attitude, in which we undertake to supervise and tell the underdeveloped countries what to do – can succeed. The word "colonial" may not be proper, but I cannot think of a better word at the moment.[71]

He added that aid was "a manifestation of the arrogance of power. Its basis, if not messianism, is certainly egotism. It assumes that the size, wealth, and power of the United States are evidence of wisdom and virtue as well … it has become a vehicle toward the involvement of the United States in matters lying beyond its proper concern." This was a full-throated embrace of the idea that foreign aid was imperialism, and even went beyond Morse's emphasis on aid to dictatorships. The solution, Fulbright suggested, was internationalizing aid to de-imperialize the process. The United States needed to stop going it alone, end its neglect of the United Nations, and listen to the "views and sensibilities of allies and other countries."[72]

Fulbright went even further in arguing that exploitative capitalism was at the heart of the problem. Businesses in the United States (and in Western Europe) had been extracting commodities from poorer countries, but not paying enough. This led to national poverty in Africa, Asia, and Latin America. To deal with that poverty the United States (and others) then sent foreign aid. This made no sense, he said. Aid was solving, or at least trying to solve, a market problem. There needed to be a way to fix markets so that poorer countries got higher prices for their commodities. He said this had worked in the United States where a system of price supports helped farmers make a living and kept them from needing other kinds of aid. In the same way, global pricing arrangements could help alleviate the need for economic aid.[73]

Morse picked up on the argument about aid and colonialism and its connections to Vietnam, but as he had in the past, said the real question was "whether we shall support dictatorships or shall not support dictatorships." Foreign aid was hypocrisy, he again explained, because "we talk a good game about freedom, and support dictatorships. We talk a good game about self-determination, and then we support dictators who trample freedom underfoot." Congress needed to do its job, adding, "American boys are dying in Asia today because the Congress of the United States has stood by and let the executive branch of the Government exercise unchecked powers." Fulbright, fully on board, then followed up. He lauded Morse and said that he had "demonstrated great foresight in the last several years in regard to our present troubles in Southeast Asia, and also I think with regard to the foreign aid program, even as disassociated from Southeast Asia." Fulbright admitted that he had "come around to a point of view that is very similar to that of the Senator from Oregon." In the words of one reporter, this shift meant the "embattled program was virtually defenceless."[74]

This critical tone dominated debates on amendments and spending. It ensured that the Senate rejected the broad five-year aid authorization authority Johnson had wanted (though senators did accept a smaller two-year plan for Alliance for Progress funding). They also changed the bill to limit the number of countries that could receive specific types of loans; only ten would be allowed the largest and most flexible types of loan (program loans), and only 40 would be allowed to receive smaller project-oriented technical assistance loans (project loans). Other amendments on the Senate floor also tried to eliminate opportunities for aid administrators to "cheat" and offer aid in ways Congress had not intended. One example was an amendment that Illinois Republican Everett Dirksen proposed (and which was passed), that said no loan could later be turned into a grant that did not need to be repaid, which had been a common practice when countries could not pay back loans. Another amendment forced the government to get the World Bank's certification that a country needed credit and was likely to repay it.[75] Morse's greatest accomplishment was an amendment similar to those he had offered in the past, and cosponsored with Javits, that halted funding for any country in Latin America if a new government came to power via a military *coup*. Perhaps the most powerful sign of change in this area was that there was no substantial discussion or debate on this issue, no senator objected, and it was adopted by a voice vote. Finally, in an unusual step, the Senate also cut $250 million from the bill, in addition to another cut recommended by the Senate Foreign Relations Committee.[76]

The victory for Morse, Fulbright, and their increasing number of allies was not complete though, and some amendments failed because Johnson's remaining allies and fiscal conservatives mobilized against them. Morse had wanted Congress, not the president, to determine if aid should begin flowing again after a *coup d'état*, but that did not pass. He also failed to pass an amendment that would have prohibited aid to any Latin American country spending more than 3.5 percent of its gross national product on its military. A Gruening amendment, which also would have led to more oversight, similarly failed. Gruening proposed that all aid-spending projects over $100,000 (which would have been almost all aid spending) be accompanied by an application that demonstrated US funds would be used in an "economically and technically sound manner." This would have greatly increased the aid bureaucracy, but also slowed it and made it more accountable to Congress and the public.[77]

As the tone in the Senate was shifting as a result of Morse's activism and Fulbright's changing view, it is important to note that many liberal and Vietnam-skeptical senators still held on to the idea that aid needed to be a vital part of US global engagement. George McGovern argued that "the wealthiest nation on the face of this earth cannot live at peace in a sea of poverty." It was not a moral position, he said, but a practical one as it made "no sense on either economic or moral grounds for us to devote $25 billion annually to put out a fire in Vietnam when we are unwilling to expend even 10 percent of that amount in the rest of the world to prevent other more dangerous fires from breaking out, fires of the same kind arising from misery and poverty in undeveloped areas."[78]

Senator Robert Kennedy (D-NY), who had been hitherto relatively silent on foreign aid, also fought for the bill and gave an impassioned plea about the moral imperatives of offering foreign aid. He explained, "we are increasingly an island of affluence and privilege in a world of desperate poverty – a world in revolution," and echoed the faith of modernization theorists, maintaining, "We have it within our power to give to millions of these young people a greater chance at a decent life." He contended, "a relatively modest investment now can make a difference, in five or ten years, to as much as half the world's people." Gruening, speaking for the new Morse/Fulbright alliance, thought Kennedy and McGovern had missed the point. He explained he had offered six amendments to improve the aid bill, and not one of them cut any money from the program. All were designed to improve its operation because it was badly constructed and did not meet its goals. More money would not help because, in his words, "the larger doses of the wrong medicine do not effect a cure."[79]

Ultimately the bill passed the Senate 66 to 27, but because of all the amendments, it was a victory for anti-aid forces.[80] It should be noted that, as in the past, fiscally minded Republicans also joined in challenging the bill and in introducing amendments that limited spending. As earlier anti-aid conservatives had argued, the Arizona Republican Paul Fannin told the Senate that "the American people are disgusted at being taken advantage of by every so-called new emerging nation that has learned from experience how to kick Uncle Sam and get dollars in return." John Tower (R) of Texas addressed the domestic side, stating, "my duty as a US Senator to my constituents and all other Americans who must pay for our foreign aid programs forces me to say 'no' to any bill which does not weed out all the weaknesses and waste that for so long have been a part of our aid programs."[81]

But Morse deserves the credit for changing the aid conversation in the mid-1960s, and setting up the debates of the later part of the decade considered in the next chapter. Before he objected, liberals had consistently backed the idea that government could transform other societies, and that those societies would be better off following their transformation. Morse did not, in essence, disagree with that. He worried about waste and inefficiency, and he was particularly concerned about the executive branch building its power, but his most powerful critique was the moral one, that the United States was backing dictatorships, and in doing so, undermining its Cold War claims about fighting for freedom against totalitarianism. His liberal internationalism was thus more powerful than his faith in liberal economic principles.

In emphasizing how aid put the United States on the wrong side of global change, Morse's political fight intersected with the anti-war movement. This is visible in Fulbright's transformation toward aid skepticism, which was part of his growing unease about US commitments in Vietnam. It was linked to Fulbright's shift from support of the effort in 1964 to doubt in 1966. In a way, however, the war also pushed the aid conversation off to the side of national foreign policy debates. This should not be surprising because the war dominated conversations about the US global role and animated a national debate about Cold War morality. Anti-war protesters were angry about commitments in Vietnam for the same essential reasons that Morse was angry about foreign aid: both were evidence of a government that had lost its moral compass. The anger of the mid-1960s had a considerable impact in encouraging citizens and political leaders to scrutinize US power, and as the following chapter will show, even as Vietnam became less of an issue (or only one of many issues), the heightened awareness led liberals to greater concerns about the implementation of US aid programs.

Notes

1 Quoted in A. Robert Smith, *The Tiger in the Senate: The Biography of Wayne Morse* (Garden City, 1962), 420; "Oregon's Former Senator Wayne Morse Succumbs at 73," *Los Angeles Times*, July 22, 1974.
2 C. Q. Unruh, "Republican Apostate: Senator Wayne L. Morse and his Quest for Independent Liberalism," *Pacific Northwest Quarterly* 82, 3 (July 1991), 82–91.
3 Smith, *Tiger in the Senate*, 24–28.
4 Ibid.
5 "Senate Nay-Sayer: Wayne Lyman Morse," *NYT*, August 8, 1964; Alden Whitman, "Senator Morse Dies," *NYT*, July 23, 1974.
6 *CR*, July 29, 1953, 10315.
7 Berni Fisher, "It's ERP or Disaster: Sen. Morse," *Newsday*, February 26, 1948; Wayne Morse, "Foreign Aid is Out of Focus," *Los Angeles Times*, October 6, 1963; "6.7 Billion Aid Bill Passed by Senate," *NYT*, July 30, 1953; William S. White, "Democrats Push Fight on Aid Bill," *NYT*, June 14, 1957; *CR*, July 29, 1953, 10315–10319; *CR*, June 13, 1957, 8966.
8 *CR*, June 13, 1957, 8964.
9 "Should Bigotry in Spain Enjoy American Subsidy," *Church & State* 11, 6 (June 1958), 6; Larry Cepair, "The Foreign Policy of Senator Wayne Morse," *Oregon Historical Quarterly* 113, 1 (Spring 2012), 6–35; Rowland Evans, "Foreign Aid Cuts Hinted by Fulbright," *New York Herald Tribune*, June 13, 1959; Robert C. Albright, "Senate Votes Spain Loan of $100 Million," *Washington Post*, August 2, 1950.
10 *CR*, May 14, 1958, 8662.
11 "Foreign AID Program Suffers Setbacks," *CQ Almanac 1963* (Washington, 1964).
12 Douglas Little, "The New Frontier on the Nile: JFK, Nasser, and Arab Nationalism," *Journal of American History* 75, 2 (September 1988), 501–527; Jessie Ferris, *Nasser's Gamble: How Intervention in Yemen Caused the Six-Day War and the Decline of Egyptian Power* (Princeton, 2013), 1–23.
13 *CR*, April 30, 1963, 7739.
14 Irving Sedar and Harold J. Greenberg, *Behind the Egyptian Sphinx: Nasser's Strange Bedfellows* (Philadelphia, 1960).
15 *CR* 1963, April 30, 1963, 7345; Leonard Farbstein (D-NY) successfully proposed a similar amendment in the House Foreign Affairs Committee, targeting Egypt, that mirrored the language Morse suggested. The amendment prohibited aid to any country engaged in, or preparing for military action against any other country receiving aid, subject to the president's determination. "Foreign AID Program Suffers Setbacks," *CQ Almanac 1963* (Washington, 1964).

16 *CR*, November 7, 1963, 21344.
17 US Senate, *Hearings Before the Committee on Foreign Relations, Eighty-Eighth Congress, First Session on S. 1276, a Bill to Further Amend the Foreign Assistance Act of 1961, as Amended, and for Other Purposes* (Washington, 1963), 128–129.
18 *CR*, August 2, 1963, 14042.
19 *CR*, July 22, 1963, 13082; *CR*, August 2, 1963, 14042.
20 *CR*, July 22, 1963, 13082; *CR*, October 28, 1963, 20337–20339.
21 Felix Belair, "Ban on Junta Aid Backed in Senate," *NYT*, October 18, 1963. The amendments had a clause that would allow the president to override them by certifying that aid was in the national interest; *CR*, October 29, 1963, 20477; *CR*, November 1, 1963, 20894; *CR*, November 5, 1963, 21110; "Foreign AID Program Suffers Setbacks," *CQ Almanac 1963* (Washington, 1964), 255–288. The part about territorial limits was designed to halt aid to aggressor states, but it was also designed to protect what the United States considered international waters.
22 Felix Belair, "Senate Refuses to Ask Deep Cut for Foreign Aid," *NYT*, November 2, 1963.
23 *CR*, November 1, 1963, 20904.
24 *CR*, October 28, 1963, 20337; "Foreign AID Program Suffers Setbacks," *CQ Almanac 1963* (Washington, 1964), 255–288.
25 Humphrey and Javits both made similar points. *CR*, October 28, 1963, 20337, 20350.
26 *CR*, November 5, 1963, 21083.
27 Ibid.
28 "Foreign AID Program Suffers Setbacks," *CQ Almanac 1963* (Washington, 1964), 255–288.
29 Foreign Aid Funds," *CQ Almanac 1963* (Washington, 1964), 288–297.
30 C. P. Trussel, "Morse Attacks Aid Bill as it is Reported to Senate," *NYT*, July 14, 1964.
31 "Few Cuts Made in Foreign Aid Program," *CQ Almanac 1964* (Washington, 1965), 296–311. John Tower (D-TX) had offered the Indonesia amendment.
32 Felix Belair, "Congress Votes $3.25 Billion Aid," *NYT*, October 3, 1964; "Wayne Morse: Serious Senator," *Los Angeles Times*, August 14, 1964.
33 "Gulf of Tonkin Resolution, August 5 and 7, 1964; The Avalon Project, avalon.law.yale.edu/20th_century/tonkin-g.asp.
34 *CR*, August 6, 1964, 18413.
35 *CR*, August 7, 1964, 18448.
36 *CR*, August 7, 1964, 18470.
37 Felix Belair, "Rusk Says Aid Cut Would Hurt U.S.," *NYT*, March, 10, 1965; Felix Belair, "Fulbright Quits as Floor Leader for Foreign Aid," *NYT*, January 28, 1965; Felix Belair, "Rusk Says Aid Cut Would Harm U.S.," *NYT*, March 10, 1965; Randall Bennett Woods, "Dixie's Dove: J. William Fulbright, The Vietnam War, and the American South," *Journal of Southern History* 60, 3 (August 1994), 533–552.
38 Felix Belair, "Fulbright Quits as Floor Leader for Foreign Aid," *NYT*, January 28, 1965; Felix Belair, "Rusk Says Aid Cut Would Hurt U.S.," *NYT*, March 10, 1965.
39 Felix Belair, "Fulbright Agrees to Direct Aid Bill," *NYT*, June 3, 1965.
40 Randall Bennett Woods, "Dixie's Dove: J. William Fulbright, The Vietnam War and the American South," *Journal of Southern History* 60, 3 (August 1994), 533–552.
41 Woods, *Fulbright: A Biography* (New York, 1995), 360–375, 381–395; Peter G. Felten, "The Path to Dissent: Johnson, Fulbright, and the 1965 Intervention in the Dominican Republic," *Presidential Studies Quarterly* 26, 4 (Fall 1996), 1009–1018; Randall Woods, "Conflicted Hegemon: LBJ and the Dominican Republic," *Diplomatic History* 32, 5 (November 2008), 749–766; Alan McPherson, "Misled by Himself: What the Johnson Tapes Reveal about the Dominican Intervention of 1965," *Latin American Research Review* 38, 2 (June 2003), 127–146; John H. Burnett, "J. W. Fulbright,

Chairman of The Senate Foreign Relations," *Arkansas Historical Quarterly* 20, 4 (Winter 1961), 318–330.

42 *CR*, June 10, 1965, 13119; *CR*, June 11, 1965, 13367–13369.

43 *CR*, August 24, 1965, 21499–21500; Felix Belair, "Senate Approves Aid Compromise," *NYT*, August 25, 1965; "Major Revision of Aid Program Rejected," *CQ Almanac 1965* (Washington, 1966), 422–441.

44 See Appendix C.

45 Felix Belair, "$3.3 Billion Foreign Aid Asked," *NYT*, January 25, 1966.

46 "Supplemental Foreign Aid Authorization," *CQ Almanac 1966* (Washington, 1967), 393–396; William Conrad Gibbons, *The US Government and the Vietnam War: Executive and Legislative Roles and Relationships, Part IV* (Princeton, 1985), 220–221.

47 Gibbons, *US Government and the Vietnam War*, 223.

48 US Senate, *Supplemental Foreign Assistance, fiscal year, 1966: Vietnam: Hearings before the Committee on Foreign Relations, Eighty-ninth Congress, second session, on S. 2793, to amend further the Foreign Assistance Act of 1961, as amended: January 28, February 4, 8, 10, 17 and 18, 1966* (Washington, 1966), 3.

49 US Senate, *Supplemental Foreign Assistance*, 50–51.

50 Ibid., 61.

51 "Senate Panel Will Conduct Broad Inquiry on Vietnam," *NYT*, February 4, 1966.

52 US Senate, *Supplemental Foreign Assistance*, 96–97, 129–130.

53 Ibid., 134–135.

54 Ibid., 182–184.

55 Ibid., 190–192.

56 Ibid., 215–216.

57 Ibid., 162.

58 Telephone Conversation #9623, Sound Recording, Lyndon B. Johnson and Larry O'Brien, February 5, 1966, 8:27am, Recordings and Transcripts of Telephone Conversations and Meetings, LBJ Presidential Library, www.discoverlbj.org/item/tel-09623 (accessed August 19, 2020).

59 Telephone conversation # 9624, sound recording, Lyndon B. Johnson and Hubert Humphrey, February 5, 1966, Recordings and Transcripts of Telephone Conversations and Meetings, LBJ Presidential Library, www.discoverlbj.org/item/tel-09624 (accessed August 19, 2020).

60 US Senate, *Supplemental Foreign Assistance*, 302.

61 Ibid., 331–336.

62 Ibid., 563–564.

63 E. W. Kenworthy, "Senators Reject Cuts in Vietnam Bill," *NYT*, March 5, 1966; E. W. Kenworthy, "Senate Panel Votes Vietnam Aid Funds," *NYT*, March 8, 1966.

64 *CR*, March 10, 1966, 5563.

65 US Senate, Temporary Select Committee to Study the Senate Committee System, *Operations of the Senate Committee System: Staffing, Scheduling, Communications, Procedures, and Special Functions, Appendix to the Second Report, Committee Print, 95th Cong., 1st Sess.* (Washington, 1977); Woods, *Fulbright*, 405.

66 Conducted by Gallup, datasets USAIPO1963–0667, USAIPO1965–0706, and USAIPO1966–0724, collected by the Roper Center for Public Opinion Research, ropercenter.cornell.edu (accessed February 14, 2018).

67 Conducted by Louis Harris & Associates, datasets USHARRIS.082464, USHARRIS.112364, USHARRIS.100465, and USHARRIS.HA071866.R2R, collected by the Roper Center for Public Opinion Research, ropercenter.cornell.edu (accessed February 14, 2018).

68 "Presidential Job Approval," APP, Gerhard Peters, ed., www.presidency.ucsb.edu/statistics/data/presidential-job-approval (accessed October 6, 2020).

69 "Aid Program Extended with Minor Changes," *CQ Almanac 1966* (Washington, 1967), 397–418; Felix Belair, "Aid Bill Debate Begun in the Senate," *NYT*, July 19, 1966; Felix Belair, "Vietnam Issue Makes Trouble for the Aid Bill," *NYT*, June 19, 1966.
70 *CR*, July 18, 1966, 16020–16023.
71 *CR*, July 18, 1966, 16023.
72 *CR*, July 18, 1966, 16065.
73 *CR*, July 18, 1966, 16023.
74 *CR*, July 18, 1966, 16029; *CR*, July 18, 1966, 16030; *CR*1966, July 18, 1966, 16034; Felix Belair, "Senate Cuts Back for Aid Loans," *NYT*, July 21, 1966.
75 Felix Belair, "Senate Rejects 2-Year Aid Plan," *NYT*, July 19, 1966; Felix Belair, "Senate Approves Two-Year Latin Aid," *NYT*, July 25, 1966; Felix Belair, "Senate Cuts Back for Aid Loans," *NYT*, July 21, 1966.
76 "Javits Asks Curb on Alliance Aid," *NYT*, July 18, 1966; *CR*, July 18, 1966, 16077; Felix Belair, "Senate Cuts Back for Aid Loans," *NYT*, July 21, 1966; *CR*, July 21, 1966, 16510.
77 "Aid Program Extended with Minor Changes," *CQ Almanac 1966* (Washington, 1967), 397–418.
78 *CR*, July 21, 1966, 16552.
79 *CR*, July 21, 1966, 16552, 16590; *CR*, July 22, 1966, 16822; *CR*, July 26, 1966, 16584; James Reston, "Revolt in the Senate," *NYT*, July 22, 1966.
80 *CR*, July 22, 1966, 17073.
81 *CR*, July 20, 1966, 16466; *CR*, July 25, 1966, 16956; *CR*, July 26, 1966, 17072–17073.

6

NIXON, DEFEATING AID, AND THE PATH TO BASIC HUMAN NEEDS

Congress undertook a series of aid reform efforts in the late 1960s and early 1970s to control and limit spending that built on Morse's objections and the continued antipathy of fiscally minded conservatives. Just a decade after Kennedy had embraced modernization theory, few in Congress continued to believe that foreign aid could transform other societies and solve global problems. Even its most ardent supporters started to think about aid's limitations, and most believed that while aid could help solve problems and help people, it would not be transformative. President Richard Nixon certainly saw aid spending this way, and proposed a new business-friendly aid framework. He hoped to reduce the government's role, and rejected the idea that the United States was responsible for development in other countries. Congressional leaders had their own ideas though, and instead opted to recast the entire aid program. Aid continued, but it increasingly reflected the views of its long-standing critics that the program had wasted money and damaged US international credibility.

Nixon and Aid

On taking office, Nixon hoped to revitalize US power and restore its global leadership in the wake of its failures in Vietnam. He believed the war had been a damaging distraction and made it harder for the United States to play a vital role in managing global affairs. As the liberals of the mid-1960s understood it, there was no real threat to vital US interests in Vietnam, and a communist victory would do little to adjust the global balance of power. The war was costly, both in financial terms and in loss of US prestige, which made it harder to fight the Cold War elsewhere. This led to Nixon's wholesale reassessment of US foreign policy, and eventually to his efforts to establish peaceful working relationships with both the Soviet Union and the People's Republic of China.[1]

Part of his reassessment also considered aid's operations and results. Nixon had been critical of aid policy in the Kennedy and Johnson administrations, generally arguing that the United States needed to emphasize helping private enterprise promote development. He contended, as many fiscally conservative legislators had, that backing foreign government's spending efforts equated to US support for socialism, and said that while other nations were free to try socialist experiments, US taxpayers should not pay the bill. He also believed that aid needed a place in US foreign policy however. He suggested it made no sense to "abolish the program or emasculate it in the name of economy," because it was one of the "indispensable tools" available for fighting communism and the Cold War, especially in poorer parts of the world. The challenge, he suggested, was figuring out how to manage a better aid program that reflected US values, strengthened US businesses, and extended US power.[2]

Reforming foreign aid was only one relatively small part of Nixon's effort to recast the Cold War and reenergize US global power. In broader terms, Nixon made his most significant statement about the United States' role in the world in July 1969, while in Guam, by introducing his "Nixon Doctrine." He did not discuss aid in his comments, but in a way the doctrine addressed ideas about US economic aid programs. Considering threats to Asian states, Nixon said, "as far as the problems of internal security are concerned, as far as the problems of military defense, except for the threat of a major power involving nuclear weapons … the United States is going to encourage and has a right to expect that this problem [security] will be increasingly handled by, and the responsibility for it taken by, the Asian nations themselves."[3] The United States needed to do less and adopt a constrained global role. This would apply to military intervention, and also to foreign aid.

Nixon advanced this idea in a November 3, 1969, speech to the nation, significant because he discussed the ways the United States would step back from its commitment to Vietnam. He explained that Johnson had "Americanized the war in Vietnam," but that his administration instead would be "Vietnamizing the search for peace." Johnson had assumed the "primary responsibility for fighting the war," but Nixon said he would ensure that the Vietnamese, with US backing, would increasingly take charge, allowing US combat forces to withdraw. Nixon explained that as "South Vietnamese forces become stronger, the rate of American withdrawal can become greater."[4] There was no explicit link to foreign aid, only a focus on extracting the United States from global conflict by working to shift responsibility to the Vietnamese, but there were implications for aid policy.

In a message to Congress on February 18, 1970, Nixon continued to explain this idea, and made a clearer connection to foreign aid. He said his "central thesis" was that "the United States will participate in the defense and development of allies and friends, but that America cannot – and will not – conceive all the plans, design all the programs, execute all the decisions and undertake all the defense of the free nations of the world. We will help where it makes a real difference and is considered in our interest." Aid had become bloated, and failed, because "Americans are a do-it-yourself people – an impatient people. Instead of teaching someone else to do a job, we like to do it ourselves." This was the essence of the Marshall Plan, which built on the understanding that "the United States was the richest and most stable country," and that without US "initiative and resources, little security or progress was possible" around the world. "This impulse" he added "carried us through into the 1960s. The United States conceived programs and ran them. We devised strategies, and proposed them to our allies. We discerned dangers, and acted directly to combat them." It was time for change, he said, as that policy led to both the Vietnam War and an overambitious and failing US foreign aid program. This was not about living in isolation, Nixon insisted, but there needed to be a "more balanced and realistic American role in the world … if American commitments are to be sustained over the long pull."[5]

It is thus unsurprising that when Nixon made his first aid proposal in 1969 to Congress, he only asked for $2.21 billion, then the lowest presidential request in the postwar era. As his predecessors had done, Nixon called his request "necessary to meet essential requirements." But reducing expenditures was only one part of his plan.[6] Reflecting his earlier criticisms, he said he wanted to restructure aid to emphasize a business-oriented "fresh approach" that would "enlist the energies of private enterprise, here and abroad, in the cause of economic development." This would stimulate "additional investment through businesslike channels, rather than offering ringing exhortations." To accomplish this goal, he asked Congress to create the Overseas Private Investment Corporation (OPIC), which would privatize US aid programming by creating a for-profit, US government-backed entity to provide seed capital and technical expertise to foreign development projects. OPIC would not replace aid, immediately, but its successes would shift the burden from the taxpayer, and ensure that the United States was advancing capitalistic growth, rather than socialistic spending.[7] Despite this historically low funding request, as with previous administrations, fiscal conservatives and disillusioned liberals united to cut the presidential request. Over the course of a long debate in 1969, both houses agreed to $1.46 billion for both the 1970 authorization and appropriation bills. Congress did authorize the OPIC though, which was a Nixon victory.[8]

The Peterson and Rockefeller Recommendations

The OPIC was only a first step to bringing in private enterprise, and to go further, Nixon commissioned a task force to transform his vision into specific policy recommendations and legislation. In September 1969, he asked Rudolph Peterson, the president of the Bank of America, to lead this committee of influential bankers, lawyers, and corporate executives. Nixon said the group's goal was to develop the "basis for an innovative and more effective foreign assistance program which will justify even greater support from the Congress and the American people." In a private meeting, explaining what he wanted the task force to do, Nixon told Peterson that "we need to get away from government-to-government aid and from aiding countries who are headed toward adoption of totalitarian socialist systems. This is not because of ideology," he noted, it was "because aid simply will not be effective in such environments," and the "success stories to date have occurred mainly in environments where the private sector played a major role." Nixon added that Peterson should ignore State Department officials who wanted to give aid to every country in the world. They were busy creating "Mickey Mouse programs" that led to failure after failure, pouring "money down ratholes." Peterson instead should listen to individuals involved in trade policy who could offer suggestions about how to link together trade and aid. The committee also met with Henry Kissinger, Nixon's national security advisor. Kissinger suggested that they should follow up on Nixon's belief, stated in Guam and elsewhere, that poorer nations need to "begin to assume an increasing share in shaping their own progress." The task force needed to emphasize that the United States could no longer "shape" the world, it could "contribute where it could help" but that was probably about it.[9]

With these marching orders, the task force delivered its report in March 1970, saying it was time to remake international development into a "truly cooperative venture," because only a "genuinely cooperative program can gain the necessary long-term support" in the United States and internationally. Its specific recommendations reflected an understanding of widespread frustrations in Congress among Passman-like critics who argued that earlier development efforts had been flawed, and that technology exports and project funding would never create economic growth. The task force argued that because foreign aid recipients were taking money and advice from external bodies who were unfamiliar with local conditions, aid disrupted local systems and, in the long run, hindered growth by causing social and cultural chaos. Even without those problems, recipient nations were just not ready. They had "unresponsive social and political systems, severe deficiencies of technical skills, poorly organized markets … and limited local savings." Drawing a contrast with the Marshall Plan, they wrote, "Modernization is a long-term and much more difficult and complex process than was the reconstruction of war-damaged industrial economies."[10]

The question, then, was how to develop programs that made sense for recipient countries and that fit within US foreign policy objectives and national resources. To start, they said aid administration should be restructured and smaller new agencies with more limited missions should replace the bloated United States Agency for International Development (USAID). They also wanted to construct an independent, US government-backed International Development Bank (to be run by both public and private sector directors), and a similarly managed International Development Institute to study best practices in development processes. The institute would, in the committee's words, help train and distribute "breakthroughs in the application of science and technology to resources and processes critical to the developing nations." Both would be similar to OPIC, but even more independent of congressional funding. Finally, they called for a managerial international development council to coordinate US development activities and ensure that aid programs were actually "directed toward long-term development purposes" and that they were "coordinated with the work of international organizations." In sum, they were calling for more private industry involvement, greater cooperation with international agencies, and the export of knowledge instead of money. While suggesting new directions in some respects, the report was conspicuous for its lack of engagement with concerns about aid to dictatorships. In its expansiveness, it did not seem to address the concerns of economy-minded critics. This was not exactly a government solution, but it was still ambitious and suggested that government actions could be transformative.[11]

Nixon also asked Nelson Rockefeller, then governor of New York and his rival for the Republican nomination in 1968, to study US aid in Latin America. Following the announcement of this effort on February 17, 1969, Rockefeller and a small staff took four trips to Latin America, most of which demonstrated to Rockefeller that US aid coming through the Alliance for Progress had done little to economically transform the region or to build cooperative relationships with pro-US democratic governments.[12] Like the Peterson recommendations, the Rockefeller Report, which Nixon received in November 1969, reflected frustration with extant aid programs, noting that sending "assistance in small and inadequate amounts to a country, where it makes little impact on development, can be a misuse and waste of funds." Aid programs had been ineffective, the report suggested, because they had been "encumbered with conditions and restrictions" by Congress. For example, US loans required that at least half of all goods purchased with aid be shipped on US-flagged vessels. This helped subsidize the US merchant marine, but it increased costs as aid money ended up in the pockets of shipping corporations. Similarly, aid agreements forced recipients to purchase goods in the United States, even if those goods might be less expensive elsewhere. There were other problematic conditions attached to aid agreements, including protections for US fishing fleets and other US businesses operating in recipient countries. These provisions, the report suggested, "appear to violate the sovereignty of other nations" and led to "waste and misuse of funds." Like the Peterson Report, Rockefeller's report was also a call to reform aid consistent with Vietnamization and the Nixon Doctrine.[13]

Using these studies, in April 1971, Nixon proposed a comprehensive administrative reorganization to eliminate the Agency for International Development and establish the replacement institutions recommended by the Peterson Report. In requesting Congress act, he said that aid had been cut year after year because it had not kept up with the changing world. He argued that the "cause of this downward drift is not that the need for aid has diminished; nor is it that our capacity to help other nations has diminished; nor has America lost her humanitarian zeal; nor have we turned inward and abandoned our pursuit of peace and freedom in the world." The reason for reduced aid, he said, was failed bureaucracy and not enough reliance on the private sector. This conclusion suggested a limited understanding of the history of congressional objections, but it was an argument for his proposals.[14]

Nixon's Plans Quickly Die in the Senate

Congressional leaders unsurprisingly saw these bills as willfully ignoring what they had been saying for the past decade, and they did not interpret them as a real change in approach.[15] This created one of the most remarkable aid fights in the Cold War era, leading to a dramatic victory for aid's opponents. In 1971, for the first time, the Senate refused to approve the foreign aid program. It would later pass a substitute bill, but the fight led to a fundamental transformation in how future US leaders would justify aid.

In initial deliberations on Nixon's proposals, the Senate Foreign Relations Committee determined that there was not enough time to hold a debate on the administrative changes, and instead decided to write a stop-gap bill for fiscal year 1972 based on earlier legislation that could pass. After all the planning, study and reports, Nixon's reform proposals died, and they would never be revived in later years. Yet, even while rejecting Nixon's ideas, there was no enthusiasm for the status quo. The committee report noted their decision to advance a stop-gap aid authorization bill to the full Senate came "more by sufferance and a lack of appealing alternatives than through true support." The report continued, "In view of the dearth of enthusiasm for the existing program, the government's fiscal crisis, and the state of our economy and society, it is remarkable that there is a foreign aid bill at all."[16]

The most notable feature of the Senate Foreign Relations bill, introduced on October 26, 1971, was an amendment offered by Idaho's Frank Church and John Sherman Cooper (R-KY) that prohibited financing of any kind that might support military operations in Laos, South Vietnam, North Vietnam, Thailand, Cambodia, or Burma without explicit congressional approval. Money could be spent for the withdrawal of US soldiers from these countries, but the amendment prohibited US forces from engaging in combat unless they were in imminent danger as they withdrew.[17] This amendment built on Cooper and Church's similar efforts the previous year, and was part of a wider congressional push to rapidly end the Vietnam War. In April 1970, following US incursion into Cambodia, Cooper and Church had introduced a bipartisan amendment to a military sales bill to cut off all funding for US forces in Cambodia (as well as military advisors and air support) after June 30, 1970. They hoped to use congressional power over spending to force Nixon to pull US troops out of Cambodia. On one hand, the amendment was not controversial as Nixon stated that he had no intention of keeping US forces in Cambodia after July 1, and that it was only a short-term mission to stop weapons from reaching communists in South Vietnam. But the amendment was significant because Congress was attempting to usurp Nixon's presidential authority as commander-in-chief of the armed forces.

The basic constitutional issues in the amendment led to months of intense debate. The Senate ultimately passed the 1970 Cooper-Church amendment in a 58 to 37 vote, and in so doing asserted the principle that they could use their budgeting power to control US foreign policy. However, Nixon's supporters were able to delay the vote until the end of June, just as US troops were leaving Cambodia, so the amendment had no practical impact.[18]

The 1971 Cooper-Church amendment was a bigger step in attempting to expand congressional foreign policy power. It was also only one of multiple efforts to rein in the president, though. Senators Mark Hatfield (R-OR) and George McGovern (D-SD) acting together, and Majority Leader Mike Mansfield (D-MT) acting alone, repeatedly tried to attach amendments to foreign policy spending bills that would have forced US withdrawal from Vietnam on an accelerated timeline. These amendments, including the 1971 Cooper-Church amendment, all failed as Nixon was able to mobilize enough support to block them, though the votes were close. The 1971 Cooper-Church amendment, for example, lost 47 to 44.[19] The issue here, to be clear, was not really about foreign aid; it was part of a larger frustration with long-term US policy in Vietnam, and the almost universal belief that Congress had made a mistake in 1964 in giving the president too much power in the Gulf of Tonkin Resolution. There was consensus on that point, and as part of the debate on the 1970 Cooper-Church amendment, the Senate had symbolically repealed the Gulf of Tonkin Resolution by an 81 to 10 margin. The few senators in the minority on this measure noted that they were only voting no because it was a pointless symbolic vote, and those kinds of votes undermined the Senate's seriousness.[20] Still, in a larger context, congressional interest in gaining control of US operations in Vietnam was important for the aid debates because it signaled something fundamental had gone awry in US foreign policy, that presidents had made disastrous decisions, and that Congress could and should fix it.

The Aid Bill and Taiwan at the United Nations

Although Vietnam was the overriding issue, other factors were pushing Congress to oppose an aid bill in 1971. The first was the United Nations' vote to seat the Beijing government, and the second was irritation about aid to Greece's military government. The UN vote alienated fiscally minded conservatives and critics that counseled reduced global engagement, and the Greece situation alienated liberals who worried about aid and national values. Both developed at the same time, which was also the moment when the foreign aid bill was moving through the Senate, and together they unified critics and helped kill the aid bill.

The government of the Republic of China (ROC) had been a charter UN member, and one of the five nations with a permanent seat on the Security Council. In 1949, that government had lost a civil war to the Chinese Communist Party, which gained control of all of mainland China and established the

People's Republic of China (PRC). At the end of the fighting, however, the ROC still retained control of Taiwan, and from there it claimed that it remained the legitimate government of all of China. It also retained control of the UN seat. Through the 1950s and 1960s, the United States, hoping to limit communist power, backed the ROC's UN claim, and in 1962 pushed the United Nations to adopt Resolution 1668, which held that it would require a two-thirds majority vote in the General Assembly to remove the Taiwan government and seat the PRC's representatives. At the time, given the number of communist states relative to non-communist ones, this seemed like a high enough barrier to protect the status quo.[21]

But Resolution 1668 was also an open invitation for governments sympathetic to the PRC to call for a vote, forcing the United States to mobilize its allies. Throughout the 1960s these votes got closer and closer. Partly this was because US allies like France and the United Kingdom had decided that backing Taiwan as the representative of all of China made little sense. France opened diplomatic relations with the PRC in 1964, and by that point the United Kingdom had already opened diplomatic offices in mainland China. A bigger problem was that the newly independent governments in Africa and Asia saw the situation through anti-colonial lenses. They thought, just as in Vietnam, the United States was acting as an imperial power trying to control the destinies of non-Europeans. In 1971, the pro-PRC nations reached a two-thirds majority, and in a 76 to 35 vote passed UN Resolution 2758, which replaced the ROC representatives with PRC ones (17 nations abstained).[22] In victory, the resolution's sponsors, the Albanians, Algerians, and Tanzanians, cheered and embraced. Other delegations joined what became a raucous celebration, capped by the Tanzanian chief delegate, Salim Ahmed Salim, leading his colleagues in an impromptu victory dance. He told reporters it was a triumph for the idea that superpowers could be defeated.[23]

Observing from Washington, many senators noted that 42 countries slated to receive aid in the coming year had voted against the United States; another 12 were among those who abstained. This made no sense to West Virginia Democrat, Jennings Randolph. He said he could not understand that the United States had sent "huge sums of money" to these nations, and then they could turn around and vote for the communists. The whole point of sending aid, he argued, was to get people to follow the US lead. The Ohio Republican William Saxbe was also frustrated, in part by the lack of gratitude, but also by the glee many nations took in voting against the United States. Using injudicious language, he told the Senate that those watching the vote on television "saw a lynching party, with the shouting and the dancing, the slapping each other on the back, the heaping of abuse upon this country, one nation after nation taking the stand and telling what great exploiters of the world we were – colonialism and imperialism. It was a regular lynching party." Moving from that point directly to the aid issue, he said, "however ill-advised our actions have been in the world, we nevertheless have been altruistic and have been well-intentioned," and it was disappointing "to find that the people to whom we have given most have turned against us, not just in the vote but also in their actions, in the way they voted, and the emotionalism to which they succumbed." Hugh Scott (PA), the Republican minority leader, was blunter. Addressing the aid bill, he said, "I think we are going to wipe off some of the smiles from the faces we saw on television during the United Nations voting the other night."[24]

With punishment in mind, the New York senator James Buckley introduced an amendment to the foreign aid authorization bill to eliminate US funding for the United Nations Development Fund and the United Nations Food and Agriculture Organization program.[25] Buckley said the Taiwan vote was an act of "grave injustice" that revealed the "nature of the organization." He continued, the "expulsion of the Republic of China was an unprincipled act taken in response to political pressures applied by Peking [Beijing] and her suitors." Therefore, the United States government could not be "expected to place a high degree of confidence" in the United Nations, and Congress should begin to reexamine its support for it.[26] Senator Strom Thurmond (R) of South Carolina echoed Buckley. He said the vote was a "defeat of the first magnitude for US foreign policy," especially as all the members of NATO voted against US interests. The United Nations was an inhospitable place, and the United States should not act with a sense of retaliation, but with a clear sense of "prudence and foresight" about what the United Nations might do in the future. James Allen of Alabama (D) was more direct in saying the Senate should punish the United Nations, and the United States needed to stop being "Uncle Sucker" in funding its programs. The UN was "morally and financially bankrupt," and the "dancing, whooping, [and] jigs" on the floor of the General Assembly after the vote proved that point. The punishment probably would not work, he said, and the UN would become increasingly hostile, but that was all the more reason to avoid sending it money.

Several senators rejected this idea. Jacob Javits (R) said his fellow New Yorker's amendment would appear "punitive" and "petulant." He argued that pulling UN funds immediately after the China vote would isolate the United States, which would be a mistake. He asked, rhetorically, "Do we want to take on the world because of the China situation, or do we want to stay in the world and work out our problems with the world?" The Alaskan, Mike Gravel (D), added that as punishment the Buckley amendment was not rational. If the United States wanted to punish someone, it should punish the countries that voted to seat the PRC, not the institution where the vote happened. It would be a clear case of isolationism if the United States punished the "only organization to offer any possible vestige of hope for peace in the world."[27]

Gravel and Javits' position carried the day as Buckley's amendment lost 55 to 28, but that number signaled danger. Buckley's supporters were traditional fiscal conservatives, some Republican and some Democrats, who had long fought foreign aid. Despite their support for Nixon, it seemed likely that many of them, if not most, would vote against a final bill. The problem was that the liberals were angry as well. Church, who was about to insert himself into the debate more aggressively, told the press that "the mood of the Senate is hot-tempered and irrational. Senators have been known to do silly things in the past, and who knows what silly thing" they might do now. Reflecting this concern, Ohio senator William Saxbe suggested that the Senate temporarily send the aid bill back to the Foreign Relations Committee, via a recommittal, and then start talking about it again after there was a calmer mood. Mansfield, the majority leader, and Hugh Scott, the minority leader, both rejected that idea, believing recommittal would get in the way of other Senate business, and without support, Saxbe withdrew his motion.[28]

The Fight About Greece as a Moral Issue

After the debate on Buckley's proposal, Allen (D-AL) offered an amendment to eliminate a restriction on offering Greece any military assistance. There had been a military coup in Greece in 1967, and beyond using repression and torture to silence its critics, the military seemed not to be making meaningful efforts to return the country to democracy. In response to this, the Senate Foreign Relations Committee's drafted bill included language that forbade sending military aid to Greece. Though Wayne Morse had not been reelected in 1968, other senators, such as Fulbright and Church, had come to accept his views about aid and democracy, and pushed to include this kind of language in the bill. The committee report explained they hoped to "demonstrate to the Greek Government, and the world, that the military dictatorship of that country does not enjoy the backing and support of the United States."[29]

Allen objected. He said Greece was a valuable ally, and the clause would be destructive to NATO, and ultimately to the United States. If war broke out, the United States might need Greece, especially its port facilities and air bases, but without military aid, the Greek government could reject US pleas, or more likely, be unable to protect itself in such a way that its facilities would be usable. He explained that Greece and Turkey were among the most strategically vital NATO allies, situated at the Soviet entrance to the Mediterranean. Greece's military had taken power to stop communists from taking power, and they should not be punished for that laudatory step. He added that the clause was hypocritical in that it cut aid to Greece's military dictatorship, but the bill still included aid for a host of other non-democratic nations including Spain, Portugal, Saudi Arabia, Syria, and Turkey.[30]

Claiborne Pell of Rhode Island (D), one of the senators who assumed Morse's role, replied simply that the Greek government had failed to promote democratic ideals in the country, but it was susceptible to US pressure to change, and the pressure should be applied. He claimed that international condemnation had already been successful in reducing the use of torture for political opponents, and aid might be able to operate similarly. Fulbright joined the conversation, and also added that limiting aid would be a way to strengthen NATO. While he agreed offering Greece more military aid might strengthen the alliance's combat strength, it would be more important to push the country to align their political structure with the democratic values of the rest of the members. Recalling the larger concerns with aid to Vietnam, it was an easy decision to come down against aid for Greece.[31]

Allen's amendment passed 49 to 31, and the language about Greece was removed from the bill. This vote led to one of the most dramatic moments in the consideration of this, or any aid bill. Church used the occasion to deliver a speech he entitled "Farewell to Foreign Aid: A Liberal Takes Leave" to explain how he had moved from aid enthusiast to aid critic to aid opponent. Widely covered in the press, Church explained that he had always thought that aid could make a better world via uplift. He believed in government's ability to improve society and felt the United States had global responsibilities to fulfill. Yet he said that he was changing his mind. At great length he reviewed an essay by John Kenneth Galbraith that labeled aid as "the disaster area of our foreign policy." Galbraith, an influential economist who had served as Kennedy's ambassador to India, suggested that the United States should have learned four lessons in its history of aid granting, but it had not. First, it should have learned that the Marshall Plan experience was not transferrable to poorer nations that lacked "Europe's pre-existing organizational, administrative, and technical capacities." Second, the United States should have seen that few people in poorer societies cared about ideological or intellectual differences between capitalism and communism, which had little impact on their daily lives. Third, it should have been obvious that the effort to shape the development of other countries required massive and intrusive bureaucracies. Finally, fourth, he argued political leaders should have seen that the aid bureaucrats would fight to increase development programming, not to advance political objectives, but to justify and secure their own positions. Church added a fifth lesson that should have been drawn from the experience of the 1960s. He said that it had become clear that, "even with enormous power and the best of intentions, there are some things we cannot do, things which are beyond our moral and intellectual resources." He continued, "it will profit us immeasurably to have learned that being richer and stronger than everybody else has not made us wiser. When it comes to wisdom, we are part of the pack."[32]

Church argued that these lessons had not been learned. US leaders, including Nixon, still hoped aid would promote global stability, but he insisted that stability would not deter communism or advance democracy, and would not automatically create allies. There was no point in developing aid programs if the goal was stability; it had to be growth, which would lead toward progress. Experience demonstrated that aid could not create growth; "all we can really do" he said, is "service the status quo in countries where it is not strongly challenged anyhow." So if stability was the goal, the only logic he could see in foreign aid, as organized, was to serve US commercial interests by helping establish favorable foreign investment climates. But this was not the government's job, and it wasted money by encouraging external, rather than domestic investment, which limited growth in the United States. Aid spending, he said, made it safer to invest abroad than to invest at home, leading to capital flight and weakened US industry.[33]

Moving back to the problem of growth, Church argued that "revolution," of one form or another, could change the status quo in Africa, Asia, Latin America, and the Middle East and lead to progress. "Thoroughgoing social revolution," he said, "is the necessary prerequisite" for economic development. The United States certainly should not promote revolution however, as that would be interventionist and imperialist. What it could do, and should do, was "stop promoting counter-revolution." If there were revolutionaries (who might be peaceful) that hoped to create more equitable societies, the United States should not help governments in stopping them. It needed to remember that "aid policy is not only an aspect of our total foreign policy, it is also a reflection of the life and values of our society."[34]

Church's argument aligned with Morse's earlier critiques, suggesting that aid policy had to reflect national principles, and that Cold War perspectives had led policymakers to overestimate its potential. Aid spending had not served US foreign policy goals, but had either been wasted, or worse, helped create a less just world. His criticism was remarkable, in part, because he was attacking core liberal views about state action – that is, the idea that the United States could create progress in other societies because of its wealth and superior knowledge about development processes. Instead of creating growth, he said, it created bureaucracy and strengthened inequality by backing the status quo. This was not a complete rejection of government power, as he certainly saw its necessity in transforming domestic society and recognized that aid might be useful if directed toward advancing justice and freedom. The speech was significant because of its finality. He did not call for reform, nor did he say the United States should just spend less, which Morse had; he said the United States should just stop giving aid altogether.[35]

Defeating Aid

After this long debate, when the Senate voted on October 29, 1971, the aid authorization bill lost, 41 to 27. Republicans split, with 15 backing the bill (and in essence Nixon, who wanted the spending despite being unable to transform aid's administration) and 19 opposing it; Democrats were also divided with 24 for and 8 against, with liberals on both sides of the vote.[36] It was the first time, going back to the Marshall Plan, that a foreign aid bill failed to pass. There had been close votes, extensive budget-cutting, and amendment after amendment that altered the bills, but it always passed. The vote shocked most senators, who seemed to have assumed that despite their own personal objections and the obvious sentiments in the chamber, the bill would nevertheless still move forward. Reporters explained that senators were "astonished" by their collective action, and seemed not to know what to do next. Church was pleased. He said the vote was "the most cleansing cathartic happening on Capitol Hill in many a year," and colorfully said his colleagues joined him because aid "has been turned into a grotesque money tree, sheltering the foreign investments of our biggest corporations and furnishing aid and comfort to repressive governments all over the world." Sam Ervin (D-NC) indicated he thought the Taiwan UN vote was behind the bill's loss and said he hoped they would all learn, as Polonius said in Shakespeare's *Hamlet*, "Loan oft loses both itself and friend."[37]

Others were disappointed, and also responded in a way that indicated their shock. Massachusetts' Edward Kennedy (D) told the press that he thought the vote was the worst taken in the Senate since it voted against joining the League of Nations in 1919.[38] Scott, the Republican minority leader and a close Nixon ally, said it was a kind of isolationism, and driven by the sentiment of telling "the world to stop because we want to get off."[39] Mansfield, the majority leader, who voted no, was more diplomatic and said that it was an event of "unusual occurrence" in the Senate, and it marked "the end of the foreign aid program as it has been enunciated" in the postwar era. Gaining his bearings, he said that everyone understood that aid would not end immediately; there was money in the foreign aid pipeline, and Congress could pass a continuing resolution that would allow additional funding at the previous years' level without passing a new authorization bill. Still, he said the Senate had issued a "clear signal" that if there would be to be a foreign aid program it would need to be based on a new model. A better aid program would "take the burden off the shoulders of this Nation … distribute it more equally … [and] do away from the grab bag and the gift gimmick which has become all too prevalent." A new program, he added, would need to be structured in such a way that individual senators could not subject it to their personal whims. With these changes, he thought the aid program "will not die suddenly, but very likely die a lingering death."[40]

The vote was bad news for Nixon. One administration official told reporters, perhaps a bit too melodramatically, that the Senate, "like Samson, pulled the pillars of the temple down." White House Press Secretary Ronald Ziegler issued a simple statement that read: "President Nixon feels this vote by the Senate is a highly irresponsible action which undoes twenty-five years of constructive bipartisan foreign policy and produces unacceptable risks to the national security of the United States … ." The statement continued, "A carefully planned foreign aid program is essential in order to continue assisting underdeveloped countries and providing urgently needed humanitarian, economic, and other assistance to friendly nations."[41]

The Agency for International Development also issued a dire warning, explaining the Senate action would undermine its global efforts. Without aid in Vietnam the war effort would "grind to a halt, and the economy would be thrown into utter chaos." Elsewhere, in Laos 300,000 refugees would be left without assistance, and there would be no way to help the 9.5 million people fleeing violence because of the conflict between Pakistan and India. The economies of Indonesia, Turkey, and multiple Latin American countries would stall without loans that facilitated purchases of raw materials and kept factories running. Nixon explained the stakes in a speech in New York City at a Republican fund-raising dinner a few days later. He said that if the United States "should determine that it will discontinue its programs of mutual assistance for countries abroad – helping them so that they can help themselves – it can only mean that the world will become much more unstable, that the dangers of war in the world will greatly increase, and that the United States will no longer be a world power respected in the world, no matter how strong we are at home."[42]

Mansfield was right, however. The vote was not the end of foreign aid. It would have been impossible to terminate a well-established program and end US global commitments. In the following days congressional leaders worked to fix the problem their vote created. As majority leader, Mansfield hoped to pass a continuing resolution (CR) to allow funding to continue without a bill on a prorated level, as determined by previous spending. Fulbright, from his position as chair of the Senate Foreign Relations Committee, opposed this idea because it avoided the issues at stake, and pushed for a full bill.[43] Mansfield then said he would back a bill, but reverting to his initial hope, only if it included an explicit clause saying that the spending was contingent on the withdrawal of all US military forces from Vietnam within six months. Thus it went nowhere, as leaders in the House and Nixon supporters in the Senate opposed this idea. It led to stalemate, and without movement to authorize future spending, and under pressure to adjourn, Mansfield and Fulbright both temporarily agreed to endorse a CR in mid-December that would fund US aid programs for two-and-a-half months without the Vietnam clause. Then, when Congress returned in January 1972, Fulbright's Senate Foreign Relations Committee produced a new aid authorization bill with a lower spending figure. By this point, no one wanted to keep fighting, and the bill, which was essentially another CR, passed both chambers easily. Mansfield claimed the Senate had served notice that it would insist on more cuts and a "complete overhaul in what has become largely an irrelevant exercise in government spending."[44]

The Aftermath of the Defeat

The fight in late 1971 and early 1972 led to a transformation in US aid, which included the long-term depoliticization of the congressional aid review process. In the short term though, it meant a bit of chaos. Throughout 1972 there were conversations about larger reform, but no movement on actually constructing a new aid paradigm, and thus senators were unwilling to pass a new bill. This led them to pass a series of short-term continuing resolutions that authorized spending for a few months at a time, but without committing to anything longer, and there was no bill in 1972.[45]

Finally, in early 1973, congressional leaders in both chambers began completely overhauling the aid bill, and in essence restructured US aid programming with the new goal of serving a "Basic Human Needs Mandate." The idea was to limit direct fund transfers to other countries and instead use US aid, coordinated with multinational organizations, to focus on alleviating poverty. The updated bill emphasized programs in three specific areas – food, health, and education – and targeted spending to people facing the direst conditions. The plan was a clear rejection of the ideas associated with the Peterson plan, which emphasized market-oriented development solutions, but it was also, in a way, a victory for Nixon in that it scaled down US ambitions; Nixon thus opted to embrace the congressional effort. Nixon's message to Congress on the fiscal year 1974 aid bill, while making the philosophical point that aid should spur recipients to "take on an increasing commitment" for their own development efforts, also highlighted that aid needed to address hunger, poverty, and disease. These conditions represented "a moral challenge to all mankind." He was quick to emphasize that this was not "pure altruism," as it would help build up trading partners and promote global stability, but it had clear altruistic elements.[46]

The emphasis on basic human needs also reflected, in part, USAID administrator John Hannah's ideas. In 1969, Nixon had tapped Hannah, who had previously been president of Michigan State University, to run USAID. Hannah believed that critics were often right about aid's failings. He told a conference of agricultural experts in 1970 that after twenty years of programs aid had not done much to alter global conditions. Poverty was just as much of a problem, and as he put it, the gap between "the haves and the have-nots" was "widening at an accelerating rate." This was the case even though many of the other "haves" had joined the United States in establishing their own aid programs.[47]

Hannah developed a different strategy that he called "New Directions." Similar to the Basic Human Needs Mandate, it emphasized providing technical assistance for food production, education, and health and family planning. In changing its focus, USAID would stop encouraging monumental infrastructure projects or providing budget assistance to other nations. A central tenet of New Directions was that decisions needed to be collaborative and, as Hannah said, that US officials needed to "lecture less and listen more" while working with other donors and recipients. This was an acknowledgment that the United States government could not make development happen and a repudiation of Rostow and Kennedy's modernization theory. But it still recognized that some problems were solvable. Hannah said, for example, that the United States could fight disease. He noted in 1970 that over a hundred million people in 19 African countries had received smallpox vaccines through a US-funded program, and that smallpox deaths had fallen almost to zero.[48]

The shift at USAID meant that as congressional leaders searched for ideas about how to recast the aid program, aid administrators were ready to help them rewrite a new bill. Reflecting its mixed heritage, reporters called the 1973 authorization both the Basic Human Needs Mandate and the New Directions legislation. The bill's transformation meant that aid would no longer be thought of as a cure-all, or even as a substantial weapon in fighting the Cold War; aid would more meaningfully become an expression of a humanitarian impulse and a responsibility that a wealthy country might have to poorer ones. It should be noted that the transformation was not total; the 1974 bill included substantial funds for selected countries where the United States had strategic concerns (most notably in Southeast Asia), and some senators wanted even larger changes in the bill.[49] Both Mansfield and Fulbright worried that the basic human needs policies were only cosmetic and did not do enough to emphasize limiting population growth, rural development, and nutrition. Church said he continued to worry that even with the new focus, US tax dollars would still "end up in the Swiss bank accounts of Cambodian generals" or be turned into "United States-built tanks used to kill Greek and Thai students."[50]

The bill had some novel features. Among the most significant came from a short amendment offered by Illinois Republican Charles Percy that directed the government to "give particular attention to those programs, projects, and activities which tend to integrate women into the national economies of foreign countries, thus improving their status and assisting the total development effort." In a brief speech, he noted that in traditional societies, as well as in the United States and other wealthy countries, women suffered discrimination, and he argued, just as Congress should be emphasizing women's equality at home, it should make that part of its foreign policy. There was no debate on the amendment, nobody objected, and it passed immediately on a voice vote.[51] Percy had been encouraged by Clara Beyer, a USAID labor specialist, who had previously worked at the Department of Labor and had a history of promoting women's equality, but the larger context for the push came from the 1970 publication of Ester Boserup's *Women's Roles in Economic Development*. Percy had been echoing Boserup's thesis (in a simplified way) that gender was central to the division of labor, and that because of colonial-era policies that limited female property rights, and because of cultural expectations about unpaid domestic labor, women in poorer agrarian societies suffered greater poverty than men. Percy's amendment led to a 1974 USAID policy decision that determined the agency needed to address women's roles in all planning and project assessment, which in the long term was the basis for the substantial US emphasis on female-oriented development policy.[52]

Another key aspect of the 1974 aid bill, and its successors, was its permanent separation of military and economic aid. Though earlier aid bills had included both categories, and although they were always technically on separate budget lines, the Vietnam experience demonstrated that there was overlap between these two parts of the bills that corrupted each other. This was not a rejection of military aid; the Senate defeated an amendment 51 to 44 that would have blocked all military aid designated for foreign intelligence and internal surveillance operations.[53] Fulbright was among those who voted to end this type of aid. He said the United States should phase out military aid on the theory that it "was a relic of the past" that deserved a "fitting burial," but most senators thought differently, and continued to see a significant role for military aid in fighting the Cold War. Yet it was close, and symbolic of an overall lack of consensus on the new approach to aid policy.

The House considered the overall legislation first and chopped the humanitarian spending from $1 billion down to $650 million, and that only passed by a narrow 188 to 183 margin. A 54 to 42 vote in the Senate was less close, as many liberals, along with most fiscal conservatives, still opposed it. Cutting aid, and voting against aid, had become a habit for many legislators, and they did not necessarily see the reconstructed aid bill as anything new.[54]

The 1974 bill addressed the questions Morse had raised during the 1960s about US support for dictatorships. It stated firmly that the president "should deny any economic or military assistance to the government of any foreign country which practices the internment or imprisonment of that country's citizens for political purposes." This was a step forward, but not a full victory for liberals given that the president would still make the final determination about what countries should get aid, and there was evidence that he would not take this kind of clause seriously. The year before, Congress had explicitly banned any aid to the Greek government, but citing an "overriding" US national security interest, Nixon used his prerogative to sell them weapons anyway.[55]

This clause, and the extensive history of liberal objections, set the stage for much more aggressive approaches in the following two years. In 1974, in considering the 1975 bill, liberals in Congress argued that Turkey's invasion of Cyprus violated the terms of its military aid grant, which by law, had specified that countries using weapons for any purpose other than internal security or self-defense would be automatically ineligible for receiving aid. To stop Turkey from receiving more military aid, liberals added enforcement amendments into bills, but Gerald Ford (who became president following Nixon's August 1974 resignation) fought them, and used a series of veto threats to keep aid flowing.[56] This was not an economic aid issue, and it was not about human rights because it focused on military aid, but it still frustrated lawmakers who could see that Ford did not take their concerns about aid recipient behavior seriously.

Following this failure, during the 1975 consideration of the aid bill, Iowa representative Tom Harkin (D), then in his first term, introduced a more authoritative amendment to solve the question about aid for dictatorship once and for all. His amendment said that aid could not be sent "to the government of any country which engages in a consistent pattern of gross violations of internationally recognized human rights, including torture or cruel, inhuman, or degrading treatment or punishment, prolonged detention without charges, or other flagrant denials of the right to life, liberty, and the security of a person." This amendment was potent, in part, because of its blanket phrasing, but it was also powerful for two other elements. It said that instead of wholly relying on the president to determine if a government was violating the human rights of its people, USAID should draw its conclusions from reviewing the investigations of international bodies such as the Red Cross, the United Nations, and the Organization of American States. The second element was that a president could officially state that for humanitarian reasons it would be appropriate to send aid to a government that did violate human rights, but that the president would need to request and obtain explicit approval from Congress to do so. This gave Congress much greater control over funding. It also left open a window for using aid to help the poorest citizens living under a brutal regime.[57]

The amendment expressed the frustration that had been building for decades about US moral authority and support for dictatorship, but it also addressed the concerns of the moment. One powerful case was US support for the brutal Chilean dictatorship that overthrew the democratically elected president, Salvador Allende, in late 1973. As observers in the United States learned about the human rights violations committed by Augusto Pinochet's military junta, Congress voted to cut aid to Chile to a relatively minuscule $25 million. Ford ignored the spirit of Congress' intent, and used creative accounting methods to send Chile over $250 million. Frustrated, Congressional leaders asked Secretary of State Henry Kissinger to explain why the United States was offering aid to governments that violated the human rights of their people. Kissinger refused to respond, which further angered liberals in Congress, and ensured that Harkin's amendment, with its requirement for congressional approval, would make it into the final bill.[58]

The Harkin amendment was not fundamentally anti-aid, and in explaining his intention to the House of Representatives he stressed that he hoped that humanitarian aid would reach people facing brutal repression. He insisted that the amendment would not be triggered by lack of democracy, only human rights violations. His goal, he said, was to improve aid and strengthen its moral backbone, and in a more significant way, build US moral authority in the international arena. In this respect, it was an extension of the basic human needs legislation that similarly aimed to disconnect aid from utilitarian Cold War objectives.[59] Harkin's bill also raised a question about the power of government to transform other societies. Some critics of aid to dictatorships hoped that withholding aid might limit brutality as recipient governments would be shamed into changing their behaviors. Alternatively, they might make strategic decisions to become less repressive because they needed aid for economic development. Aid, in this case, would still be a political tool, but one wielded in the cause of humanitarianism rather than anti-communism.

This goal was still a far cry from the grandiose claims in the Truman and Kennedy administrations that aid might create a better world via economic uplift, however. The same is true, and perhaps even more accurate, in thinking about the Basic Human Needs Mandate. Here, aid was being granted not to create long-term development, but to alleviate the worst suffering. In theory, the idea was that once suffering had been eliminated, economic growth might be possible, but it lacked the ambition and the faith in government solutions. That makes sense of course, because advocates of government power could see, with the exception of the Marshall Plan, that economic aid had not transformed the world; they had little choice but to accept that it was not money well spent, even when it was not going to repressive dictatorships. Basic human needs emerged, and became a consensus idea, because nobody was willing to stand up for a grander view about development ideologies. No one, it seemed, wanted to argue that if Congress had given the various presidents from Truman to Nixon the full amounts they had requested, aid might have had more meaningful economic and political impacts.

Even with the transformations in aid policy and aid legislation, they still reflected a sense that the United States had global responsibilities, and that it still needed to be engaged. Church had counseled stopping aid altogether, partially on the theory that aid was more destructive than constructive, but the other congressional liberals who took up Morse's mantle rejected that idea and argued that the United States still needed to be globally active, and that it had responsibilities it could not abandon. The United States just had to do a better job of making sure that its spending did not undermine its values.

Notes

1 Daniel Sargent, *A Superpower Transformed: The Remaking of American Foreign Relations in the 1970s* (New York, 2015), 42; Stephen Ambrose, *The Triumph of a Politician, 1962–1972* (New York, 1987); David Greenberg, *Nixon's Shadow: The History of an Image* (New York, 2003); Richard Reeves, *President Nixon, Alone in the White House* (New York, 2001).

2 "Nixon Rips Kennedy's Foreign Policy," *Chicago Tribune*, April 21, 1963; Godfrey Sperling, "Nixon Blueprints Policy Views for 1968," *Christian Science Monitor*, August 22, 1967.

3 Jeffrey Kimball, "The Nixon Doctrine: A Saga of Misunderstanding," *Presidential Studies Quarterly* 36, 1 (March 2006), 59–74; Denise Bostdorff, "The Evolution of a Diplomatic Surprise: Richard M. Nixon's Rhetoric on China, 1952-July 15, 1971," *Rhetoric and Public Affairs* 5, 1 (Spring 2002), 31–56; Richard Nixon, "Informal Remarks in Guam with Newsmen, July 25, 1969," Gerhard Peters and John T. Woolley, eds, APP, www.presidency.ucsb.edu/node/239667 (accessed on October 22, 2020); Ruttan, *United States Development Assistance Policy*, 96.

4 Richard Nixon, "Address to the Nation on the War in Vietnam, November 3, 1969," Gerhard Peters and John T. Woolley, eds, APP, www.presidency.ucsb.edu/node/240027 (accessed on October 22, 2020).

5 Richard Nixon, "First Annual Report to the Congress on United States Foreign Policy for the 1970's, February 18, 1970," Gerhard Peters and John T. Woolley, eds, APP, www.presidency.ucsb.edu/node/240665 (accessed on October 22, 2020).

6 Felix Belair, "President to Ask Vast Changes in $2,6 Billion Bill," *NYT*, May 25, 1969; Godfrey Sperling, "How Nixon Will Divide Foreign Aid," *Christian Science Monitor*, May 24, 1969; "Foreign Aid Authorization Lowest in Program's History," *CQ Almanac 1969* (Washington, 1970), 434–447; Richard Nixon, "Special Message to the Congress on Foreign Aid, May 28, 1969," Gerhard Peters and John T. Woolley, eds, APP, www.presidency.ucsb.edu/node/239278 (accessed on October 22, 2020).

7 Richard Nixon, "Special Message to the Congress on Foreign Aid"; "Foreign Aid Authorization Lowest in Program's History," *CQ Almanac 1969*; Felix Belair, "President

Asks $2.6 Billion Aid to Foster Peace," *NYT*, May 29. 1969; Robert Young, "Nixon Request on Foreign Aid a Record Low," *Chicago Tribune*, May 29, 1969; Carroll Kilpatrick, "Nixon Foreign Aid Goal $2.6 Billion," *Washington Post*, May 29, 1969.

8 Hedrick Smith, "Senator Church Warns on Aid Bill," *NYT*, August 15, 1969; E. W. Kenworthy, "Congress: Flap Over a 'Top Secret' Military Agreement with Thailand," *NYT*, August 17, 1969; Felix Belair, "Foreign Aid Bill Facing Hurdles," *NYT*, October 19, 1969; Felix Belair, "House Committee Approves Aid Bill of $2.19 Billion," *NYT*, October 30, 1969; Felix Belair, "House Heeds Nixon and Bars Deep Cut In Foreign Aid Bill," November 21, 1969; Felix Belair, "Foreign Aid Plea Clears a Hurdle," *NYT*, December 3, 1969; "Foreign Aid is Cut by 2 Committees," *NYT*, December 9, 1969; Felix Belair, "Senate Approves $1.9 Billion in Aid," *NYT*, December 13, 1969; Felix Belair, "Senate-House Conferees Agree to $1.97-Billion-a-Year Ceiling on Foreign Aid," *NYT*, December 18, 1969; Warren Weaver, "Congress Avoids Tie-Up on Rights, Prepares to Quit," *NYT*, December 23, 1969; Felix Belair, "Foreign Aid, Under Fire, Faces Further Cutbacks," *NYT*, December 29, 1969; David Francis, "Fresh Views on Foreign Aid?," *Christian Science Monitor*, January 26, 1970; Felix Belair, "$1.8 Billion for Overseas Aid Set by Conferees," *NYT*, January 27, 1970.

9 Greenwald to Rogers, "NSSM 4-Choices in Foreign Aid, March 25, 1969," Document 4, *Foreign Relations of the United States, 1969–1976, Volume IV, Foreign Assistance, International Development, Trade Policies, 1969–1972* (Washington, 2001); "Memorandum of Conversation, Nixon, Peterson, Kissinger, Bergson, September 2, 1969," Document 120, *Foreign Relations of the United States, 1969–1976, Volume IV, Foreign Assistance, International Development, Trade Policies, 1969–1972* (Washington, 2001); "Memorandum of Conversation, Kissinger, Members of the Peterson Task Force, Bergsten, October 16, 1969," *Document 120, Foreign Relations of the United States, 1969–1976, Volume IV, Foreign Assistance, International Development, Trade Policies, 1969–1972* (Washington, 2001); Felix Belair, "Foreign Aid, Under Fire, Faces Further Cutbacks," *NYT*, December 29, 1969.

10 *U.S. Foreign Assistance in the 1970s: A New Approach,* Peterson Report (Washington, 1970), 1–2.

11 Richardson to Nixon, "Foreign Aid Review-Issues for the NSC Meeting, March 25, 1970," Document 131, *Foreign Relations of the United States, 1969–1976, Volume IV, Foreign Assistance, International Development, Trade Policies, 1969–1972* (Washington, 2001); *U.S. Foreign Assistance in the 1970s*, 4–5; Ruttan, *United States Development Assistance Policy*, 96; *U.S. Foreign Assistance in the 1970s*, 3–4.

12 Taffet, *Foreign Aid as Foreign Policy*, 186; "Nixon Announces Rockefeller Will Make a Series of Trips to Latin America," *NYT*, February 18, 1969; "Nixon and Latin's Mood," *NYT*, October 31, 1969; "President Urges Latins Take Lead to Spur Progress," *NYT*, November 1, 1969.

13 *Quality of Life in the Americas* (the Rockefeller Report), included as an appendix to US Senate, *Hearing Before the Subcommittee on Western Hemisphere Affairs of the Committee on Foreign Relations, Ninety-First Congress, First Session, November 20, 1969* (Washington, 1970), 140.

14 Richard Nixon, "Special Message to the Congress Proposing Reform of the Foreign Assistance Program, September 15, 1970," Gerhard Peters and John T. Woolley, eds, APP, www.presidency.ucsb.edu/node/240510 (accessed on October 22, 2020); Lancaster, *Foreign Aid*, 75–76; Ruttan, *United States Development Assistance Policy*, 97; US Senate, *Hearings Before the Committee on Foreign Relations, Ninety-Second Congress, First Session, on S. 1656 and S. 1657* (Washington, 1971), 2–143.

15 US Senate, *Hearings Before the Committee on Foreign Relations, on S. 1656 and S. 1657* (Washington, 1971).

16 US Senate, *Committee on Foreign Relations, Report together with Supplemental Views to accompany H.R. 9910* (Washington, 1971), 6, 18, 62–90; "Foreign Aid: Senate Rejection of 24-Year Program," *CQ Almanac 1971* (Washington, 1972).

17 John Finney, "Senate, 47 to 44, Kills Fund Curb on Vietnam War," *NYT*, October 29, 1971.
18 US Senate, *Report to Accompany H.R. 9910*, 56–58; *CR*, October 26, 1970, 37525, 37528; Philip Warden, "Senate Rejects War Curb, Reduction in Funds for U.N.," *Chicago Tribune*, October 27, 1971; David Schmitz, *Thank God They're on Our Side: The United States and Right-Wing Dictatorships, 1965*–1989 (New York, 1990), 121; Julian Zelizer, "Congress and the Politics of Troop Withdrawal," *Diplomatic History* 34, 3 (June 2010), 529–541; Robert David Johnson, "Congress and the Cold War," *Journal of Cold War Studies* 3, 2 (Spring 2001), 76–100.
19 John Finney, "Senate Sets Vote Tuesday on Cooper-Church Proposal," *NYT*, June 26, 1970; "Vote in Senate," *NYT*, September 2, 1970; John Finney, "Senate, 55 to 42, Defeats McGovern-Hatfield Plan," *NYT*, June 17, 1971; Mansfield had also proposed cuts to US forces in Europe. Henry Kissinger, *White House Years* (Boston, 1979), 938–949.
20 John Finney, "G.O.P. Acts to End Cambodia Debate," *NYT*, June 24, 1970; John Finney, "Senators, 81 T0 10, Vote For Repeal Of Tonkin Action," *NYT*, June 25, 1970.
21 1080th Plenary Meeting, Friday December 15, 1962, Volume 2: October 19–December 15, 1961, UNA(01)/R3, 1067–1072, Plenary Meetings, Official Records of the General Assembly, United Nations, New York.
22 Richard C. Bush, *At Cross Purposes: U.S.-Taiwan Relations Since 1942* (Armonk, NY, 2004), 103–117; Sigrid Winkler, "Taiwan's UN Dilemma," Brookings, June 20, 2012, www.brookings.edu/opinions/taiwans-un-dilemma-to-be-or-not-to-be (accessed August 20, 2020).
23 Tad Szulc, "Peking's Backers Jubilant Over Vote," *NYT*, October 26, 1971.
24 *CR*, October 26, 1971, 37535, 37553, 37727, "Nixon Deplores Jubilation of Delegates," *NYT*, October 28, 1971.
25 Buckley had been elected to the Senate in 1970 as a member of the Conservative Party of New York State, defeating the Charles Goodell, the incumbent Republican, and Democratic representative Richard Ottinger. He caucused with Republicans.
26 *CR*, October 28, 1971, 38018; John H. Averill, "Senate: U.N. Foes Seek to Cut Aid for World Body," *Los Angeles Times*, October 27, 1971.
27 *CR*, October 28, 1971, 38019–38024.
28 *CR*, October 28. 1971, 38019–38024; "UN Vote Denounced in the Senate," *Associated Press*, October 27, 1971; Spencer Rich, "Various Moves to Cut U.N. Funds Face Trouble on Hill," *Washington Post*, October 27, 1971; Frank Starr, "His Critics Praise Nixon Asia Policy," *Chicago Tribune*, October 28, 1971; John Averill, "Senate Rejects First Retaliatory Move to Slash Funds for U.N.," *Los Angeles Times*, October 29, 1971.
29 US Senate, *Report to accompany H.R. 9910*, 41–42.
30 *CR*, October 29, 1971, 38231–38233, 38240, 10/29/71, Buckley, in supporting Allen offered a larger, but still incomplete, list of US aid recipients with questionable records on aid, Argentina, Brazil, Haiti, Nicaragua, Iran, Iraq, Syria, Turkey, Burma, Ethiopia, Ghana, Sudan, and Tunisia.
31 *CR*, October 29, 1971, 38236.
32 *CR*, October 29, 1971, 38241–38254. Church was citing John Kenneth Galbraith, *Economics, Peace and Laughter* (Boston, 1971), 170–175.
33 *CR*, October 29, 1971, 38255.
34 *CR*, October 29, 1971, 38258. Mansfield reaction to Church's speech was, "I welcome him to the club." *CR*, October 29, 1971, 38259.
35 Robert A. Pastor, *Congress and the Politics of Foreign Economic Policy* (Berkeley, 1980), 278.
36 The floor vote was 27–41. Because of absences there were many paired and announced votes, and including stated preferences, the vote would have been 39–52. Russell Long had been vocal in opposing the bill, but did not have a recorded vote,

and it is inconceivable that Barry Goldwater (R-AZ) or Karl Mundt (R-SD) would have voted yes. One pattern was that Southern Democrats voted no in a bloc, almost, with only John Sparkman (AL) voting yes. *CR*, October 29, 1971, 38283.

37 *CR*, October 29, 1971, 38283, 38286; Philip Warden, "Strange Grouping of Old Foes Brings an End to Foreign Aid," *Chicago Tribune*, October 30, 1971; Philip Warden, "Senate Kills Foreign Aid," *Chicago Tribune*, October 30, 1971; Robert Barkdoll, "$51 Billion Aid in Next 5 Years," *Los Angeles Times*, October 30, 1971; John Finney, "A Possible End to Bilateral Aid," *NYT*, October 30, 1971.

38 Bernard Gwertzman, "Senate Reaction is Astonishment," *NYT*, October 31, 1971.

39 "Ax for Foreign Aid," *NYT*, October 31, 1971.

40 Bernard Gwertzman, "Senate Reaction is Astonishment," *NYT*, October 31, 1971; "Ax for Foreign Aid," *NYT*, October 31, 1971; *CR*, October 29, 1971, 38283; "Ax for Foreign Aid," *NYT*, October 31, 1971.

41 "Statement by Press Secretary Ronald L. Ziegler on the Senate's rejection of the foreign aid bill." Released by the White House on October 30, 1971, printed in the *Weekly Compilation of Presidential Documents* 7 (Washington, 1971), 1457; "Foreign Aid: Senate Rejection of 24-Year Program," *CQ Almanac 1971* (Washington, 1971), 387–407. James Naughton, "Proposals for Reform Likely to Gain," *NYT*, October 31, 1971.

42 "AID Lists Work Periled by Senate," *NYT*, November 4, 1971; Richard Nixon, Remarks at a "Salute to the President" Dinner in New York City. Gerhard Peters and John T. Woolley, eds, APP, www.presidency.ucsb.edu/node/241209 (accessed October 28, 2020).

43 Felix Belair, "Senate Democrats Balk at 90-day extension for Aid," *NYT*, November 3, 1971; Felix Belair, "Fulbright Threatens to Fight Extension on Aid," *NYT*, November 9, 1971; Bernard Gwertzman, "State Department Says New Senate Aid Proposals Would Cripple South Vietnam," *NYT*, November 6, 1971.

44 "Conferees Fail Again on Aid Bill," *NYT*, December 4, 1971; John Finney, "Congress Passes Extension of Aid," *NYT*, December 17, 1971; Felix Belair, "Foreign Aid Bill is Voted by House," *NYT*, January 25, 1972; John Finney, "Foreign Aid Survives Obituary," *NYT*, March 4, 1972.

45 John Finney, "Fund Bill for Aid Passed by House," *NYT*, September 22, 1972; Senate Slashes Foreign Aid Bill," *NYT*, October 17 1972; John Finney, "Congress Passes Bill on Benefits," *NYT*, October 18 1972; "Congress Passes Extension of Aid," *NYT*, March 1, 1973.

46 Ruttan, *United States Development Assistance Policy*, 94; Nick Cullather, *The Hungry World: America's Cold War Battle Against Poverty in Asia* (Cambridge, MA, 2010), 234–252; Carol Lancaster, *Foreign Aid: Diplomacy, Development, Domestic Politics* (Chicago, 2007), 76–77; "Overhauling Aid," *NYT*, June 05, 1973; Richard Nixon, "Special Message to the Congress Transmitting Proposed Legislation for Funding of Foreign Assistance Programs in Fiscal Year 1974, May 1, 1973," Gerhard Peters and John T. Woolley, eds, APP, www.presidency.ucsb.edu/node/255386 (accessed October 29, 2020); Richard Nixon, "Fourth Annual Report to the Congress on United States Foreign Policy, May 3, 1973," Gerhard Peters and John T. Woolley, eds, APP, www.presidency.ucsb.edu/node/255404 (accessed October 29, 2020); "Mutual Cooperation," *NYT*, June 25, 1973.

47 John A. Hannah, "New Directions in Foreign Aid for the 1970s," *American Journal of Agricultural Economics* 52, 2 (May 1970), 302–307.

48 Hannah, "New Directions"; P. David Searles, *The Peace Corps Experience: Challenge and Change, 1969–1970* (Lexington, KY, 1997); Larry Nowels, "Foreign Aid Reform Commissions, Task Forces, and Initiatives: From Kennedy to Present," in Lael Brainard, ed., *Security by Other Means: Foreign Assistance, Global Poverty, and American Leadership* (Washington, 2007).

49 Ruttan, *United States Development Assistance Policy*, 111–113.
50 "Senate Unit Votes Aid Bill," *NYT*, July 15 1973.
51 *CR*, October 2, 1973, 32583–32584.
52 Ester Boserup, *Women's Roles in Economic Development* (London, 1970); B. L. Turner and Marina Fischer-Kowalski, "Ester Boserup: An Interdisciplinary Visionary Relevant for Sustainability," *Proceedings of the National Academy of Sciences of the United States of America* 107, 51 (December 10, 2010), 21963–21965; Lourdes Benería and Gita Sen, "Accumulation, Reproduction, and 'Women's Role in Economic Development': Boserup Revisited," *Signs* 7, 2 (Winter 1981), 279–298; Joanne Meyerowitz, "Clara Beyer's Gen(d)erations," *Radcliffe Magazine* (Summer 2016), www.radcliffe.harvard.edu/news/in-news/clara-beyers-genderations (accessed October 29, 2020); Karen Garner, *Gender and Foreign Policy in the Clinton Administration* (Boulder, CO, 2013); *GAO Report: U.S. Has Made Slow Progress in Involving Women in Development* (Washington, 1993).
53 "Fulbright Seeks End to Arms Aid," *NYT*, April 04, 1973; "Curb On Foreign Aid Fails Senate Test," *NYT*, October 02, 1973.
54 "Foreign Aid Bill Passed by House," *NYT*, July 27, 1973; David Binder, "Senate, 54 to 42, Votes $1.2 Billion for Foreign Aid," *NYT*, October 03, 1973; John Finney, "Compromise Set on $2.4 Billion Aid Bill," *NYT*, November 15, 1973.
55 Ruttan, *United States Development Assistance Policy*, 103, 114; Brian H. Smith, *The Politics of Private Foreign Aid* (Princeton, 1990), 69–70; Benjamin Welles, "US Plans to Sell Arms to Greece," *NYT*, March 4, 1972.
56 "Turkey: Still Ineligible," *NYT*, October 13, 1974; David Binder, "House Approves Foreign Aid Bill," *NYT*, December 19, 1974.
57 *CR*, September 10, 1975, 28306.
58 .John P. Salzberg, "A View from the Hill: US Legislation and Human Rights," in David Newsom, ed., *The Diplomacy of Human Rights* (Lanham, MD, 1986), 17; "House Votes to Ban Foreign Aid for Human-Rights Violations," *NYT*, September, 11, 1975; Leslie Gelb, "Realism vs. Idealism in American Foreign Policy," *NYT*, November 30, 1975; Bernard Gwertzman, "Senate Unit Approves Over $4 Billion Aid," *NYT*, December 20, 1975.
59 *CR*, September 10, 1975, 28309.

CONCLUSION

US foreign aid programs from the Marshall Plan through the early 1970s had their roots in optimism about the power of money and expertise to transform the world. Planners believed aid would bring technology and economic growth to poorer people and transform them into modernized and enthusiastic allies. This would help the United States win the Cold War, benefit US businesses, and permanently secure US-style global capitalism.

Historians have been rightfully critical of these foreign aid programs. They have explained that using aid to create self-sustaining growth did not work. Although some aid may have been impactful, especially on the small scale, global inequality remained severe. Economic aid planners over-promised and under-delivered. Foreign aid also failed to have a meaningful and positive political impact. People in recipient nations, generally, did not recognize an implied *quid pro quo* when receiving aid, and they did not become appreciably more pro-US. Instead, aid's inherent interventionism strained political relationships and alienated allies. Economic aid to military regimes further damaged the United States' global reputation by offering communists an easy opportunity to argue that the United States was anti-democratic. Finally, it is clear that foreign aid contained imperialist presumptions about US superiority. Aid planners assumed the United States was objectively better than other countries because of its relative development, and that it could solidify its place in the world by implanting its systems and values in other nations.[1]

Aid critics saw these problems and more, and fought hard and lonely battles to limit US ambitions. The passage of the aid bills in the 1970s with historically low spending levels, and the inclusion of the Basic Human Needs Mandate in 1973 and the Harkin Amendment in 1975, were substantial victories for them. It was not the end of fighting about aid budgets, and it was certainly not the end of debates about aid's place in US foreign policy. But the bills mark the end of an era, with a final and permanent blow to Cold War, Marshall Plan and modernization theory visions about how aid could remake the world. Aid continued, and some US leaders continued to argue that the United States needed to spend more to create stability, and as a wealthy country, it had a responsibility to the poor. This occurred with tamped-down expectations about what kinds of transformations were possible. The era of grandiose rhetoric had conclusively ended.[2]

In the late 1970s and beyond, US leaders still believed aid could reflect national values, yet still disagreed on what those values were. William Michael Schmidli's work, for example, demonstrates how President Jimmy Carter's administration used foreign aid with the clauses Congress had put into aid bills to try to stop the brutally repressive Argentine military junta from continuing its widespread human rights violations. However, Carter's successor, President Ronald Reagan, saw the relationship between aid and morality differently. Reagan argued that aid to military dictators was moral and in the national interest because it was a way to fight the greater evils of communism. His policy flowed from the conclusions that Jeanne Kirkpatrick, who served as his ambassador to the UN, had explored in her 1979 essay, "Dictatorships and Double Standards." Kirkpatrick argued that communist dictatorships were worse than non-communist ones. Both were repressive, but communist regimes were more likely to block economic and religious freedom, which she argued were the building blocks of all liberty, and they were less likely to transition to democracies.[3] Thus Reagan argued it was moral to use aid to support anti-communist dictatorships, just as Carter had argued it was immoral. The issue was not really about aid, though. It was not a question of whether aid was good or bad, effective or ineffective, or necessary or unnecessary; it was how could aid be used to strengthen other policy decisions.

The Mexico City/Global Gag Rule is another example of how aid programming changed over time because of contested political views and ethical stances. In 1984 the Reagan administration strengthened already extant regulations that prohibited US foreign aid from funding abortion services. Its new rule, introduced at a conference in Mexico City, barred aid recipients from providing family planning advice that included information about abortion, even if the money used came from other aid sources. Bill Clinton rescinded the policy in 1993, reflecting his domestic stance on abortion. Then, in 2001 George W. Bush reinstated it, and eight years later in 2009 Barack Obama again rescinded it. Donald Trump predictably reinstated it in 2017, and in 2019, further strengthened its provisions to bar aid recipients from making grants to other organizations that provided family planning services that mentioned abortion. Of course, Joe Biden changed the policy once more in 2021, and rescinded these regulations. Here too, these were not disputes about aid's necessity; rather, they were disagreements about how to implement a program. They were not the debates that had defined the earlier disputes about government power and international engagement, but they were about values, and how aid spending reflected US society.[4]

Aid and National Political Change

Exploring aid opposition from the late 1940s to the early 1970s is valuable for developing a fuller understanding of political change afterwards. It provides context for Carter's concerns about the ethical use of national power, and it can help in exploring how conservatives understood foreign policy.

Jimmy Carter's emphasis on promoting human rights rested on numerous foundations. Most obviously it came from frustrations with Watergate and Vietnam. Carter said, in accepting the Democratic presidential nomination in 1976, that the nation had "been shaken by a tragic war abroad and by scandals and broken promises at home;" the country needed to be better and live up to its promise and values.[5] This view, that something had gone wrong in US politics and society, had also animated Congress in the early 1970s. In 1973, Representative Donald M. Fraser (D-MN) opened hearings on US failures to promote human rights as chair of the Foreign Affairs' Subcommittee on International Organizations and Social Movements, and then in 1975, the Senate launched the Select Committee to Study Governmental Operations with Respect to Intelligence Activities. This Senate committee, led by Frank Church, investigated Central Intelligence Agency (CIA) operations, and in case after case revealed that the agency had undermined constitutional and legal processes in other countries. Both committees concluded that US policy was inconsistent with democratic principles.[6]

These concerns, as the text explained, were not new in the 1970s. They were central to the objections that Wayne Morse had used about giving foreign aid to support dictatorships. Long before Carter, or even Church, Morse was fighting a lonely battle to convince his colleagues that US foreign policy needed to rest on something other than anti-communism. As Carter would years later, Morse saw that repressive anti-communist leaders were poor allies, and by backing them, the United States was not only acting immorally, but destroying its credibility. Rather than helping the nation win the Cold War, it was making that fight harder by alienating people and suggesting that the United States was not a voice for liberty, justice, freedom, or economic development. Morse did not believe, as other aid critics did, that aid could never be done well. However, he saw substantial problems in its execution that limited aid's utility and thought it was a key factor pulling the United States into the Vietnam War. With these concerns, he and followers like Church pushed for substantial cuts in aid spending and greater legislative power over US programs. It is a stretch to argue that Morse's actions were wholly responsible for the long-term shifts in US foreign policy and the wider acceptance of these ideas in the 1970s. It is reasonable to suggest, however, that he sparked the process.

Morse's position was similar to Henry Wallace's earlier response to the Marshall Plan. Wallace had also rejected the idea that the United States should ground its aid programs in anti-communism, and he similarly believed that aid could unite the world together and advance democratic values. He believed in global engagement, but worried that the Truman administration's unwillingness to cooperate with the Soviet Union and its allies had made the world less safe. Like Morse, and later Carter, he saw Cold War mentalities as destructive and dangerous, and thought that aid in the service of anti-communism would destroy its utility for constructing global community. Wallace, Morse, and Church all came to believe that US foreign aid was doing more harm than good.

In a different way, the story about aid opposition helps explain the evolution of conservative foreign policy ideas. Here, there is not a causal link. Ideas about aid did not drive conservative ideologies, nor were they a substantial factor in the movement's development. Yet, studying aid opposition highlights how conservatives approached foreign policy questions and how their ideas intersected with their domestic views. It allows for a fuller, more nuanced understanding of the postwar evolution of the conservative movement.

Passman's views demonstrate this point. He was the most important legislator focusing on waste, inefficiency, and incompetency in foreign aid programming, and his positions resonated with his colleagues because of the substantial evidence that they were valid. With so much failure, it was easy to argue that aid budgets needed to be much smaller. Year after year, aid administrators came to his subcommittee asking for money, and he reasonably replied that the evidence suggested aid was not a good investment. He insisted money would be better off in the hands of taxpayers than bureaucrats. His position was similar to the ones made by conservatives attacking domestic social welfare spending as inefficient and wasteful. Just as government could not alleviate poverty in the United States, it was failing abroad. This is the point that Henry Hazlitt had made, and in a milder variant, that Eisenhower and Nixon had made. It was also the case Taft had made in fighting the Marshall Plan and Point Four. They all suggested a version of the argument that state intervention in the economy would damage, rather than advance, economic development.

The most virulent anti-communist conservatives, who saw the Soviet Union as an immediate existential danger, added two additional dimensions. If communists were dedicated to global conquest and destruction of the United States, economic aid would be a half measure in challenging them. Aid was a long-term proposition to advance development, but the Soviet threat was immediate. Thus, domestic military spending would be much more important in helping win the Cold War than aid. Even worse though, because aid was reliance on government power, it veered toward socialism, and from there it was only a short leap to actual communism. Aid planners, either wittingly or unwittingly, were not fighting the Cold War; they were undermining it by advancing the enemies' economic ideas. Real patriots needed to stop foreign aid to win the Cold War.

But Passman also made another case, that aid was dangerous because it relied on external values systems and tried to transform traditional societies. Here he was expressing the anger and frustration of white Southerners facing the Civil Rights Movement, and taking the natural position that foreign aid was its international analogue. Both aid and the Civil Rights Movement rested on the principles that some societies were regressive, and that it was the responsibility of progressives, who had the capability to make change happen, to fix backward traditionalism in the name of modernization and justice. Conservative critics said this was not progress, it was merely an effort of one group of people to force its value system on another. The fight against aid then, as described, was parallel to the domestic conservative fight about the preservation of traditional values. The same white Southerners who most aggressively fought against Civil Rights were similarly the most antagonistic to aid spending.

Conservative aid opponents were not a monolith, however. Some conservative opponents, especially outside the South, borrowed from prewar isolationist ideas and suggested the United States should not worry about problems outside its borders. They argued that, if government was going to promote economic growth, it should spend that money at home. Some liberals made the same case, arguing that helping people in other countries was a luxury, while helping people at home was a necessity. Of course, it needs to be restated that these opponents were usually in the minority, though their power grew over time. Most liberals backed aid, and as a group they were slow to recognize the weight of what Wallace and Morse were saying. By the early 1970s, though, there was a significant switch and most had adopted those positions. Conservatives too, to a lesser extent, often backed aid as a reasonable way to fight the Cold War. Making this more complex, what it meant to be conservative shifted during this era. Republicanism and conservatism were not the same things, just as Democrats and liberals were not synonymous. Eisenhower's approach, for example, incorporated some elements of conservative aid skepticism, but recognized aid's utility, leading him to eventually embrace it as a vital part of Cold War foreign policy. Exploring ideas about foreign aid, then, is helpful in explaining the evolution of political philosophies, but suggests that using political labels in that process should be done with caution.

Aid and US History

This text attempts to explain that both aid planners and aid critics, in making assessments about the world and the most appropriate way to fight the Cold War, were not operating in a historical vacuum. Aid planners' optimism rested on beliefs about the power of government to transform society, and on a missionary sense of US global responsibility. Aid opponents questioned the idea that change was automatically good or that the United States should be globally engaged.

None of the ideas raised in the postwar world about foreign aid were new, each had roots in earlier moments of US history, and some rejected the philosophies that drove US foreign aid. Wallace and Morse were not the first to worry that the United States might be using its power immorally and that its global engagement violated national values. Abraham Lincoln in challenging war with Mexico, the Mugwumps in questioning rising imperialism, and the many pacifists before the world wars all argued, similarly, that the United States had a special responsibility to eschew power politics and hold itself to a higher ethical standard because of its idealistic foundations. For these critics, the United States needed to avoid global engagement, as it would lead to imperialism.

Other aid opponents built on George Washington's framework that the United States would only be damaged by entangling itself in the affairs of other countries. Even if they thought the United States could and should trade internationally, the US should not assume responsibility for political change in other countries. This view drove prewar isolationism, and also promoted opposition to the Marshall Plan and Point Four. In this period, not only were the ideas the same, but it was often the same people, like Robert Taft, involved with both efforts. In fighting aid, they argued that the United States was endangering itself by attaching its destiny to that of other nations. Aid opponents mostly believed that US economic power and victory in World War II carried some responsibility to help restore European economies, but that was limited; it did not follow that the United States was responsible for every poor person in every country around the world.

Aid opponents had consistent views about government and believed in Jeffersonian notions about the dangers of an activist state. They argued that the United States could not, and should not, use its power to transform other countries, and built on historical fears that urbanization and modernization might corrupt society's traditional values. Most visibly, they rehashed the arguments that Republicans such as Warren G. Harding had advanced in the 1920s, that government planning would destroy ambition and undermine the individualistic and capitalistic values that had built the nation. Aid opponents making an economic argument also advanced a simpler case. Aid spending meant more taxation, and more taxation meant less money in citizens' pockets. It was bad enough that their taxes funded domestic welfare programs, but much worse in that their money was being spent abroad on programs destined to fail.

This is a final point to emphasize, that foreign aid spending was spending. It was taking hard-earned taxpayer money sending it abroad to help people in other countries. Legislators and taxpayers understandably and appropriately wanted to know if that money was being well spent, if that money was advancing US security and stability, and if that money was helping the US economy grow.

They were right to ask if aid programs were working, and right to worry about waste and inefficiency. They were right to wonder if aid was supporting governments that implemented policies antithetical to their own understandings of national values. Their job was to make sure money was being spent well, and to a large extent this is a story about how they tried to do that.

Bringing aid's opponents into a conversation about aid, and noting their impact in cutting spending year after year, highlights that there was discord rather than unanimity about how to approach the world. It also demonstrates the wide differences in how the people engaged in these debates understood the nation. Aid's advocates argued that the United States government could make change happen, and that in doing so it could make the world better. Aid's opponents rejected that, though not for the same reasons. No matter what their objections were, they too wanted to live in a better world, as they defined it, and believed that aid spending was not the right medicine.

Notes

1 Nick Cullather explored this vast literature in "Development? It's History," *Diplomatic History* 24, 4 (Fall 2000), 641–653, and it has expanded since that essay's publication.

2 Lars Schoultz, *In Their Own Best Interest: A History of the U.S. Effort to Improve Latin Americans* (Cambridge, MA, 2018), 240.

3 William Michael Schmidli, "Institutionalizing Human Rights in U.S. Foreign Policy: U.S.-Argentine Relations, 1976–1980," *Diplomatic History* 35, 2 (April 2011), 351–377; William Michael Schmidli, *The Fate of Freedom Elsewhere: Human Rights and Cold War Policy Toward Argentina* (Ithaca, NY, 2013); Jeane J. Kirkpatrick, "Dictatorships and Double Standards," *Commentary* 68, 5 (November 1979), 34–45.

4 Yana van der Meulen Rodgers, The Global Gag Rule and Women's Reproductive Health: Rhetoric Versus Reality (New York, 2018); "The Mexico City Policy: An Explainer," Kaiser Family Foundation, www.kff.org/global-health-policy/fact-sheet/mexico-city-policy-explainer (accessed November 12, 2020).

5 Jimmy Carter, "Address Accepting the Presidential Nomination, July 15, 1976," Gerhard Peters and John T. Woolley, eds, APP, www.presidency.ucsb.edu/node/244286 (accessed November 18, 2020).

6 Sarah Snyder, "'A Call for U.S. Leadership': Congressional Activism on Human Rights," *Diplomatic History* 37, 2 (April 2013), 372–397.

Appendix A: Path from Initial Eisenhower Request to Final Appropriation, FY1954–FY1961

	1954	*1955*	*1956*	*1957*	*1958*	*1959*	*1960*	*1961*
Presidential Request	5.8–5/5/53, 0.5 for economic, the rest for military[1]	3.51–1/20/54, 0.769 for economic, the rest for military[2]	3.53–1/18/55, 1.5 for economic, the rest for military[3]	4.860–3/19/56, 1.6 for economic, the rest for military[4]	4.4–1/16/57, 1.95 for economic, the rest for military,[5] 3.865–5/21/57, 1.065 for economic, the rest for military[6]	3.942–2/19/58, 1.307 for economic, the rest for military[7]	3.93–1/19/59, 2.33 for economic, the rest for military[8]	4.175–2/16/60, 2.175 for economic, the rest for military[9]
Senate Foreign Relations Committee authorization proposal	5.313–6/10/53[10]	3.1–7/12/54[11]	3.408–5/26/55[12]	4.458–6/18/56[13]	3.637–6/7/57[14]	3.763–5/21/58[15]	3.93–3/18/59,[16] 4.165–6/15/59[17]	4.146–4/20/60[18]
House Foreign Affairs Committee authorization proposal	4.999–6/18/53[19]	3.471–6/27/54[20]	3.286–6/22/55[21]	3.891–5/22/56[22]	3.242 – 7/1/57[23]	3.543–4/23/58[24]	3.642–5/26/59[25]	4.038–3/31/60[26]
Senate Authorization Bill	5.319–7/1/53[27]	2.731–8/3/54[28]	3.53–6/2/55[29]	4.517–6/29/56[30]	3.637–6/14/57[31]	3.713–6/6/58[32]	3.543–7/8/59[33]	4.105–5/2/60[34]
House Authorization Bill	4.999–6/19/53[35]	3.369–6/30/54[36]	3.286–6/30/55[37]	3.800–6/11/56[38]	7/19/57–3.117[39]	3.602–5/14/58[40]	3.542–6/18/59[41]	4.038–4/21/60[42]
Conference Committee/ Final Authorization Bill	5.157–7/16/53[43]	3.054–8/4/54[44]	3.285–7/8/55[45]	4.014–7/18/56[46]	3.367–8/14/57[47]	3.676–6/27/58[48]	3.556–7/22/59[49]	4.086–5/12/60[50]
House Appropriations Subcommittee on Foreign Affairs proposal[51]	4.433–7/16/53[52]	2.896–7/24/54[53]	2.639–7/8/55[54]	3.700–7/4/56[55]	2.525–8/14/57[56]	3.07–6/27/58[57]	3.03–7/24/59[58]	3.384–6/13/60[59]
House Appropriations Bill	4.439–7/22/53[60]	3.054–8/9/54[61]	2.639–7/11/55[62]	3.655–7/11/56[63]	3.192–8/15/57[64]	3.078–7/2/58[65]	3.186–7/29/59[66]	3.584–6/17/60[67]
Senate Appropriations Bill[68]	4.562–7/30/53[69]	2.79–8/14/54[70]	3.206–7/22/55[71]	4.111–7/13/56[72]	3.693–8/27/57[73]	3.518–8/24/58[74]	3.282–9/15/59[75]	3.989–8/24/60[76]
Conference Committee/ Final Appropriations Bill	4.531–8/3/53[77]	2.781–8/19/54[78]	2.703–7/28/55[79]	3.767–7/28/56[80]	3.436–8/30/57[81]	3.298–8/24/58[82]	3.226–9/15/59[83]	3.722–8/25.60[84]

Figures in billions of US dollars, rounded to nearest million. Figures represent only new budget requests, not funding reauthorizations or reappropriations from prior years. Fiscal years indicated ran from July 1 to June 30, and the fiscal year started in the previous year (i.e. FY 1954 began on July 1, 1953). Dates refer either to when a vote occurred or when a committee introduced a draft bill.

Notes

1 Felix Belair, "Eisenhower Urges 5.8 Billion in Aid," *NYT*, May 6, 1954. Presidential request is later specified as $5.474 billion. This table, and the subsequent appendices B and C almost exclusively use figures from the *New York Times*, mostly because they reported frequently on them, and also to ensure all comparisons are "apples to apples;" because of the complexity of these bills, publications often calculated numbers differently.
2 Paul P. Kennedy, "President Charts Foreign Aid Slash," *NYT*, January 22, 1954; "3.5 Billions in Aid Asked Congress," *NYT*, April 7, 1954. Presidential request is later specified as $3.497 billion, and then as $3.500 billion.
3 Dana Adams Schmidt, "New Foreign Aid Set at 3.5 Billion," *NYT*, January 18, 1955.
4 W. H. Lawrence, "Eisenhower Asks Foreign Aid Fund of $4,559,975,000," *NYT*, March 20, 1956. The presidential request is later specified as $4.909 billion.
5 Edwin Dale, "President Asks 71.8 Billion Budget," *NYT*, January 17, 1957.
6 William S. White, "Eisenhower Sets 3.8 Billion Floor for Foreign Aid," *NYT* May 10, 1957; W. H. Lawrence, "President Offers Reduced Aid Plan," *NYT*, May 22, 1957; "House Unit Votes $3,242,333,000 Aid," *NYT*, July 10, 1957.
7 William S. White, "President Seeks 3.9 Billon in Aid," *NYT*, February 20, 1958.
8 Edwin Dale, "Budget is Balanced at 77 Billion," *NYT* January 20, 1959.
9 Felix Belair, "President Urges 4.1 Billion in Aid," *NYT*, February 17, 1960.
10 Felix Belair, "Senate Unit Votes $5,312,732,500 Aid," *NYT*, June 11, 1953.
11 Clayton Knowles, "Bill on Aid Gains," *NYT*, July 13, 1954.
12 "Senate Unit, 13–2, Supports Aid Bill," *NYT*, May 27, 1955.
13 William S. White, "$4,457,575,000 Aid Plan Approved by Senate Unit," *NYT*, June 19, 1957.
14 William S. White, "Senators Favor Giving President 3.6 Billion in Aid," *NYT*, June 8, 1957.
15 Allen Drury, "$200,000,000 Cut in Aid Restored by Senate Group," *NYT*, May 22, 1958.
16 "Foreign Aid Bill Given to the Senate," *NYT*, March 19, 1959.
17 Russel Baker, "Aid Bill is Voted by Senate Group," *NYT*, Jun 16, 1959.
18 "4.1 Billion in Aid Gaining in Senate," *NYT*, April 21, 1960.
19 Felix Belair, "Foreign Aid Fight is Begun in House," *NYT*, June 19, 1953.
20 "$3,470,608.000 Aid is Urged on House," *NYT*, June 27, 1954.
21 "House Group Votes 3.2 Billion Aid Bill," *NYT*, June 23, 1955.
22 William S. White, "Foreign Aid Bill Cut $1,109,000,000 by House Group," *NYT*, May 23, 1956; "Aid Bill Cleared House Action," *NYT*, May 24, 1956.
23 William S. White, "House Unit Kills Ban It Imposed on Foreign Aid," *NYT*, July 2, 1957; "House Unit Votes $3,242,333,000 Aid," *NYT*, July 10, 1957.
24 "House Group Cuts Foreign Aid Bill," *NYT*, April 24, 1958.
25 John D. Morris, "House Unit Votes to Cut Foreign Aid to 3.6 Billion," *NYT*, May 27, 1959.
26 "House Panel Bids U.S. End Cuba Aid," *NYT*, April 1, 1960.

27 Felix Belair, "Senate Approves Foreign Aid Bill," *NYT*, July 2, 1953.
28 Clayton Knowles, "Senate Chops Aid by Half a Billion, Then Passes Bill," *NYT*, August 4, 1954.
29 John D. Morris, "Senate Approves 3.5 Billion in Aid President Asked," *NYT*, June 3, 1955.
30 William S. White, "4.5 Billion in Foreign Aid Voted by Senate," *NYT*, June 30, 1956.
31 William S. White, "Senate Approves Aid Funds Intact by Vote of 57–25," *NYT*, June 15, 1957
32 Allen Drury, "Senate Approves Foreign Aid Bill by Vote of 51–17," *NYT*, June 7, 1958.
33 Russell Baker, "Senate Approves Foreign Aid Bill," *NYT*, July 9, 1960.
34 Russell Baker, "Senate Votes Aid Outlay," *NYT*, May 3, 1960.
35 Felix Belair, "Aid Bill Approved as Democrats Save Measure in House," *NYT*, June 20, 1953.
36 William S. White, "$3,368,608,000 Aid is Voted by House," *NYT*, Jul 1, 1954.
37 Russell Baker, "Foreign Aid Bill Passed by House," *NYT*, July 1, 1955.
38 William S. White, "Aid Bill is Passed by House with 1.1 Billion Reduction," *NYT*, June 12, 1957.
39 Allen Drury, "Rebellious House Cuts 747 Million from Foreign Aid," *NYT*, July 20, 1957.
40 Allen Drury, "Foreign Ad Voted by House, 259–134," *NYT*, May 15, 1958.
41 Russell Baker, "House Approves 3.5 Billion in Aid," June 19, 1959.
42 C. P. Trussell, "House Approves 4 Billion in Aid," *NYT*, April 22, 1960.
43 Felix Belair, "Aid Bill is Passed," *NYT*, July 14, 1953; PL 118, Mutual Security Act of 1953, July 16, 1953, www.govinfo.gov/content/pkg/STATUTE-67/pdf/STATUTE-67-Pg152.pdf#page=1 (accessed December 7, 2020).
44 Clayton Knowles, "Conferees Raise Foreign Aid Fund Sliced by Senate," August 5, 1954.
45 Allen Drury, "Conferees Agree on 3 Billion in Aid," *NYT*, July 7, 1955; Allen Drury, "House Group Cuts Military Aid Bill," *NYT*, July 9, 1955.
46 William S. White, "Conferees Accept 4 Billion Aid Bill," *NYT*, July 7; "President Signs Foreign Aid Bill," *NYT*, July 18, 1956.
47 W. H. Lawrence, "President Warns of Session on Aid," *NYT*, August 14, 1957; Allen Drury, "3.3Billion in Aid Set," *NYT*, August 9, 1957; "Major Bills in Congress," *NYT*, August 10, 1957.
48 "Eisenhower Signs Foreign Aid Bill," *NYT*, June 30, 1958.
49 Russell Baker, "Congress Passes 3.5 Billion in Aid," *NYT*, July 23, 1959.
50 Tom Wicker, "White House Gets Foreign Aid Bill," *NYT*, May 13, 1960.
51 Subcommittee chairs: Taber for 54 and 55, Passman for the following years.
52 Felix Belair, "House Unit Ignores Eisenhower Appeal," *NYT*, July 16, 1953.
53 John D. Morris, "House Unit Pares 13% of Foreign Aid Eisenhower Asked," *NYT*, July 25, 1954. This is the figure proposed by the full Appropriations Committee.
54 Allen Drury, "House Group Cuts Military Aid Bill," *NYT*, July 9, 1955.
55 "Big Cut in Aid Funds Bill," *NYT*, July 5, 1956.
56 W. H. Lawrence, "President Warns of Session on Aid," *NYT*, August 14, 1957.
57 Edwin Dale, "President Scores 872 Million Slash from Foreign Aid," *NYT*, June 28, 1958.
58 "726-Million Cut in Aid Bill Voted by House Group," *NYT*, July 25, 1959.
59 C. P. Trussel, "House Panel Cuts Aid Fund," *NYT*, June 14, 1960.
60 Felix Belair, "House Spurns Plea by President, Votes Aid Cut 288–115," *NYT*, July 23, 1953.
61 William S. White, "Recess of Senate is Again Delayed," *NYT*, August 10, 1954.
62 "House Approves 2.6 Billion in Aid with Arms Slash," *NYT*, July 12, 1955.
63 William S. White, "House Approves 3.6 Billion Fund," *NYT*, July 12, 1956.

64 John D. Morris, "Aid Slash Passed by Congress," *NYT*, August 16, 1957.
65 Allen Drury, "Eisenhower Loses Foreign Aid Vote," *NYT* July 3, 1958.
66 Russell Baker, "Aid Bill is Passed by House," *NYT*, July 30, 1959.
67 Russell Baker, "House Approves Foreign Aid Bill," *NYT*, June 18, 1960.
68 There was also a Senate Appropriations Subcommittee for Foreign Operations that had a role similar to the Passman Committee, but it was consistently in lockstep with the full Appropriations Committee, and did not play an independent role, so it has not been included here.
69 "6.7 Billion Aid Bill Passed by Senate," *NYT*, July 30, 1953.
70 John D. Morris, "Senate Approves Foreign Aid Bill After Deeper Cut," *NYT*, August 15, 1954.
71 Allen Drury, "Senate Restores $567,100,000 Cut in Voting Aid Bill," *NYT*, July 23, 1955.
72 William S. White, "Senate Approves 4.1 Billion in Aid," *NYT*, July 25, 1956.
73 "Senate Approves 3.6 Billion in Aid," *NYT*, August 28, 1957.
74 Allen Drury, "Aid Bill is Voted as 85th Congress Winds Up Session," *NYT*, August 24, 1958.
75 Allen Drury, "Senate to Debate Final Issue Today", *NYT*, September 14, 1959.
76 Tom Wicker, "Senate Restores House Cut in Aid," *NYT*, August 25, 1960.
77 "White House Gets Foreign Aid Bill," *NYT*, August 4, 1953.
78 John D. Morris, "Foreign Aid Bill Passes Congress," *NYT*, August 20, 1954.
79 "Congress Passes Foreign Aid Bill," *NYT*, July 29, 1955.
80 William S. White, "Congress Quits After Approving Foreign Aid Fund," *NYT*, July 29, 1956.
81 "Senate Approves Foreign Aid Fund," *NYT*, August 30, 1957; "The 'Foreign Aid' Bill," *NYT*, August 30, 1957.
82 Allen Drury, "Aid Bill is Voted as 85th Congress Winds Up Session," *NYT*, August 24, 1958.
83 Russell Baker, "Congress Agrees on Rights Plan in Wind Up Rush," *NYT*, September 15, 1959; Allen Drury, "Accord Reached on Aid Measure," *NYT*, September 15, 1959.
84 Felix Belair, "Congress Ignores Eisenhower Plea," *NYT*, August 27, 1960.

Appendix B: Path from Initial Kennedy Request to Final Appropriation, FY1962–FY1964

	1962	*1963*	*1964*
Presidential Request	4.0–3/22/61, 2.4 for economic, the rest for military[1] 4.535–5/25/61, 2.9 for economic, the rest for military[2]	4.878–3/13/62, 3.378 for economic, the rest for military[3]	4.95–1/14/63, 3.45 for economic, the rest for military[4] 4.525–4/2/63, 3.12 for economic, the rest for military[5]
Senate Foreign Relations Committee recommended authorization	4.326–7/24/61[6]	4.662–5/21/62[7]	4.202–10/18/63[8]
House Foreign Affairs Committee recommended authorization	4.355–7/27/61[9]	4.668–5/23/62[10]	4.087–8/1/63[11]
Senate Authorization Bill	4.076–8/18/61[12]	4.662–6/6/62[13]	3.7–11/16/63[14]
House Authorization Bill	4.355–8/18/61[15]	4.668–7/23/62[16]	3.502–8/23/63[17]
Conference Committee/ Final Authorization Bill	4.253–8/31/61[18]	4.672–7/24/62[19]	3.599–12/9/63[20]
House Appropriations Subcommittee on Foreign Affairs recommendation (Passman Committee)	3.357–8/29/61[21]	3.427–9/17/62[22]	2.8–12/13/63[23]
House Appropriations Committee recommendation	3.357–8/31/61[24]	3.627–9/18/62[25]	2.8–12/14/63[26]
House Appropriations Bill	3.657–9/4/61[27]	3.627–9/20/62[28]	2.8–12/16/63[29]
Senate Appropriations Committee recommendation	4.196–9/12/61[30]	4.423–9/26/62[31]	3.3–12/17/63[32]
Senate Appropriations Bill[33]	4.196–9/15/61[34]	4.422–10/2/62[35]	3.272–12/19/63[36]
Conference Committee/ Final Appropriations Bill	3.914–9/26/61[37]	3.928–10/7/62[38]	3.0–12/30/63[39]

Figures in billions of US dollars, rounded to nearest ten million. Figures represent only new budget requests, not funding reauthorizations or reappropriations from prior years. Fiscal years indicated ran from July 1 to June 30. Dates refer either to when a vote occurred or when a committee introduced a draft bill.

Notes

1 John F. Kennedy, "Special Message to the Congress on Foreign Aid," March 23, 1962
2 E. W. Kenworthy, "$535,000,000 Rise in Aid Requested," *NYT*, May 26, 1961.
3 Gerhard Peters and John T. Woolley, eds, The American Presidency Project, https://www.presidency.ucsb.edu/node/236977.
4 Felix Belair, "Kennedy to Ask for 4.9 Billion Fund for Foreign Aid," *NYT*, January 16, 1963.
5 Felix Belair, "President Cuts Foreign Aid Plea," *NYT*, April 3, 1963.
6 Felix Belair, "Aid Measure Sent to Senate Floor," *NYT*, July 25, 1961; E. W. Kenworthy, "Fulbright Terms Aid Bill Best Yet," *NYT*, August 5, 1961.
7 Felix Belair, "4.6 Billion Voted by Senate Panel," *NYT*, May 23, 1962.
8 Felix Belair, "Senate Panel Bars Aid Cut," *NYT*, October 19, 1963.
9 Felix Belair, "House Unit Backs Aid Bill," *NYT*, July 28, 1961; E. W. Kenworthy, "Fulbright Terms Aid Bill Best Yet," *NYT*, August 5, 1961.
10 Felix Belair, "4.6 Billion Aid Bill Voted by House Unit," *NYT*, May 25, 1962.
11 Felix Belair, "Foreign Aid Bill Cut 430 Million," *NYT*, July 12, 1963; Felix Belair, "4-Billion Ceiling on Foreign Aid Approved by House Committee," *NYT*, August 2, 1963.
12 E. W. Kenworthy, "Congress Votes Conflicting Bills on Long Term Aid," *NYT*, August 19, 1961.
13 Felix Belair, "Aid Bill Voted By Senate," *NYT*, June 8, 1962.
14 Felix Belair, "Senate Approves Aid Bill," *NYT*, November 16, 1963.
15 E. W. Kenworthy, "Congress Votes Conflicting Bills on Long Term Aid," *NYT*, August 19, 1961.
16 . "Passman Asks Cut in Foreign Aid," *NYT*, July 26, 1962; Felix Belair, "House Supports Kennedy's Power to Aid Red Lands," *NYT*, July 13, 1962.
17 Felix Belair, "Kennedy Decries House Aid Slash as Irresponsible," August 24, 1963.
18 E. W. Kenworthy, "Congress Passes Aid Bill," *NYT*, September 1, 1961.
19 C. P. Trussel, "4-Billion Aid Bill Sent to Kennedy," *NYT*, Jul 25, 1962.
20 Felix Belair, "Conferees Bank 3.6 Billion Limit for Foreign Aid," *NYT*, September 6, 1963; "$3.6 Billion in Aid is Voted by House," *NYT*, December 10, 1963.
21 E. W. Kenworthy, "House Unit Backs Foreign Aid Cut," *NYT*, September 2, 1961.
22 Felix Belair, "House Unit Votes $1,500,000,000 Cut for Aid Program," *NYT*, September 18, 1961.
23 Felix Belair, "House Panel Cuts Aid $800 Million," *NYT*, December 14, 1963.
24 E. W. Kenworthy, "House Unit Backs Foreign Aid Cut," *NYT*, September 2, 1961.
25 Felix Belair, "1.1-Billion Aid Cut is Sent to House," *NYT*, September 19, 1962.
26 Felix Belair, "Johnson Brands Foreign Aid Cuts 'Setback' for U.S.," *NYT*, December 15, 1963.
27 Felix Belair, "House Restores Most of Arms Aid Committee Cut," *NYT*, September 5, 1961.
28 Felix Belair, "House Approves Foreign Aid Bill," *NYT*, September 21, 1962.
29 "House Approves $2.8 Billion in Aid," *NYT*, December 16, 1963.
30 Felix Belair, "533-Million Cuts in Aid Restored by Senate Panel," *NYT*, September 13, 1961.

31 Felix Belair, "792 Million Cut in Aid Restored by Senate Group," *NYT*, September 28, 1962.
32 Felix Belair, "$500 Million Aid Put Back in Bill by Senate Panel," *NYT*, December 18, 1963.
33 There was also a Senate Appropriations Subcommittee for Foreign Operations that had a role similar to the Passman Committee, but it was consistently in lockstep with the full Appropriations Committee, and did not play an independent role, so it has not been included here.
34 Felix Belair, "Conferees Fail to Agree to Sum for Foreign Aid," *NYT*, September 25, 1961.
35 Felix Belair, "Senate Approves 4.4 Billion in Aid," *NYT*, October 3, 1962.
36 Felix Belair, "Senate Kills Ban on Grain Credit; Votes Aid Funds," *NYT*, December 20, 1963.
37 Felix Belair, "Congress Votes Aid Compromise," *NYT*, September 27, 1961.
38 John D. Morris, "Foreign Aid Bill Goes to Kennedy," *NYT*, October 9, 1962.
39 Felix Belair, "Congress Adjourns Until Jan. 7 After Senate Votes Foreign Aid," *NYT*, December 31, 1963

Appendix C: Path from Initial Johnson Request to Final Appropriation, FY1965–FY1969

	1965	*1966*	*1967*	*1968*	*1969*
Presidential Request	3.5–1/21/64, 2.4 for economic, the rest for military[1]	3.38–1/14/65, 2.21 for economic, the rest for military[2]	3.386–1/24/66, 2.469 for economic, the rest for military[3]	3.126–1/24/67, 2.53 for economic, the rest for military[4]	3.04–2/8/68, 2.53 for economic, the rest for military[5]
Senate Foreign Relations Committee recommended authorization	3.467–7/2/64[6]	3.352–4/14/65[7]	3.24–7/7/66[8]	2.724–7/27/67[9]	1.946–6/25/69[10]
House Foreign Affairs Committee recommended authorization	3.5–5/26/64[11]	3.368–5/4/65[12]	3.400–6/16/66[13]	3.16–8/2/67[14]	2.36–6/19/68[15]
Senate Authorization Bill	3.3–9/24/64[16]	3.24–6/14/65[17]	2.852–7/27/66[18]	2.6–8/17/67[19]	1.946–7/31/68[20]
House Authorization Bill	3.517–6/10/64[21]	3.367–5/25/65[22]	3.4–7/14/66[23]	2.87–8/25/67[24]	1.994–9/19/68[25]
Conference Committee/Final Authorization Bill	3.25–10/2/64[26]	3.36–8/17/65[27]	3.5–9/19/66[28]	2.67–11/8/67[29]	1.971–9/10/68[30]
House Appropriations Subcommittee on Foreign Affairs recommendation (Passman Committee)	3.317–6/23/64[31]	3.36–8/26/65[32]	3.09–9/15/66[33]	2.200–11/6/67[34]	1.619–9/16/68[35]
House Appropriations Committee recommendation	3.317–6/25/64[36]	3.280–9/2/65[37]	3.090–9/17/66[38]	2.200–11/6/67[39]	1.619–9/19/68[40]
House Appropriations Bill	3.317–7/1/64[41]	3.280–9/8/65[42]	3.040–9/20/66[43]	2.200–11/17/67[44]	1.619 – 9/19/68[45]
Senate Appropriations Bill[46]	3.300–9/29/64[47]	3.140–9/23/65[48]	2.936–10/5/66[49]	2.730–12/7/67[50]	1.930–10/4/68[51]
Conference Committee/Final Appropriations Bill	3.250–10/2/64[52]	3.218–10/5/65[53]	2.940–10/7/66[54]	2.290–12/15/67[55]	1.750–10/11/68[56]

Figures in billions of US dollars, rounded to nearest million. Figures represent only new budget requests, not funding reauthorizations or reappropriations from prior years. Fiscal years indicated ran from July 1 to June 30. Dates refer either to when a vote occurred or when a committee introduced a draft bill.

Notes

1 Felix Belair, "$3.4 Billion for Aid Reflects Sharp Cut," *NYT*, January 22, 1964. $3.5 billion is used later as request figure.
2 Felix Belair, "President Urges Foreign Aid Fund of $3.38 Billion," *NYT*, January 15, 1965.
3 Felix Belair, "$3.3 Billion Foreign Aid Asked," *NYT*, January 25, 1966.
4 Felix Belair, "Goal for Foreign Aid Increases by $400 Million," *NYT*, January 25, 1967; other figures, including $3.46 billion were used at later dates.
5 Felix Belair, "President Asks 3.04 Billion Aid," *NYT*, February 9, 1968.
6 Felix Belair, "Senate Unit Cuts Aid Fund Lightly," *NYT*, July 3, 1964.
7 Felix Belair, "Aid Fund Sent to Senate," *NYT*, April 15, 1965.
8 Felix Belair, "Senate Unit Puts Aid at 3.2 Billion," *NYT*, July 7, 1966.
9 Felix Belair, "Foreign Aid Bill Cut $736 Million," July 28, 1967.
10 Felix Belair, "Smallest Aid Authorization Approved by Senate Panel," *NYT*, July 26, 1968.
11 Felix Belair, "House Unit Backs Full Foreign Aid Asked by Johnson," *NYT*, May 26, 1964.
12 Felix Belair, "House Unit Banks $3.37 Billion Aid," *NYT*, May 5, 1965.
13 Felix Belair, "Panels of Senate and House Split Over Cuts" *NYT*, June 17, 1966.
14 Felix Belair, "House Unit Cuts Aid $305 Million," *NYT*, August 3, 1967.
15 Felix Belair, "$600 Million Cut in Aid Bill Voted," *NYT*, June 19, 1968.
16 Felix Belair, "Senate Approves $3.3 Billion Plan for Foreign Aid," *NYT*, September 25, 1964.
17 "Washington Proceedings," *NYT*, June 15, 1965.
18 Felix Belair, "Military Aid Bill of $792 Voted by Senate," *NYT*, July 28, 196; Felix Belair, "$2 Billion Aid Bill Passed by Senate." *NYT*, July 27, 1966. The Senate passed two bills, the figure given is for both.
19 Felix Belair, "Foreign Aid Bill Cut $100 Million, Passed by Senate," *NYT*, August 18, 1967.
20 Felix Belair, "Senate Approves Slashed Aid Bill," *NYT*, August 1, 1968.
21 Felix Belair, "House Approves $3.5 Billion Aid by 230–175 Vote," *NYT*, June 10, 1964. $3.517 billion indicated as presidential request
22 Felix Belair, "House Approves Foreign Aid Bill by 249–148 Vote," *NYT* May 26, 1965.
23 Felix Belair, "House Votes Aid Measure," *NYT*, July 15, 1966.
24 Felix Belair, "House, Led by GOP, Cuts Foreign Aid," *NYT*, August26, 1966.
25 Felix Belair, "$1.6 Billion in Aid Passed by House," *NYT*. September 20, 1968.
26 Felix Belair, "Congress Votes $3.25 Billion Aid," *NYT*, October 3, 1964.
27 Felix Belair, "Conferees Settle Foreign Aid," *NYT*, August 18, 1965; Felix Belair, "Senate Approves Aid Compromise," *NYT*, August 25, 1965.
28 "$3.5 Billion Aid Bill Signed by President," *NYT*, September 20, 1965.
29 Felix Belair, "$2.67 Billion Aid Set by Conferees," *NYT*, November 2, 1967; Felix Belair, "Congress Votes Aid Compromise," *NYT*, November 9, 1967.
30 "Conferees Vote Lowest Aid Fund," *NYT*, September 10, 1968.
31 Felix Belair, "House Unit Votes $3.3 Billion in Aid, Defying Passman," *NYT*, June 24, 1964.

32 Felix Belair, "House Unit Votes 75 Million Aid Cut," August 26, 1965.
33 Felix Belair, "House Panel Cuts Aid by 295 Million," *NYT*, September 16, 1966.
34 Felix Belair, "House Panel Cuts Billion in Aid Bill," *NYT*, November 7, 1966. Committee voted on figure previously, introduced it to Appropriations Committee on this date.
35 Warren Unna, "House Unit Cuts Foreign Aid," *Washington Post*, September 17, 1968.
36 Felix Belair, "Full Committee Balks Passman," *NYT*, June 26, 1964.
37 "House Unit Votes $3.28 Billion Aid," *NYT*, September 3, 1965.
38 Felix Belair, "House Panel Votes $3.09 Billion in Aid," *NYT*, September 17, 1966.
39 Felix Belair, "House Panel Cuts Billion in Aid Bill," *NYT*, November 7, 1966.
40 Crowther Rodney, "House Gives Lowest Sum Ever to Aid," *Baltimore Sun*, September 20, 1968.
41 Felix Belair, "House Approves $3.3 Billion Aid, Backing Johnson," *NYT*, July 2, 1964.
42 John D. Morris, "Foreign Aid Bill Voted by House," *NYT*, September 9, 1965.
43 Felix Belair, "Foreign Aid Bill is Voted by House," *NYT*, September 21, 1966.
44 John W. Finney, "House Slashes Foreign Aid," *NYT*, November 17, 1967.
45 Felix Belair, "$1.6 Billion in Aid Passed by House," *NYT*. September 20, 1968.
46 There was also a Senate Appropriations Subcommittee for Foreign Operations that had a role similar to the Passman Committee, but it was consistently in lockstep with the full Appropriations Committee, and did not play an independent role, so it has not been included here.
47 "Senators Provide $3.3 Billion in Aid," *NYT*, September 30, 1964.
48 Felix Belair, "Foreign Aid Bill Clears Senate," *NYT*, September 24, 1965.
49 "Washington Proceedings," *NYT*, October 6, 1966.
50 Felix Belair, "Senate Restores Many Cuts in Aid," *NYT*, December 8, 1967.
51 "$1.9 Billion in Aid Voted by Senate," *NYT*, October 5, 1968.
52 John D. Morris, "Congress Blocks Appalachia Bill," *NYT*, October 3, 1964.
53 Felix Belair, "Senate Approves Aid Compromise," *NYT*, October 6, 1965.
54 "Aid Bill Approved Lowest in 9 Years," *NYT*, October 8, 1966.
55 John Herbers, "Congress Clears Four Major Bills and Ends Session," *NYT*, December 16, 1967.
56 Marjorie Hunter, "Congress Defers Plan to Adjourn," *NYT*, October 12, 1968.

Appendix D: Annual Foreign Aid Cycle

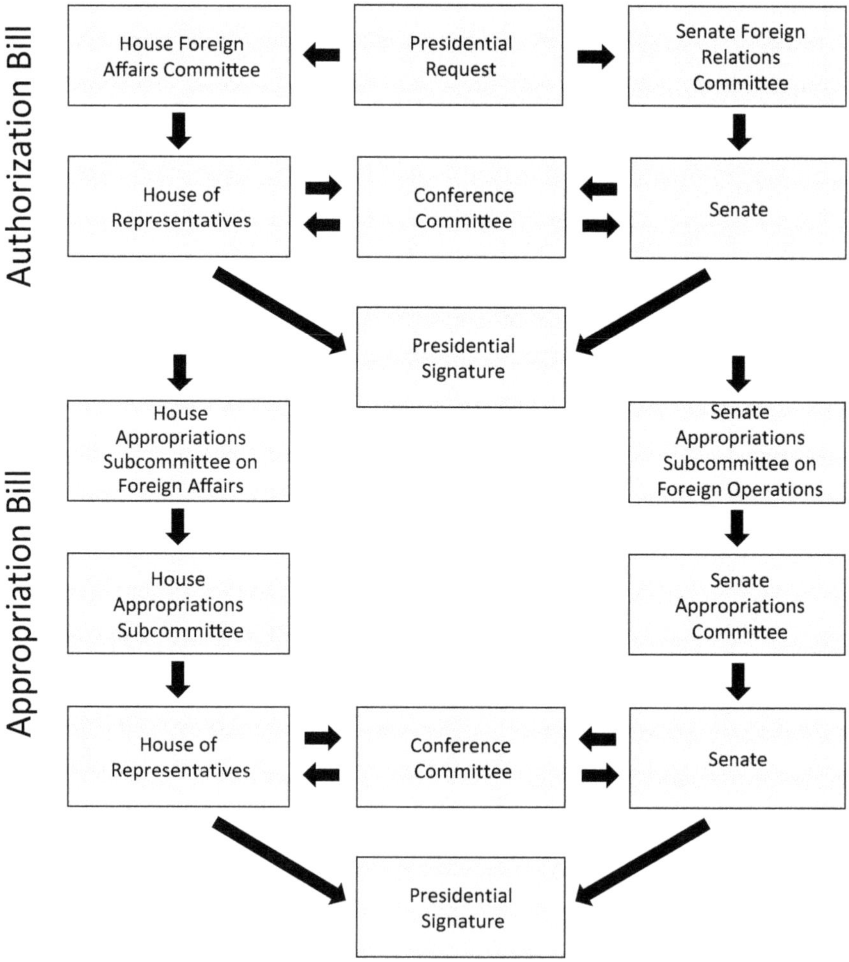

INDEX

www.ingramcontent.com/pod-product-compliance
Ingram Content Group UK Ltd.
Pitfield, Milton Keynes, MK11 3LW, UK
UKHW020134200926
475702UK00005B/747
* 9 7 8 1 1 3 8 3 4 5 2 7 0 *